THE GOLDEN FEAST

The song arose to the Golden Feast:
the Eternal Man rejoic'd.

WILLIAM BLAKE, *The Four Zoas*, Night IX, 690

BY

ROY WALKER

THE MACMILLAN COMPANY · NEW YORK · 1952

THE GOLDEN FEAST

A PERENNIAL THEME IN POETRY

EDEN AND COCKAIGNE

THE antithesis between The Garden of Eden and the Land of Cockaigne, or Fools' Paradise, is implicit throughout the book and is discussed in the chapter on the Earthly Paradise.

The Cockaigne picture, agreeing in detail with folk tradition, is by Pieter Brueghel the Elder and is now at Munich. Brueghel was influenced by Hieronymus Bosch, whose visionary picture of "The Garden of Delights" is also mentioned in the third chapter.

The Eden picture, now at The Hague, is the work of two artists. Rubens is responsible only for the figures of Adam and Eve. The Garden and its animals are by Jan Brueghel, one of the sons of the painter of the Cockaigne picture, who made several other studies of the subject in which the human figures were placed in distant perspective, animals, trees and fruit occupying the foreground.

Thus, although the pictures were chosen for this book when Jan Brueghel's part in the latter was not known to the author, it happens that the son painted the perfected life on Earth implied by his father's condemnation of a debased sensuality.

[Pictures reproduced by permission of the Mauritshuis, The Hague, and the Alte Pinakothek Collection, Munich]

69066

MADE AND PRINTED IN GREAT BRITAIN
BY THE CAMELOT PRESS LTD.
LONDON AND SOUTHAMPTON

TO MY AMERICAN FRIENDS
Richard Gregg
Helen and Scott Nearing
Agnes Ryan and Henry Bailey Stevens

*New England writers who share the Golden Feast
and who shared it with me in summer, 1949,
and to the memory of Mrs. M. R. L. Freshel,
this American edition is dedicated in friendship*

B

CONTENTS

ACKNOWLEDGMENTS

IN addition to the many particular obligations acknowledged in the appended References, I am indebted to Howard Williams' *The Ethics of Diet* (1883) for a number of quotations, and to J. A. Stewart's *Myths of Plato*, kindly presented to me by my old friend, Illit Grondahl. I should have made much fuller use of Alfred Nutt's long and learned essays printed in *The Voyage of Bran* and of Henry Bailey Stevens' important anthropological synthesis *The Recovery of Culture* if these books had come earlier into my hands. A number of other recent books bear in different ways on practical aspects of my theme, among which I would particularly mention Fairfield Osborn's *Our Plundered Planet* and William Vogt's *Road to Survival* and two books more akin to poetry, John Stewart Collis's *The Triumph of the Tree* and Richard St. Barbe Baker's *Green Glory*.

I have been generously helped by busy scholars and writers. Gilbert Murray gave me valuable references on Orphism. E. V. Rieu saved me from mistaking a piece of Pope's pastiche for authentic Homer. Robert Graves wrote from Spain about the Argonautic literature and Celtic folk-lore. W. F. Jackson Knight vouchsafed an apocalyptic glimpse into the Roman poets. Professors James and Bullough kindly replied to enquiries about Cockaigne. My friend Giovanni Pioli of Milan helped me to check facts about Petrarch. Kenneth Muir recalled the Samuel Daniel version of Tasso's Shepherds' Chorus, read the book in draft and made several excellent suggestions. G. Wilson Knight gave me the quotation from Dryden's *Don Sebastian*, directed me to Byron's *Cain*, and through his production and performance of *Timon of Athens* drew my attention to the scene quoted. Marjory Fausset kindly made an excellent version in hexameters of the untranslated lines by Lamartine. Alexander McKinley Terhune generously drew on his special knowledge of FitzGerald's unpublished correspondence. Patric Dickinson recalled references to Pythagoras in Yeats's *Last Poems*. Geoffrey Grigson also answered enquiries for possible modern allusions to my theme. My friend Charles Heriot helped in many ways. No one but myself, of course, is responsible for the use I have made of the material.

I wish also to thank the following authors, editors, executors, translators and publishers of copyright material for permission to quote:

Andrew Dakers, Ltd.:
—and the author: Jack Lindsay's *Song of a Falling World.*
Cambridge University Press: Geoffrey L. Bickersteth's translation of Leopardi, Jane Harrison's *Prolegomena to Greek Religion,* Kenneth Jackson's *Studies in Early Celtic Nature Poetry.*
Chatto & Windus:
—and Columbia University Press: Basil Willey's *The Eighteenth Century Background.*
—and Harper & Brothers, New York: Aldous Huxley's *Themes and Variations.*
—and The Macmillan Company, New York: E. M. W. Tillyard's *Milton.*
Constable & Co. Ltd.: Bernard Shaw's *Farfetched Fables.*
Faber and Faber, Ltd.: W. H. Auden's *For the Time Being,* T. S. Eliot's *The Waste Land,* W. F. Jackson Knight's *Roman Vergil.*
—and Richard Steele & Son, for the author: Fairfield Osborn's *Our Plundered Planet.*
George Allen and Unwin, Ltd.:
—and Oxford University Press, Inc., New York: Gilbert Murray's translations of *Hippolytus* and *The Bacchae.*
—and Simon and Schuster, Inc., New York: Bertrand Russell's *History of Western Philosophy.*
Hogarth Press, Ltd.: J. B. Leishman's translation of Rilke, *Sonnets to Orpheus.*
J. M. Dent & Sons, Ltd.:
—and E. P. Dutton & Co. Inc., New York: W. E. Leonard's translation of Lucretius, *Of the Nature of Things,* T. F. Royds's translation of Vergil, *The Eclogues and Georgics.*
Johns Hopkins Press:
—and Humphrey Milford, O.U.P.: G. Boas and A. O. Lovejoy, *Primitivism and Related Ideas in Antiquity.*
Jonathan Cape, Ltd.:
—and Oxford University Press, Inc., New York: C. Day Lewis's *The Poetic Image.*

Loeb Classical Library: C. B. Gulick's translation of Athenaeus, *Deipnosophistae*, M. Heseltine's translation of Petronius, *Satyricon*.

Macmillan & Co. Ltd.: Sir C. M. Bowra's *From Vergil to Milton* and *The Creative Experiment*.

—and A. P. Watt & Son, for Mrs. Yeats: W. B. Yeats's *The Celtic Twilight* and *Last Poems*.

Methuen & Co. Ltd.: W. K. C. Guthrie's *Orpheus and Greek Religion* and E. J. Urwick's *The Message of Plato*.

Open Court Publishing Co.: W. E. Leonard's translation of Empedocles.

Oxford University Press:

—and University of North Carolina Press: Odum and Johnson, *Negro Workaday Songs*.

—and University of Minnesota Press: Blegen and Ruud, *Norwegian Emigrant Songs and Ballads*.

Penguin Books, Ltd.:

—and the translator: Robert Graves's version of Apuleius, *The Golden Ass*.

Sidgwick & Jackson, Ltd.:

—and the author: Dr. W. W. Greg's *Pastoral Poetry and Pastoral Drama*.

The Clarendon Press, Oxford: F. M. Cornford's translation of Plato's *Republic* and Sloss and Wallis ed. *The Prophetic Writings of William Blake*.

The Council of Trinity College, Cambridge, and Macmillan & Co. Ltd.: Sir James Frazer's *The Golden Bough*.

Pearn, Pollinger & Higham, Ltd. for the author:

—and Penguin Books: Dr. Edith Sitwell's *Alexander Pope*.

Miss Magdalene Stewart on behalf of the family of the author: J. A. Stewart's *The Myths of Plato*.

The author: G. Wilson Knight's *The Starlit Dome* and *The Burning Oracle*.

The extracts from *Farfetched Fables* by Bernard Shaw are reproduced with the permission of the Public Trustee and the Society of Authors.

It has proved impossible to trace the Executors of the late A. F. Murison, whose *Horace in English Verse*, published by Longmans Green & Co. Ltd. is also quoted.

PROLOGUE

"THE Golden Age has existed intermittently throughout the history of civilization as a tradition of poetry, a world of ideas, a dynamic urge to the reconstruction of the social fabric and an inspiration to the heart of man", wrote H. W. Massingham. The seven chapters of this book trace that tradition of poetry, that social, dynamic and personal inspiration through Greece, Rome, Mediaeval and Renaissance Europe, and through the Puritan, Augustan and Romantic eras of English literature, until the stream broadens again to irrigate France, Germany, Italy and America. Much of the poetry is consciously written in a literary tradition, and consequently with greater and less degrees of imaginative vitality. After Hesiod in Greece, three others—Ovid, Milton and Blake, an otherwise varied trio—virtually recreate the essential vision from their own poetic resources. Concentration on English poetry for the three hundred years that end on the threshold of the nineteenth century is justified by the course of the tradition and the general character of our national literature. As W. J. Courthope says, "though the history of English poetry furnishes a clear mirror of the intellectual growth of the nation, this progress is to be regarded, not from a mere insular point of view, exhibiting the march of the Anglo-Saxon, or any other element in the constitution of the people, but rather in its European aspect, which shows us the gradual blending of many spiritual forces into the organic conscience that now directs our national life".

Arthur Golding, the Elizabethan poet who made the first English translation of Ovid's *Metamorphoses*, and wisely observed that "Not only in effect he dooth with Genesis agree", introduces it with some apt lines:

> These fables out of every book I have interpreted,
> To show how they and all the rest may stand a man in stead:
> Not adding over curiously the meaning of them all,
> For that were labour infinite, and tediousness not small.

Here, too, superfluous minor instances and elaborate exegesis would be fatal. "Poets", in C. M. Bowra's lucid words, "try to present complex states with a faithful regard for their emotional and imaginative significance. They must do more than convey ideas: they must re-create certain states for their readers as they have themselves known them." This book aspires to be a composite poetic image, and thus to convey in its many facets a single experience more widely shared by representative poets in all ages than has been recognised or acknowledged.

Within fairly strict limits, the interspersed commentary may direct attention to this constant which is the measure of superficial divergencies, of individual modulations and the distinctive coloration of the spirit of an age. It ventures beyond appropriate literary and historical details to a sketch of the currents of religious or philosophical thought—Orphism, Pythagoreanism and Platonism —or rather of the leading exponents of such beliefs who directly influenced the poets. And there are plunges into Hindu, Persian, Chinese, Slavonic and Celtic as well as classical mythology since the dividing lines between aetiological myth and the poetry that evokes a remote past are almost non-existent and such myths throw much light upon the poems with which we are primarily concerned.[1] There was a temptation, too, to make forays into the social sciences, which has for the most part been resisted as likely to transpose the discussion from the plane of creative imagination to that of analytical controversy. But a few authorities are quoted in the Anthropological Epilogue to indicate the nature of the evidence.

The issue cannot, however, be altogether evaded at the outset. Invocation of religion, philosophy and mythology is a warning that we are not dealing with amiable efforts to disguise stark reality in pretty but perishable verbal garlands, but with what often purports to be authentic vision of the human past. What must be made of such claims? Any possibility that the poetic vision of the Golden Age has immemorial natural roots must radically alter our judgment of the meaning and validity of the dream that has haunted Europe, and not only Europe, since the dawn of history. Although, as Sidney said, Nature's world is brazen and "the poets only deliver a golden", between the poetic and the scientific view of Nature there may be

---

[1] See Bibliographical Note, p. **xxi**.

a qualitative difference of vision rather than a disagreement about what is to be seen.

In some such prehistorical Golden Age not only eminent scientists but modern authors such as H. W. Massingham and Edward Carpenter have firmly and rationally believed. But the importance of the evidence from a remote past lies mainly in the conclusions we draw about essential human nature in its relationship with the total natural environment. We may prefer to leave that vexed question to the archaeologists and try instead to understand human nature here and now, only to find with Rousseau that it is virtually undiscoverable amid the habits and vices of a man-modified environment. Like those economists who once turned to hypothetical desert islands to simplify a complex problem, we may deport an imaginary Swiss Family Robinson to a fertile solitude and await the emergence of primal purity or barbarity, or both: but that is open to the opposite objection of dismissing the whole achievement of civilization as arbitrarily as the most fanatical primitivist. Modern writers have therefore usually preferred Utopian visions of a streamlined future where environment has been stamped with the pattern guaranteed to release the highest potential for human happiness, and contact with Nature is usually no more organic than a picnic in a National Park: but this sort of speculation is actually no less confined within contemporary limitations, and the result is so obviously inferior in truth, goodness and beauty to Hesiod's or Ovid's vision of a "barbaric" past—to say nothing of Genesis—as to remind us sharply that our present starting-point is not central but perversely eccentric to natural order. "By their fruits" is, in every sense, a good criterion. Formerly, we should have been more likely to tackle our problem by removing man altogether from the earth, though not necessarily from the flesh, by imagining for him a life after death in some paradisal place. If the starting-point was not inspiration but the usual yearnings of *l'homme moyen sensuel*, that too had a way of coming round to much the same thing; and disembodied spiritual survival and bliss has for many people an air of abstraction, even if credible at all.

All these directions, past, present, future and eternal, are explored in the poetic tradition we are considering. The quest is always the same, the answer of the true poet is always the same, because the truth is always the same truth. And the whole point of taking the poets seriously is that it is a truth we are not very good at discovering for ourselves, though we may recognise it when we are initiated by them. The poets adventure into a world, actually or mythically in the past, mystically or remotely present, imminent or far off in the future or beyond the grave, where there is peace of mind, peace with all men and—what we have lost to our shame and peril—peace with Nature celebrated at each day's feast.

The poets have written thus as "unacknowledged legislators" irrespective of their own habits and social and intellectual environment, though the insight is always the beginning of growth towards its realisation, conception in the full organic sense. The law is not of their invention but of their perpetual rediscovery. It is there. We transgress it at our own risk and not without penalty. The insight of which the Golden Feast is the sufficient symbol—it was seen as such before it was found in Blake—is vital to a complete view of human life within the natural order. Urban and industrialised existence, for all its triumphs, alienates us from the world in which ultimately all life is lived, so that our civilization is inwardly becoming the wilderness, the waste land of T. S. Eliot's poem:

> What are the roots that clutch, what branches grow
> Out of this stony rubbish? Son of man,
> You cannot say, or guess, for you know only
> A heap of broken images, where the sun beats,
> And the dead tree gives no shelter, the cricket no relief,
> And the dry stone no sound of water.

The same primordial-prophetic note sounds in the closing lines of Aldous Huxley's *Themes and Variations*: "The Golden Rule is to be applied to animate and inanimate Nature as well as to our fellow men. Treat Nature with charity and understanding, and Nature will repay you with unfailing gifts. Treat Nature aggressively, with greed and violence and incomprehension: wounded Nature will turn and destroy you. Theoretically, at least, the ancients understood these truths better than ourselves. The Greeks, for example, knew very well that hubris against the essentially divine order of Nature would be followed by its appropriate nemesis. The Chinese taught that the Tao, or indwelling Logos, was present on every level from the physical and the biological up to the spiritual; and they knew that outrages against Tao, in Nature no less than in man, would lead to fatal results. We have to recapture some of this old lost wisdom. If we fail to do this—we condemn ourselves and our children to misery and deepening squalor and the despair that finds expression in the frenzies of collective violence."

Can we indeed look forward to a future in which man seeks peace with Nature and the creatures as well as with all his fellow men, or is that only one of Bernard Shaw's *Farfetched Fables*? Certainly the fable has come far, it carries us back beyond Methuselah and forward as far as thought can reach. This book is mainly a procession of travellers towards that promised land. Its only claim is to throw open a window through which is visible a longer stretch of that road than can be seen from most urban dwellings nowadays. And borne upon the air is a scent of eternal spring, and the sound of a divine voice singing to the lute.

ROY WALKER

GREENWICH,
   January, 1951.

BIBLIOGRAPHICAL NOTE

THE GOLDEN FEAST attempts to reconstruct an important and strangely neglected tradition to which most of the greatest poets of Western civilization have contributed, and by so doing to throw light upon the poems in that tradition. The emphases that emerge are not those of orthodox academic and critical opinion among my contemporaries, who may therefore suspect ingenious special pleading. It therefore seems timely to draw attention to independent research in a kindred field which has come to my notice only since my book was completed but which goes far to corroborate the conclusions drawn from poetic evidence.

Primitivism and Related Ideas in Antiquity by G. Boas and the author of the remarkable volume of William James lectures at Harvard on *The Great Chain of Being*, A. O. Lovejoy, published by the Johns Hopkins University Press at Baltimore in 1935, remarks that "There is some reason to think that this background is not universally familiar to those whose special fields of study lie within the period from the Renaissance to our own time; it is in any case certain that without a fairly full acquaintance with it a good many passages in modern writings, and the ideas contained in them, cannot be seen in their true historical perspective. Even in the works of learned authors it is sometimes possible to find indications of the supposition that primitivism was essentially a novelty in the seventeenth or the eighteenth century; and in the minds of the less learned the belief appears still widely to prevail that it was a queer paradox introduced chiefly by Rousseau—the fact being that it was then beginning to go (temporarily) out of fashion, and that Rousseau contributed something to bring about its obsolescence." The last remark is perhaps more true of political philosophy than romantic poetry.

The 1935 volume was intended to be the first of four that would comprise *A Documentary History of Primitivism and Related Ideas*, but the Second World War wrought havoc with this plan as with so many others. It was not until 1948 that Boas published a much smaller volume of *Essays on Primitivism and Related Ideas in the Middle Ages,* in which he expresses the hope that this work will have driven the piles for a study of the same theme in Renaissance literature, and that others may yet be found to complete the *History* to the end of the eighteenth century as originally planned. Earlier Miss Lois Whitney, with the encouragement of Professor Lovejoy, had produced in 1934 an interesting study of *Primitivism and the Idea of Progress in English Popular Literature of the Eighteenth Century,* but as the title indicates this is a subsidiary work concerned chiefly with "unclassified popular documents" of the period, so that Pope, Thomson and the Wartons, for example, find no place in the index. To Boas's essays on the Middle Ages may now be added the volume by Howard Rollin Patch, *The Other World,* issued in 1950 from the Harvard University Press.

In the single volume of the Boas-Lovejoy history, then, there exists an independent, encyclopaedic and scholarly research study of the development in the classical period of the theme with which *The Golden Feast* is concerned. Its evaluation substantially agrees with the conclusions here drawn solely from a study of the poetry. Empedocles, to take but one example, is quoted to demonstrate the tradition in which "the essential is that primitive man was better than contemporary man, chiefly by reason of his vegetarianism and the absence of animal sacrifices and of war." Yet even so great a scholar as Newman Ivey White, with the poetry before him, could only write off Shelley's vegetarianism as one of his *Miscellaneous Tastes, Traits and Peculiarities*! The extent and meaning of similar preoccupations among the Christian Fathers and monastic orders, on which there are some remarks in my fifth chapter, is a main theme in the later Boas volume of essays.

But if the history of ideas is thus coming to the rescue of an adventurous interpreter sailing his cockleshell consciousness across the high seas of poetry, some of his courses remain uncharted. Boas and Lovejoy, noticing a common element of something like indolence, do not seem to realise the extent to which Eden or the Golden Age and Cockaigne are antithetical conceptions, a point that is strongly brought out in these pages. And perhaps my own explorations of Renaissance, eighteenth- and nineteenth-century poetry in the same tradition may make some incidental contribution to the later volumes of the *History* those learned authors began and which it is left to others to complete.

These studies in primitivism are concerned with what has been thought and said and not, even where primitivism takes the form of chronological assertion about the past rather than cultural discussion of the present and future, with what is correct or incorrect. In the *Anthropological Epilogue* a number of authorities in different fields are quoted as to the historicity of the Golden Age, or something like it, and notably the anthropological synthesis by Henry Bailey Stevens, of the University of New Hampshire, *The Recovery of Culture*. Looking back over what I have written towards the end of this book about the visions that Coleridge entertained of an American Earthly Paradise, of the purposes that sent Henry David Thoreau to live in the woods by Walden Pond, of the idealist communities in the same tradition and such latter-day pioneers as the sometime university professor Scott Nearing, I cannot help being struck by the extent to which the same area of New England is producing to-day the only substantial research studies on the subject, including not only those already mentioned but the survey of *Backwoods Utopias* 1663-1829 by Arthur Eugene Bestor, Jr., published by the University of Pennsylvania Press, 1950. The New World must be constantly rediscovered; perhaps after all there are still things nearer Heaven than the skyscraper. Mark Holloway's study of Utopian communities in America 1680–1880, *Heavens on Earth,* has been recently published in England by Turnstile Press, Ltd.

THE ORPHIC SONG

ORPHEUS! It is a ripple of musical air rather than a name. "Orpheus of the golden lyre, father of lays", Pindar sang, and that light from the past pierces a more ancient darkness, transfiguring the primal minstrel whose touch sends forth a harmonious zephyr that faintly blows forever across the lands of Europe, ravishing the souls of those that have ears to hear.

For love's sake this fabulous being descended into Hell, trod the dark road presently followed by Odysseus, Aeneas with the golden bough, and by Dante on the terrible journey to salvation. By his fatal backward glance from resurrection to death, Orpheus lost his beloved Eurydice, and not finding in earthly women a like divinity was torn to pieces in their Bacchanalian orgy.

Orpheus! This quivering air spans the octave from Heaven to Hell and enchants it to harmony. When Orpheus played and sang, birds of the air, the fish in the streams, wild beasts, even trees, rocks and hills, gathered round him to listen. In this divine music of creation, inanimate and animate Nature, man and beast, were resolved into a single chord.

Orpheus modulates from music through myth into history. Is it worth the while of modern man, in Browning's phrase, to "puzzle out who Orpheus was"? Vergil assigns him a place in the first rank of the just in the Elysian paradise; Dante relegates him to the first circle of the Inferno. He is regarded with anger and contempt as an impostor by Christian apologetics, and yet survived in Christian art to be metamorphosed into the Good Shepherd with his sheep. His influence has been pervasive, but his poems are all lost. The same mist shrouds the tradition that Orpheus was among the Argonauts. If they voyaged in space beyond the known world, Orpheus sailed through time, bringing his companions to a vision of the Golden Age when the harmony of Nature, beast and man was not an old song echoing in racial memory but living reality.

The reputed teacher of Pythagoras, Pherecydes, writing in the middle of the sixth century B.C., counted Orpheus among the Argonauts. Introducing a modern prose narrative closely based on classical sources, Robert Graves is doubtful about it, but includes Orpheus if only because the sailors need a musician to keep the peace. After leaving the island of sensual indulgence that prefigures Armida's and Cockaigne, the sailors ask Orpheus to purge their souls by a song of the Creation, and he sings of the first race of men who were herdsmen, whose food was milk, honey, nuts and fruit, who neither tilled the soil nor engaged in warfare and knew nothing of the use of metals. So ended the first Age.

Translating the *Argonautica* written by Apollonius Rhodius in the third century B.C., Preston quotes and comments on another record of the voyage possibly traceable to Orpheus himself:

"The account of *Orpheus*, or whoever was the ancient poet, whether *Onomacritus*, or any other, who composed the account of the *Argonautic* expedition, which has reached us, and is certainly of very remote antiquity, and borrowed in great measure from the *Orphic* fables and traditions, differs, in many circumstances, from the narrative of *Apollonius*; and particularly with respect to the route, which the adventurers pursued, on their return from Colchis to Greece." Preston then translates a dozen pages of this account, in which the following passage occurs:

"When the sixth morn arose, enlightener of man, we came, with short interval, to a race rejoicing in wealth and affluence, the *Macrobians* they are called—they live for many years—twelve chiliads of months of a hundred years of the full moon, without any of the troublesome concomitants of age. But, when at last they have reached the month, appointed by fate, they sink in a sweet and tranquil slumber, and find the boundaries of life. Nor thoughts of food, nor other cares and toils that molest the generality of man, breed in them the least solicitude. On sweet and fragrant herbs they feed amid the verdant and grassy pastures, and drink ambrosial dew, divine potation. All resplendent alike, in coeval youth, a placid serenity forever smiles on their brows, and lightens in their eyes, the consequence of a just temperament of mind and disposition, both in parents and in sons, perpetually disposing them to act what is just, and speak what is prudent. Through the populous region of these we past (*sic*) by land, and reached another shore. . . ."

In *The Life and Death of Jason,* a long poem mainly about the Argonauts and originally planned for inclusion in *The Earthly Paradise,* William Morris also placed Orpheus aboard the *Argo.* His rôle there is important and agrees with the treatment by successive poets of the theme studied in this book. Morris's expansion of the myth is unerring and must therefore be very fully treated here, not only for its own sake but because it admirably elucidates the rest of this chapter.

The Argonauts come ashore at dusk in a lonely land. After the usual sacrifice of flesh and wine, some of the meat is handed round as food, the leaders being served first, among them "the godlike singer".

> But into him his harp did Orpheus reach,
> And smote the strings, and through the ancient trees
> Rang the heart-piercing honied melodies:—

> "Alas! for Saturn's days of gold,
> Before the mountain men were bold
> To dig up iron from the earth
> Wherewith to slaughter health and mirth,
> And bury hope far underground,
> When all men needed did abound
> In every land; nor must they toil,
> Nor wear their lives in strife to foil
> Each other's hands, for all was good,
> And no man knew the sight of blood.

> "With all the world man had no strife,
> No element against his life
> Was sworn and bitter; on the sea,
> Dry-shod, could all walk easily;
> No fire there was but what made day,
> Or hidden in the mountains grey;
> No pestilence, no lightning flash,
> No over-mastering wind, to dash
> The roof upon some trembling head.

3

"Then the year changed, but ne'er was dead,
Nor was the autumn-tide more sad
Than very spring; and all unclad
Folk went upon the harmless snow,
For not yet did midwinter know
The biting frost and icy wind,
The very east was soft and kind.

"And on the crown of July days,
All heedless of the mid-day blaze,
Unshaded by the rosy bowers,
Unscorched beside the tulip flowers,
The snow-white naked girl might stand;
Or fearless thrust her tender hand
Amidst the thornless rose-bushes.

"Then, 'mid the twilight of the trees
None feared the yellow beast to meet;
Smiling to feel their languid feet
Licked by the serpent's forkéd tongue.
For then no clattering horn had rung
Through those green glades, or made afraid
The timid dwellers in the shade.
No lust of strength nor fear of death
Had driven men, with shortened breath,
The stag's wide-open eyes to watch;
No shafts to slay, no nets to catch,
Were yet; unyoked the neat might play
On untilled meads, and mountains grey,
Unshorn, the silly sheep might rove.

"Nor knew that world consuming love,
Mother of hate, or envy cold,
Of rage for fame, or thirst for gold,
Or longing for the ways untried,
That ravening and unsatisfied,
Draw shortened lives of men to Hell.

"Alas! what profit now to tell
The long unweary lives of men
Of past days—threescore years and ten,
Unbent, unwrinkled, beautiful,
Regarding not death's flower-crowned skull,

4

But with some damsel intertwined
In such love as leaves hope behind.

"Alas, the vanished days of bliss!
Will no God send some dream of this,
That we may know what it has been?

"Oh, thou, the chapleted with green,
Thou purple-stained, but not with blood,
Who on the edge of some cool wood
Forgettest the grim Indian plain,
And all the strife and all the pain,
While in thy sight the must foams out,
And maid and man, with cry and shout,
Toil while thou laughtest, think of us,
And drive away these piteous,
Formless and wailing thoughts, that press
About our hour of happiness.

"Lyaeus, King! by thee alone
To song may change our tuneless moan,
The murmur of the bitter sea
To ancient tales be changed by thee.
By thee the unnamed smouldering fire
Within our hearts turns to desire
Sweet, amorous, half-satisfied;
Through thee the doubtful years untried
Seem fair to us and fortunate,
In spite of death, in spite of fate."

He ceased, and bent his head above the wine;
Then, as he raised his eyes they saw them shine
In the red torchlight with unwilling tears,
And their hearts too, with thoughts of vanished years
Were pensive.

In Book XIV, the ship passes by the shore where seductive Sirens
sing to the mariners. The Sirens, with their long hair blown across
white bodies half-hidden with golden spray, bear a certain deceptive
resemblance to the maidens in the Garden of the Hesperides,
presently to be seen by the same voyagers. Jason, struggling to
overcome temptation, staggers to the helm to steer the vessel away
from this fatal coast, and shouts to Thracian Orpheus:

5

> Minstrel shall we die,
> Because thou hast forgotten utterly
> What things she taught thee that men call divine,
> Or will thy measures but lead folk to wine,
> And scented beds, and not to noble deeds?

Orpheus, turning from the sight of the Sirens, begins a long antiphonal struggle with them. He warns his companions that, "To have no thought of good or ill, Yet feed your fill of pleasure still" is an "idle dream". The meaning is plain. There is a merely sensual indulgence that is living death. But Orpheus himself sings the July delights of carefree love beneath the green trees of Greece. There is no general repudiation of sensuous delights. The distinction between sacred and profane love is not, in the Orphic tradition, a choice between indulgence and abstinence, good and bad are more subtly discriminated. That love is most joyous and creative which is not enjoyed at the cost of man's highest purposes. The tendency to identify the good life with denial and austerity—of which we shall presently find not a few poetic examples[1]—is not approved. But the problem of the good life and unbounded love is not solved, and remains to perplex the poets of the Renaissance and to be variously repressed, avoided or resolved by later poets.

Orpheus triumphs over the Sirens, but as the ship sails away into the night its crew "Have small delight in life all empty of that promised bliss". There follows the discovery of the true Earthly Paradise, a vision of what "In days past, all the world has been". The episode illuminates many aspects of our theme and is quoted in full:

> Yet as night died, and the cold sea and grey
> Seemed running with them toward the dawn of day,
> Needs must they once again forget their death,
> Needs must they, being alive and drawing breath,
> As men who of no other life can know
> In their own minds again immortal grow.
>
> But toward the south a little now they bent,
> And for awhile o'er landless sea they went,

---

[1] E.g. "ladies of the Hesperides"—properly, as in this poem of Morris's, an image of primal delight—becomes in Milton's *Paradise Regained*, II, 357, one of the snares set for Christ in the Wilderness by the Tempter. The Serpent was perhaps an associative link.

6

But on the third day made another land
At dawn of day, and thitherward did stand;
And since the wind blew lightly from the shore,
Somewhat abeam, they feared not with the oar
To push across the shallowing sea and green,
That washed a land the fairest they had seen,
Whose shell-strewn beach at highest of the tide
'Twixt sea and flowery shore was nowise wide,
And drawn a little backward from the sea
There stood a marble wall wrought cunningly,
Rosy and white, set thick with images,
And over-topped with heavy-fruited trees,
Which by the shore ran, as the bay did bend,
And to their eyes had neither gap nor end;
Nor any gate: and looking over this,
They saw a place not made for earthly bliss,
Or eyes of dying men, for growing there
The yellow apple and the painted pear,
And well-filled golden cups of oranges
Hung amid groves of pointed cyprus trees;
On grassy slopes the twining vine-boughs grew,
And hoary olives 'twixt far mountains blue,
And many-coloured flowers, like as a cloud
The rugged southern cliffs did softly shroud;
And many a green-necked bird sung to his mate
Within the slim-leaved, thorny pomegranate,
That flung its unstrung rubies on the grass,
And slowly o'er the place the wind did pass
Heavy with many odours that it bore
From thymy hills down to the sea-beat shore,
Because no flower there is, that all the year,
From spring to autumn, beareth otherwhere,
But there it flourished; nor the fruit alone
From 'twixt the green leaves and the boughs outshone,
For there each tree was ever flowering.

Nor was there lacking many a living thing
Changed of its nature, for the roe-deer there
Walked fearless with the tiger, and the bear
Rolled sleepily upon the fruit-strawn grass,
Letting the coneys o'er his rough hide pass,

7

With blinking eyes, that meant no treachery.
Careless the partridge passed the red fox by;
Untouched the serpent left the thrushes brown,
And as a picture was the lion's frown.

But in the midst there was a grassy space,
Raised somewhat over all the flowery place,
On marble terrace-walls wrought like a dream;
And round about it ran a clear blue stream,
Bridged o'er with marble steps, and midmost there
Grew a green tree, whose smooth grey boughs did bear
Such fruit as never man elsewhere had seen,
For 'twixt the sunlight and the shadow green
Shone out fair apples of red gleaming gold.
Moreover round the tree, in many a fold,
Lay coiled a dragon, glittering little less
Than that which his eternal watchfulness
Was set to guard; nor yet was he alone,
For from the daisied grass about him shone
Gold raiment wrapping round two damsels fair,
And one upon the steps combed out her hair,
And with shut eyes sung low as in a dream;
And one stood naked in the cold blue stream,
While on the bank her golden raiment lay;
But on that noontide of the quivering day,
She only, hearing the seafarers' shout,
Her lovely golden head had turned about,
And seen their white sail flapping o'er the wall,
And as she turned had let her tresses fall,
Which the thin water rippling round her knee
Bore outward from her toward the restless sea.

Not long she stood, but looking seaward yet,
From out the water made good haste to get,
And catching up her raiment hastily,
Ran up the marble stair, and 'gan to cry:
"Wake, O my sisters, wake, for now are come
The thieves of Aea to our peaceful home."

Then at her voice they gat them to their feet,
And when her raiment all her body sweet
Once more had hidden, joining hand to hand,
About the sacred apples did they stand,

While coiled the dragon closer to the tree,
And raised his head above them threateningly.

Meanwhile, from Argo many a sea-beat face
Gazed longingly upon that lovely place,
And some their eager hands already laid
Upon the gangway. Then Medea said:—
"Get back unto the oars, O Minyae,
Nor loiter here, for what have such as we

To do herein, where, 'mid undying trees,
Undying watch the wise Hesperides,
And where the while they watch, scarce can a God
Set foot upon the fruit-besprinkled sod
That no snow ever covers? therefore haste,
Nor yet in wondering your fair lives waste;
For these are as the Gods, nor think of us,
Nor to their eyes can ought be glorious
That son of man can do; would God that I
Could see far off the misty headland lie,
Where we the guilt of blood shall wash away,
For I grow weary of the dashing spray,
And ceaseless roll of interwoven seas,
And fain were sitting 'neath the whispering trees
In homely places, where the children play,
Who change like me, grow old, and die some day."

She ceased, and little soothly did they grieve,
For all its loveliness, that land to leave,
For now some God had chilled their hardihead,
And in their hearts had set a sacred dread,
They knew not why; but on their oars they hung
A little longer as the sisters sung.[1]

"O ye, who to this place have strayed,
That never for man's eyes was made,
Depart in haste, as ye have come,
And bear back to your sea-beat home
This memory of the age of gold,
And for your eyes, grown over-bold,
Your hearts shall pay in sorrowing,
For want of many a half-seen thing.

---

[1] In Hesiod's *Theogony*, "Th' Hesperian virgins sing with shrill sweet voice"—line 621 in Elton's translation.

"Lo, such as is this garden green,
In days past, all the world has been,
And what we know all people knew,
But this, that unto worse all grew.

"But since the golden age is gone,
This little place is left alone,
Unchanged, unchanging, watched of us,
The daughters of wise Hesperus.

"Surely the heavenly Messenger
Full oft is fain to enter here,
And yet without must he abide,
Nor longeth less the dark king's bride
To set red lips unto that fruit
That erst made nought her mother's suit.
Here would Diana rest awhile,
Forgetful of her woodland guile,
Among these beasts that fear her nought.
Nor is it less in Pallas' thought,
Beneath our trees to ponder o'er
The wide, unfathomed sea of lore;
And oft-kissed Citheraea, no less
Weary of love, full fain would press
These flowers with unsandalled feet.

"But unto us our rest is sweet,
Neither shall any man or God
Or lovely Goddess touch the sod
Where-under old times buried lie,
Before the world knew misery.
Nor will we have a slave or king,
Nor yet will we learn anything
But that we know, that makes us glad;
While oft the very Gods are sad
With knowing what the Fates shall do.

"Neither from us shall wisdom go
To fill the hungering hearts of men,
Lest to them three-score years and ten
Come but to seem a little day,
Once given, taken soon away.
Nay, rather let them find their life
Bitter and sweet, fulfilled of strife,

Restless with hope, vain with regret,
Trembling with fear, most strangely set
'Twixt memory and forgetfulness;
So more shall joy be, troubles less,
And surely when all this is past,
They shall not want their rest at last.

"Let earth and heaven go their way,
While still we watch from day to day,
In this green place left all alone,
A remnant of the days long gone."

There in the wind they hung, as word by word
The clear-voiced singers silently they heard;
But when the air was barren of their song,
Anigh the shore they durst not linger long,
So northward turned forewearied Argo's head,
And dipping oars, from that fair country sped,
Fulfilled of new desires and pensive thought,
Which that day's life unto their hearts had brought.

This deep contentment of heart and mind is the opposite of the restless melancholy with which the Argonauts reluctantly parted from the Sirens at Orpheus's bidding. That is the difference between the two worlds of human longing. The Hesperides gives no immediate sensuous fulfilment, only a vision and an assurance that "They shall not want their rest at last".

Only two pages of this book of the poem remain. In them the vessel is brought to Greece. The sudden appearance of the voyagers in a great hall where people are feasting causes alarm, and Jason cries out:

Laconians, fear ye not,
Nor leave the flesh-meat while it yet is hot
For dread of us

—and all sit down together. Next morning upon the headland milk-white bulls are slain and wine is poured upon the sacrificial fire. The Argonauts are again in the Age of Heroes, remote from the immortal island of the Age of Gold where no blood is shed and all living things are at peace one with another. The Age of Heroes is short-lived. As the book closes, the voices round the sacrificial fire are swept by the wind—

> Unto the dashing of the conquered sea,
> That far below thrust on by tide and wind
> The crumbling bases of the headland mined.

In the middle of the ninth century before the Christian era, Homer brought together in the *Iliad* the savage and brutal customs, the animal and human bloodshed of the "Heroic" Age immediately preceding his own. "Who can be so prejudiced in their favour as to magnify the felicity of those ages, when a spirit of revenge and cruelty, joined with the practice of rapine and robbery reigned through the world?" cried Alexander Pope, in the Preface to his translation of the epic. At the beginning of Book XIII of Pope's version, Jove, turning away from war and slaughter, contemplates a happy, long-lived people who love peace and the bloodless feast—

> where the far-famed Hippomolgian strays,
> Renown'd for justice and for length of days;
> Thrice happy race! that, innocent of blood,
> From milk, innoxious, seek their simple food;
> Jove sees delighted; and avoids the scene
> Of guilty Troy, of arms, and dying men:
> No aid, he deems, to either host is given,
> While his high law suspends the powers of Heaven.

But, as will be evident from a discussion of Pope's poetry in a later chapter, this is largely a reflection of the translator's own opinions.[1]

In the *Odyssey*, however, Homer treats themes of an Orphic character that later reappear in Hesiod. Arguing that the connection between war and flesh-eating has been known since time immemorial, Rousseau points out in *Emile* that "Homer makes his flesh-eating Cyclops a terrible man while his Lotus-eaters are so delightful that those who went to trade with them forgot even their own country to dwell among them". This is hardly convincing, but careful comparison of Homer's brief descriptions of the remote

---

[1] E. V. Rieu writes: "My rendering of the Hippomolgi passage is: 'the lordly Hippomolgi who drink mare's milk, and the Abii, the most law-abiding folk on earth. Not another glance of his bright eyes did he give to Troy.' That is all. The only permissible variation is to take 'Abii' not as the proper name of another tribe, but as an additional epithet of the Hippomolgi, meaning 'needy'. But this rendering has been abandoned by recent scholars. Pope's translation—especially the last two lines you quote, about 'guilty Troy', etc.—is an excellent example of the extent to which he *embroidered* Homer."

terrestrial Elysian plain, the heavens and the fruitful orchard-garden of Alcinous that lent Milton an image for Eden, shows that Rousseau was not at fault in glimpsing his ideal in the *Odyssey*. The promise of Elysium to Menelaus is made in significant contrast to the fate of Ulysses, then prisoner of the amorous Calypso:

> But oh, beloved by Heaven! reserved to thee
> A happier lot the smiling Fates decree:
> Free from that law, beneath whose mortal sway
> Matter is changed, and varying forms decay,
> Elysium shall be thine: the blissful plains
> Of utmost earth, where Rhadamanthus reigns.
> Joys ever young, unmix'd with pain or fear,
> Fill the wide circle of the eternal year:
> Stern winter smiles on that auspicious clime:
> The fields are florid with unfading prime;
> From the bleak pole no winds inclement blow,
> Mould the round hail, or flake the fleecy snow;
> But from the breezy deep the blest inhale
> The fragrant murmurs of the western gale.
> This grace peculiar will the gods afford
> To thee, the son of Jove, and beauteous Helen's lord.

The conception of the abode of the gods themselves in Book VI is closely similar:

> Then to the palaces of heaven she sails,
> Incumbent on the wings of wafting gales;
> The seat of gods; the region mild of peace,
> Full joy, and calm eternity of ease.
> There no rude winds presume to shake the skies,
> No rains descend, no snowy vapours rise;
> But on immortal thrones the blest repose;
> The firmament with living splendours glows.
> Hither the goddess winged the aërial way,
> Through heaven's eternal gates that blazed with day.

In the following book these lovely but insubstantial and remote paradisal places develop into the more terrestrial and Orphic vision of the orchard of Alcinous:

> Close to the gates a spacious garden lies,
> From storms defended and inclement skies.

13

Four acres was the allotted space of ground,
Fenced with a green enclosure all around.
Tall thriving trees confess'd the fruitful mould:
The reddening apple ripens here to gold.
Here the blue fig with luscious juice o'erflows,
With deeper red the full pomegranate glows:
The branch here bends beneath the weighty pear,
And verdant olives flourish round the year.
The balmy spirit of the western gale
Eternal breathes on fruits, untaught to fail:
Each dropping pear a following pear supplies,
On apples apples, figs on figs arise:
The same mild season gives the blooms to blow,
The buds to harden, and the fruits to grow.

Nevertheless, Homer is substantially the poet of the Heroic Age, and it is to Hesiod about a century later that we must look for the clearest Orphic images of similar remote and immediate earthly paradises, as also for the first clear chronology of ages, which shows that the abode of the gods is akin to the terrestrial Golden Age when men lived "like gods".

Hesiod indeed is the poet of peace and the countryside rather than of bloodshed and the city-state. Plutarch mentions a tradition that Homer and Hesiod were contemporaries and there is at least a legend of contest between them. Homer is nowhere named in *Works and Days*, which would be remarkable if he had lived a century earlier. But whatever the historical facts may be the essential opposition of these two great poets is real enough.

Not much is definitely known about Hesiod's life. Like Orpheus he is mostly music and myth, and we shall see that the Golden Age and other elements of his chronology were adopted by the Orphics if not derived by him from lost writings of Orpheus. Other circumstances about Hesiod remind us of Orpheus. Was there some partial identification in popular imagination? The warning in *Works and Days* against loose women and the care needed in choosing "from those that round thee dwell" a wife who is not "feast-frequenting" and inordinately passionate suggest the vengeful Bacchic women who murdered Orpheus. Hesiod also met a violent end associated with sexual crime. His fellow-traveller insulted the daughter of their host, and the girl's brothers murdered both men. Hesiod's body was thrown into the sea and wafted back to the coast of Aetolia, just as the remains of Orpheus were cast into the sea and the head and lyre were miraculously carried to a distant island. Some versions represent the assassins as promptly perishing by lightning or shipwreck sent to avenge the poet's death. Shipwreck, we shall find, would have been the apt poetic justice.

> When gods alike and mortals rose to birth,
> Th' immortals form'd a golden race on earth
> Of many-languaged men; they lived of old
> When Saturn[1] reign'd in heaven; an age of gold.
> Like gods they lived, with calm, untroubled mind,
> Free from the toil and anguish of our kind:
> Nor e'er decrepid age mis-shaped their frame,
> The hand's, the foot's proportions, still the same.
> Pleased with earth's unbought feasts; all ills removed,
> Wealthy in flocks, and of the bless'd beloved.
> Death as a slumber press'd their eyelids down;
> All nature's common blessings were their own.
> The life-bestowing tilth its fruitage bore,
> A full, spontaneous, and ungrudging store:
> They with abundant goods, midst quiet lands,
> All willing shared the gatherings of their hands.
> When earth's dark breast had closed this race around,
> Great Jove as demons raised them from the ground.
> Earth-hovering spirits, they their charge began,
> The ministers of good, and guards of man.
> Mantled with mist of darkling air they glide,
> And compass earth, and pass on every side;
> And mark, with earnest vigilance of eyes,
> Where just deeds live, or crooked wrongs arise;
> And shower the wealth of seasons from above,
> Their kingly office, delegate from Jove.
> The gods then form'd a second race of man,
> Degenerate far, and silver years began;
> Unlike the mortals of a golden kind,
> Unlike in frame of limbs, and mould of mind,—

[1] Saturnus is the presiding spirit of the Italian Golden Age, the Titan ruler whose defeat is a major ·eme of Keats's poem in this tradition, *The Fall of Hyperion*. His myth and attributes are otherwise so ·in to those of the Greek Cronus that the two were for long considered identical. Strictly speaking, this "a mistake which recent research has set right".—A. S. Murray, *Manual of Mythology*, New York, 1935, 27.

Yet still a hundred years beheld the boy,
Beneath the mother's roof, her infant joy,
All tender and unform'd: but when the flower
Of manhood bloom'd, it wither'd in an hour.
Their frantic follies wrought them pain and woe;
Nor mutual outrage would their hands forego:
Nor would they serve the gods, nor altars raise,
That in just cities shed their holy blaze.
Them angry Jove ingulf'd; who dared refuse
The gods their glory and their sacred dues:
Yet named the second bless'd, in earth they lie,
And second honours grace their memory.

    The sire of heaven and earth created then
A race, the third, of many-languaged men:
Unlike the silver they; of brazen mould,
Strong with the ashen spear, and fierce, and bold;
Their thoughts were bent on violence alone,
The deed of battle, and the dying groan.
Bloody their feasts, with wheaten food unbless'd;
Of adamant was each unyielding breast.
Huge, nerved with strength, each hardy giant stands,
And mocks approach with unresisted hands.
Their mansions, implements, and armour shine
In brass; dark iron slept within the mine.
They by each other's hands inglorious fell,
In freezing darkness plunged, the house of hell.[1]
Fierce though they were, their mortal course was run;
Death gloomy seized and snatch'd them from the sun.
Them when th' abyss had cover'd from the skies,
Lo! the fourth age on nurt'ring earth arise:
Jove form'd the race a better, juster line;
A race of heroes, and of stamp divine:
Lights of the age that rose before our own;
As demigods o'er earth's wide regions known.
Yet these dread battle hurried to their end;
Some where the seven-fold gates of Thebes ascend,
The Cadmian realm; where they with fatal might
Strove for the flocks of Oedipus in fight.

---

[1] In the light of the modern theory that the Ice Ages brought about a perversion of the Golden Age culture, it is interesting to find that Hesiod's hell is a freezing darkness, and two thousand years later Dante in the lowest circle of Hell sees those who had betrayed their benefactors wholly covered with ice. At the level of poetic imagery Hesiod's frozen Hell is, of course, the antithesis of the sun-warmed, fruitful earth of the Golden Age.

Some war in navies led to Troy's far shore;
O'er the great space of sea their course they bore,
For sake of Helen with the beauteous hair;
And death for Helen's sake o'erwhelm'd them there.
Them on earth's utmost verge the god assign'd
A life, a seat, distinct from human kind;
Beside the deepening whirlpools of the main,
In those bless'd isles where Saturn holds his reign,
Apart from heaven's immortals: calm they share
A rest unsullied by the clouds of care;
And yearly thrice, with sweet luxuriance crown'd,
Springs the ripe harvest from the teeming ground.
   Oh! would that Nature had denied me birth
Midst this fifth race, this iron age of earth;
That long before within the grave I lay,
Or long hereafter could behold the day!
Corrupt the race, with toils and griefs oppress'd,
Nor day nor night can yield a pause of rest:
Still do the gods a weight of care bestow,
Though still some good is mingled with the woe.
Jove on this race of many-languaged man
Speeds the swift ruin, which but slow began;
For scarcely spring they to the light of day,
E'er age untimely strews their temples gray.
No fathers in the sons their features trace;
The sons reflect no more the father's face:
The host with kindness greets his guest no more;
And friends and brethren love not as of yore.
Reckless of Heaven's revenge, the sons behold
The hoary parents wax too swiftly old,
And impious point the keen dishonouring tongue,
With hard reproofs, and bitter mockeries hung;
Nor grateful in declining age repay
The nurturing fondness of their better day.
Now man's right hand is law; for spoil they wait,
And lay their mutual cities desolate.
Unhonour'd he, by whom his oath is fear'd,
Nor are the good beloved, the just revered.
With favour graced, the evil doer stands,
Nor curbs with shame nor equity his hands;

> With crooked slanders wounds the virtuous man,
> And stamps with perjury what hate began.
> Lo! ill-rejoicing Envy, wing'd with lies,
> Scattering calumnious rumours as she flies,
> The steps of miserable men pursue,
> With haggard aspect, blasting to the view:
> Till those fair forms, in snowy raiment bright,
> Quit the broad earth, and heavenward soar from sight:
> Justice and Modesty, from mortals driven,
> Rise to th' immortal family of heaven:
> Dread sorrows to forsaken man remain;
> No cure of ills; no remedy of pain.

Hesiod's narrative, then, records the fall of mankind from the paradisal Golden Age, of which some vestige remains in the terrestrial paradise beyond the sea, the blessed isles whither the heroes slain in battle are transported, though one cannot help agreeing with the translator, C. A. Elton, that their claim to beatitude is not very obvious. Hesiod's despair at being born into the Iron Age rather than long before *or long after*, plainly suggests a cyclic theory in which the Golden Age of the remote past would some day return. Not only is the Golden Age past, and present—though geographically remote—it is also future, and this extra-temporal character of the tradition is a vital point in understanding the later European poetry in the same tradition. Moreover, some radiance of the Golden Age is shed by the earth-hovering spirits on the virtuous here and now, "still some good is mingled with the woe". After another forty lines of invective against the degenerate age in which he lives, figured as a hawk that seizes a nightingale and cries, "I rend my banquet", Hesiod shows what is bestowed upon the good, before returning to denunciations of fallen mankind in which we need not follow him much farther:

> But they, who never from the right have stray'd,
> Who as the citizen the stranger aid,
> They and their cities flourish; genial Peace
> Dwells in their borders, and their youth increase:
> Nor Jove, whose radiant eyes behold afar,
> Hangs forth in heaven the signs of grievous war.
> Nor scathe nor famine on the righteous prey;
> Feasts, strewn by earth, employ their easy day:

The oak is on their hills; the topmost tree
Bears the rich acorn, and the trunk the bee:
Burden'd with fleece their panting flocks: the face
Of woman's offspring speaks the father's race:
Still prosper they, nor spread in ships the sail;
For life's abundance gifts the fruitful vale.
But o'er the wicked race, to whom belong
The thought of evil and the deed of wrong,
Saturnian Jove, of wide-beholding eyes,
Bids the dark signs of retribution rise:
States rue the wrongs a sinful man has done,
And all atone the wickedness of one.
The god sends down his angry plagues from high,
Famine and pestilence; in heaps they die.
He smites with barrenness the marriage bed,
And generations moulder with the dead:
Again in vengeance of his wrath he falls
On their great hosts, and breaks their tottering walls;
Arrests their navies on the ocean plain,
And whelms their strength with mountains of the main.

Just as there is doubt about whether or not Orpheus sailed in the *Argo*, so there is a contradiction in the poetic tradition. On the one hand it is the Argonauts who, as in Morris's poem already quoted, are vouchsafed the vision of the Hesperides, "This memory of the age of gold". On the other the virtuous of the succeeding age do not "spread in ships the sail" while the navies of the wicked are sunk at sea. But the contradiction is not very difficult of resolution. The arboreal or even the agricultural society is essentially the *rooted* society, its life and its whole harmony with Nature is related to the organic cycle of its own place in the world. Seafaring, beginning with the ominous cutting-down of the tree—and the modern world turning its forests into pulp to print trash has still to awaken to the disaster it is preparing—is a still more rootless life than that of the nomad and his grazing herd. It leads in due course to the dependent economy, the implication in foreign wars, and sometimes to an over-populated homeland caught in the trap its own past "prosperity" has laid. The point is one worth the earnest consideration of the people of a great seafaring island whose rule of the waves is fast declining. We shall presently see that even at the end of the

Elizabethan age the true poet's image of England was another Eden, not Drayton's Virginia treasure trove. So much for this Coleridgean curse upon the voyager. The city too becomes at least suspect as the proliferation of mechanical principles and technical potentialities rather than an organic development within the total natural environment. But when the fatal breach with Nature has been made, the Orphic harmony smithered into discords, as in Hesiod's Iron Age, or Morris's industrialised nineteenth century, then the poet must have another image of journey, to convey the distance that now separates the Golden Age, shrunk to a fabled island from all that area on which urban anthropocentric cultures are pursuing their vicious and ultimately insane extractive economies destroying plant and animal, making a desert and calling it civilization since it is no longer possible to call it peace. That is the inner meaning of the voyage in this poetic tradition. One might say that it is the symbol of the New World's imaginative rediscovery of the Old World.

Orpheus himself, so the legend runs, was torn to pieces by other human beings in a Bacchanalian orgy. But the end of Orpheus was the beginning of Orphism, and we must notice a few essential facts about that development in order to understand what is being said by the great Greek poets and seers who came later.

"All over the world, at a different stage of religious evolution sacred animals and human beings were ceremonially killed and eaten", writes Bertrand Russell. "In different regions, this stage occurred at very different dates. Human sacrifice usually lasted longer than the sacrificial eating of human victims; in Greece it was not yet extinct at the beginning of historical times." The powerful cult of Dionysus or Bacchus "contained many barbaric elements such as tearing wild animals to pieces and eating the whole of them raw". "It was not in this form that it influenced the philosophers but in the spiritualised form attributed to Orpheus, which was ascetic." The beneficent influence of the Orphic reformers became apparent in the sixth century before Christ, and gold burial plate have been found in Italy and Crete which date from the centuries immediately following, bearing such Orphic verses as—

> Hail, hail to thee journeying the right hand road
> By holy meadows and groves of Persephone.

"There was no Orphic church but there existed a number of conventicles of initiates into the Orphic mysteries, all having a similar doctrine and rules of life, but lacking any sort of federal organisation and probably having no common standard of ortho-doxy. . . . The rules of purity included abstinence from animal food of all kinds."

W. K. C. Guthrie authoritatively emphasises the tradition of the Golden Age common to Hesiod and Orphism, the associated abstinence from flesh foods and the likelihood that belief in such a primal state is historically correct:

"Both Plato and Empedokles refer to an age of innocence, before the sin of meat-eating was known among men, as having actually existed in past times. This too they would find in Orphic writings. The idea of the *Saturnia regna*, the Golden Age when before the coming of Zeus to power a race of men lived on earth in happiness and plenty and goodness under the kindly rule of Kronos, was a familiar one to the Greeks, and made immortal for them by the poetry of Hesiod. There is a tradition that the Orphics adopted the succession of ages and adapted and altered it to fit their own scheme . . . as Proklos reports. . . . 'The religious poet (*theologos*) Orpheus gives us three races of men: first the golden, which he says was founded by Phanes, second the silver . . . third the Titanic. . . .' We may be sure that when Plato speaks of the tradition of a past age in which men thought it impious to eat flesh or to offer it to the gods, and compares this custom to the Orphic life, then it was a characteristic attributed in some Orphic writings themselves to a pre-Titanic age. These Orphic verses, themselves lost to us, have found their reflection in the philosophers of the classical age, and a more distant echo of them persists in the poetry of Vergil." "Not so easily suppressed", he adds, "was the association of the Golden Age with the abstinence from flesh", and notes that "this notion of a past age in which sacrifices were bloodless is perhaps historically correct, a dim recollection of a state of things which once existed".

Russell says it is certain that Orphic doctrines contain much that seems to have its source in Egypt, and it was chiefly through Crete that Egypt influenced Greece. Other authorities consider that the doctrines include certain religious speculations characteristic of that age, and probably resulting from the contact of Greece with the

East. There is a strong resemblance between Orphic observances and the Ordinance of Manu that, "having considered the source of flesh, and the slaughter and confinement of animals, one should cease from eating all flesh". And there is such close agreement between Hesiod and Hinduism on the subject of the Golden Age that we must briefly consider the possible influence of Vedic, Buddhist and Jaina traditions on the Greeks in general and on Plato and Pythagoras in particular.

In a standard work on Indian mythology, A. Berriedale Keith points out that the Vedic tradition of ages of the world "has both striking points of contrast with and affinity to the idea of the four ages set forth in Hesiod". Keith's assumption that Hesiod had no intuition of a recurrent cycle of ages is questionable, but as to the affinity there can be no doubt. "This is the golden age of the world, in which all is perfect. Neither gods nor demons of any kind yet exist, and sacrifices are unknown, even bloodless offerings. The Vedas themselves have no existence, and all human infirmities, such as disease, pride, hatred and lack of mental power, are absent." Keith cites Manu and the Puranas.

The epic and didactic *Mahabharata*, parts of which may be as late as the earliest centuries of the Christian era, is the source of the charming Indian play *Shakuntala* by the fifth-century poet Kalidasa, which has remained a favourite in its own country and has been translated into most Western languages. Its values are those of the older Indian traditions. The King is forbidden to shoot a deer,[1] and is entertained with fruits in the sacred grove where trees are tended and animals protected. He is to guard the hermits from flesh-eating devils. In the grove he meets the hermit-girl at one with Nature and is eventually reunited with her on the Gold Peak where he first sees their son, a boy who is good to all animals and to whom the wild beasts are tame. We are reminded of Orpheus and the Hindu musician-god Krishna with his flute which entrances all who hear it, and of the Indian *Hitopadesa*, the source of the didactic animal fables of Aesop and others.

---

[1] It is interesting to compare this tale with the tradition that the second-century Roman martyr, St Eustace, or Eustachius, was converted by a vision as he was hunting in the forest, of a cross between the antlers of a stag, while a voice cried to him: "Why persecutest thou me?" After being exposed in vain to the lions in the amphitheatre, Eustace and his family are said to have been burned to death in a oven shaped like a stag.
Compare Schiller's *The Alp Hunter*, where the spirit of the deep protects the hind and demands why he seeks the life of animals when "There's room upon the earth for all". That poem, too, is founded upon legend, from the Valley of Ormond, in the Pays de Vaud.

Arthur W. Ryder, the translator of *Shakuntala*, remarks that "Kalidasa understood in the fifth century what Europe did not learn until the nineteenth, and even now comprehends only imperfectly: that the world was not made for man, that man reaches his full stature only as he realises the dignity and worth of life that is not human." This, of course, is fundamental Hindu doctrine, and in the third book of the *Mahabharata* we are briefly reminded that:

> The constant virtue of the Good is tenderness and love
> To all that live in earth, air, sea—great, small—below, above:
> Compassionate of heart, they keep a gentle will to each:
> Who pities not, hath not the Faith. Full many a one so lives.

The *Bhagavad Gita*, which forms part of the *Mahabharata* and is often called the New Testament of Hinduism, discriminates between three basic human types to which are assigned appropriate diets in harmony with this basic principle, and the whole development is epitomised in our time by the life and faith that Mahatma Gandhi based upon the teaching of the *Gita*.

The century in which Orphic activity appears in Greece, the century of Pythagoras and of Aesop, is also the century when Mahavira and Gautama were teaching harmlessness and its dietary implications in India[1]—doctrines connected with belief in transmigration of souls derived from the still earlier Brahmanism; and that belief also now enters our Greek story. Criticising the widespread assumption that "relations between Greece and India did not begin, or rather did not assume appreciable importance until the time of Alexander's conquests", René Guénon observes that "the

[1] "The Buddhists declare that the Lord Buddha was prayed to forbid animal food absolutely, but he would not. It is argued that in the flesh itself, when the life is gone from it, there is nothing particularly sacred: therefore it is permissible to sustain life on it. Your servants may buy meat ready for sale in the market: it would be there just the same if you did not send to buy it, but you ought not to tell them to give an order for some sort of meat which is not on sale; still less should you incite people to snare or shoot wild animals for your table."

"Among the Jainas, however, whose scriptures were first collected from aural report and written down by a learned man in the sixth century A.D. . . . this rigid rule is followed by every Jaina to this day, be he monk or layman. The vegetarian principle involved in *Ahimsa* is observed rigorously by all—clearly with no bad effect on health after a trial of about twenty-four centuries, for the Jaina's physique is excellent, and they are less subject to disease than the other communities."

"For a long time Europeans believed the two religions to have but one source, and Jainism was dismissed as a Buddhist sect. The Jainas, however, always strongly held that they had a founder of their own, namely, Mahavira, and they even declared that Buddha was not his master but his disciple. After much research, Professor Jacopi decided the case in their favour by assigning to them a separate origin. Both Sakya Muni and Mahavira are generally believed to have flourished in the sixth century B.C."—Countess Evelyn Martinengo Cesaresco, *The Place of Animals in Human Thought*, 1909, pp. 193, 172, 169.

In 1931 the Jains numbered about one and a quarter million.

The Bible of the World records that Mahavira began his ministry c. 590 B.C., some thirty years earlier than Buddha but therefore at the time of his birth, since Gautama retired to the forest at the age of twenty-nine. Mahavira, the editors point out, is thus virtually contemporary with the founders of three other great living religions, Confucius, Lao-Tze and Zoroaster (or Zarathustra), and also Jeremiah, Ezekiel and Isaiah.

points of resemblance which can be established with the doctrines of India are much more striking and numerous in the pre-Socratic age than in subsequent periods", and thinks that "the early Greek philosophers may even have been acquainted not only with the Hindu but also with the Buddhist doctrines, for they certainly did not live earlier than Buddhism. Furthermore, Buddhism soon spread outside India into Asiatic regions lying nearer to Greece, which were therefore more accessible; this circumstance would appear to strengthen the argument, which is quite a tenable one, that borrowings were made chiefly, though not exclusively, from the Buddhist civilisation."

Yet, whatever developments in Greece had in common with Buddhism at first, their later course remained separate to a remarkable degree. That Eastern tradition hardly reappears in English poetry before the publication in 1879 of Sir Edwin Arnold's Buddhist poem, *The Light of Asia*, "which has become a classic in its kind". It is not highly esteemed by literary historians but its nobility of purpose and wide popular influence is conceded. Through it shines a light that has illuminated the lives of millions of Asia's people and does so still. "In India", wrote Rabindranath Tagore, who was probably thinking mainly of the Jainas, "a whole people who were once meat-eaters gave up taking animal food to cultivate the sentiment of universal sympathy for life, an event unique in the history of mankind." But to the Hindus also the cow is the living symbol of the bounty of Nature and though shamefully neglected in a land where famine is never far away it may not be slaughtered.

In Arnold's poem, Gautama the Buddha intervenes in an animal sacrifice:

> But Buddha softly said,
> "Let him not strike, great king!" and therewith loosed
> The victim's bonds, none staying him, so great
> His presence was. Then, craving leave, he spake
> Of life, which all can take but none can give,
> Life, which all creatures love and strive to keep,
> Wonderful, dear, and pleasant unto each,
> Even to the meanest: yea, a boon to all
> Where pity is, for pity makes the world
> Soft to the weak and noble for the strong.

Unto the dumb lips of his flock he lent
Sad pleading words, showing how man, who prays
For mercy to the Gods, is merciless,
Being as God to those: albeit that Life
Is linked and kin, and what we slay have given
Meek tribute of the milk and wool, and set
Fast trust upon the hands that murder them.
Also he spake of what the holy books
Do surely teach, how that at death some sink
To bird and beast, and these rise up to man
In wanderings of the spark which grows purged flame.
So were the sacrifice new sin, if so
The fated passage of a soul be stayed.
Nor, spake he, shall one wash his spirit clean
By blood: nor gladden gods, being good, with blood;
Nor bribe them, being evil; nay, nor lay
Upon the brow of innocent bound beasts
One hair's weight of that answer all must give
For all things done amiss or wrongfully,
Alone, each for himself, reckoning with that
The fixed arithmic of the universe,
Which meteth good for good and ill for ill,
Measure for measure, unto deeds, words, thoughts;
Watchful, aware, implacable, unmoved;
Making all futures fruits of all the pasts.
Thus spake he, breathing words so piteous,
With such high lordliness of ruth and right,
The priests drew down their garments o'er the hands
Crimsoned with slaughter, and the King came near,
Standing with clasped palms reverencing Buddh;
While still our Lord went on, teaching how fair
This earth were if all living things be linked
In friendliness and common use of foods,
Bloodless and pure; the golden grain, bright fruits,
Sweet herbs which grow for all, the waters wan,
Sufficient drinks and meats. Which when these heard,
The might of gentleness so conquered them,
The priests themselves scattered their altar flames
And flung away the steel of sacrifice;
And through the land next day passed a decree
Proclaimed by criers, and in this wise graved

25

On rock and column: "Thus the King's will is:—
There hath been slaughter for the sacrifice
And slaying for the meat, but henceforth none
Shall spill the blood of life nor taste of flesh,
Seeing that knowledge grows, and life is one,
And mercy cometh to the merciful."
So ran the edict, and from those days forth
Sweet peace hath spread between all living kind,
Man and the beasts which serve him, and the birds,
On all those banks of Gunga where our Lord
Taught with his saintly pity and soft speech.

Direct Indian influence on the greatest of the Greek philosophers
is boldly claimed by E. J. Urwick. Believing that "the Platonic
doctrines are not easily understood without reference to the Indian
teaching", he gives a full exposition of *The Republic* as a Western-
ised adaptation of Vedantic teaching on righteousness, which may
at least call attention to a neglected influence. Urwick likewise
contends that "Every one of the doctrines, which we know formed
the 'gospel' of Pythagoras and the Pythagorean brotherhood at
Crotona, was an almost exact reproduction of the cardinal doctrines
of the Indian Vidya and the Indian Yoga—so much so that Indian
Vedantins to-day do not hesitate to claim Pythagoras as one of
themselves, one of their great expounders, whose very name was
only the Greek form of the Indian title, Pitta Guru, or Father-
teacher."

Whatever Pythagoras, who lived later in the sixth century B.C.
than Gautama, may have drawn from Buddhism, Jainism or Vedic
sources, whether directly or during his sojourn of more than twenty
years in Egypt, the immediate influence on his life and faith was that
of the Orphic priesthood that first became widely active in the same
century. The ways of life of Orphism and Pythagoreanism were
similar, says W. K. C. Guthrie, "the abstention from meat was the
foremost requirement of both, and both proclaimed the same end,
katharsis or the purification of the soul". "The influence of Orphism
on Pythagoreanism, was very great", records another authority, "so
that it is often impossible to separate the two, although one was
primarily a religion, the other a system of philosophy." Iamblichus,
one of the Neoplatonist biographers of Pythagoras, considered it

beyond doubt that Pythagoras had received "auxiliaries from Orpheus" when composing his lost *Sacred Discourse*, which is said to have contained "the flower of the most mystical place in Orpheus".

Moreover, Pythagoras is believed to have embodied many of the more remarkable qualities of Orpheus himself. Relating how Pythagoras, on the way from Samos to Crotona, paid some fishermen to throw back alive into the sea the fish they had caught, how he stroked a wild bear, fed it on maize and acorns and successfully enjoined it to desist from harming living creatures, and how he called down and stroked an eagle, Iamblichus declares that, "Through these things, therefore, and other things similar to these, he demonstrated that he possessed the same dominion as Orpheus, over savage animals, and that he allured and detained them by the power of voice proceeding from the mouth". For the training of his disciples, Pythagoras evokes a divine music, from the lyre and the human voice, whose special virtue is drawn from "the sublime symphonies of the world", celestial music that he alone can hear. His own divinity is suggested in the story of his showing his golden thigh to the Hyperborean Abaris, to show him he was not wholly mistaken in that assumption.

Pythagoras "forbade the most contemplative of philosophers, and who have arrived at the summit of philosophical attainments, the use of superfluous and unjust food, and ordered them never to eat anything animated, nor in short, to drink wine, nor to sacrifice animals to the Gods, nor by any means to injure animals, but to preserve most solicitously justice towards them. And he himself lived after this manner, abstaining from animal food, and adoring altars undefiled with blood", records Iamblichus. "He was likewise careful in preventing others from destroying animals that are of a kindred nature with us, and rather corrected and instructed savage animals through words and deeds than injured them through punishment. And farther still, he also enjoined those politicians that were legislators to abstain from animals. . . . He permitted, however, others whose life was not entirely purified, sacred and philosophic, to eat of certain animals; and for these he appointed a definite time of abstinence." These laymen were forbidden for various reasons to eat the heart or brain of any animal, mallows, beans and the fishes melanurus and erythinus. "And he established as laws other precepts

27

similar to these, beginning through nutriment to lead men to virtue", an attitude restated two thousand five hundred years later by Tolstoy in his essay *The First Step*, where also restraint from killing and eating sentient creatures is made the essential starting-point of all advance towards virtue. Plato, as we shall see, argues for very much the same point in *The Laws*.

"Pythagoras likewise ordered abstinence from animal food, for many other reasons", Iamblichus resumes later, "and likewise because it is productive of peace. For those who are accustomed to abominate the slaughter of animals as iniquitous and preternatural, will think it to be much more unlawful to kill a man, or engage in war. But war is the leader and legislator of slaughter. For by this it is increased and becomes strong and powerful." There is a manifold variety of natural food at man's disposal. "For there are an infinite number of fruits, and an infinite multitude of roots, which the human race uses for food. It likewise uses all-various kinds of flesh; and it is difficult to find any terrestrial, aerial or aquatic animal, which it does not taste. It also employs all-various contrivances in the preparation of these, and manifold mixtures of juices. Hence it properly follows that the human tribe is insane and multiform, according to the motion of the soul. For each kind of food that is introduced into the body becomes the cause of a certain peculiar disposition." This was probably the theoretical basis of those Pythagoreans who, on their return from exile, "applied themselves to medicine, and restored health to those that were sick by a certain diet; of which methods of cure they were themselves the authors".

There are conflicting accounts of the disaster that overtook the Pythagorean community at Crotona in the lifetime of Pythagoras but it seems that almost all of the disciples were trapped in a friend's house and deliberately burnt to death by their supposedly civilized neighbours. Some accounts say that Pythagoras also perished in the burning house, others that he was saved from the fire by the heroism of his disciples but was pursued and murdered, others that he was killed elsewhere or that he voluntarily relinquished life at a later date after a prolonged fast. But as with Orpheus himself, and to a less extent Hesiod, and in our own time Gandhi, there seems to have been a sudden and bloody end to a peaceful and dedicated life at the hands of a hostile world.

Like Orpheus, Pythagoras left no surviving treatise, but like Orpheus too he left an unquestioned tradition of teaching, of which a popular exposition published some three hundred years after his death, and later entitled *The Golden Verses of Pythagoras,* is believed to epitomise the sage's doctrines of self-control:

> learn to conquer these:
> Thy belly first; sloth, luxury, and rage.
> Do nothing base with others or alone,
> And, above all things, thine own self respect.
>
> . . . . .
>
> Nor shouldést thou thy body's health neglect,
> But give it food and drink and exercise
> In measure; that is, to cause it no distress.
> Decent, without vain show, thy way of life:
> Look well to this, that none thou envious make
> By unmeet expense, like one who lacks good taste.
> No niggard be: in all the mean is best.

Some of these lines are embarrassingly like the few precepts that Polonius borrowed from Lyly. But there is an echo of something finer in this:

> Eat not the foods proscribed, but use discretion
> In lustral rites and the freeing of thy soul:
> Ponder all things, and stablish high thy mind
> That best of charioteers.

The last phrase is more reminiscent of one of the central images of the *Bhagavad Gita.* The simile may be older than *The Golden Verses* though the *Gita* is now considered to belong to the early centuries of the Christian era. At that later time, five hundred years after Pythagoras had taught in Southern Italy, his doctrines were given a living monument by the poet Ovid, not otherwise a very Pythagorean figure. The last and greatest book of the *Metamorphoses* is devoted to the Pythagorean philosophy and bears that title. We shall presently quote from Dryden's fine translation and discuss its influence on English poets of the Restoration and the eighteenth century.

Empedocles, the fifth-century B.C. Greek philosopher-statesman of Agrigentum in Sicily—then one of the most splendid cities in the world—who is said to have declined kingship but longed for deification and to have died, as in Matthew Arnold's dramatic poem, *Empedocles on Etna*, by leaping into a volcano, was also a Pythagorean. Diogenes Laertius says, on the evidence of Timaeus, that Empedocles "was a pupil of Pythagoras, adding that, having been convicted at that time of stealing his discourses, he was, like Plato, excluded from taking part in the discussions of the school". Diogenes Laertius then cites a passage in which some suppose Empedocles is referring to Pythagoras himself in terms of veneration, and then quotes Neanthes as saying that "down to the time of Philolaus and Empedocles all Pythagoreans were admitted to the discussions. But when Empedocles himself made them public property by his poem, they made a law that they should not be imparted to any poet. He says the same thing also happened to Plato, for he too was excommunicated." This may well explain why *The Golden Verses of Pythagoras* have about them the air of being a third-rate imitation of a noble teaching.

It is therefore doubly unfortunate that we do not possess the greater part of the long poem in which Empedocles is said to have imparted the essence of the Pythagorean teaching as he received it at first hand from the sage himself. Some such source, we must suppose, was the basis of Ovid's very full treatment of the tradition.

W. E. Leonard, who has translated the surviving fragments of Empedocles' poems into English verse, writes that he "seems to have conceived a period when love was predominant, and all the elements formed one great sphere. Since that period discord gained more sway. . . . As man, animal and plant were composed of the same elements in different proportion they have an identity in nature. They all have sense and understanding, mind in man being always dependent upon the body. Hence the precepts of morality are with Empedocles largely dietetic." Another authority observes that "Empedocles belongs to . . . the generation of Sophocles, and lived in the West where the Orphic-Pythagorean beliefs in transmigration of souls and the blessed life of the good had gained a firm hold. This accounts for the union of science and mysticism in his work. . . . At the same time his picture of the four-element world as being alternatively pulled together by love and torn apart by hate is also a development under Orphic-Pythagorean influences of the Hesiodic idea of degeneration from the age of gold to the age of iron."

Among the fragments of the poem *On Nature* are three lines—

> Trees have perennial fruit, perennial fronds,
> Laden with fruit the whole revolving year,
> Since fed forever by a fruitful air

that call up a vision of the balmy days of the Golden Age, of which the same poet sings in *The Purifications*:

> not then with unmixed blood
> Of many bulls was ever an altar stained;
> But among men 'twas sacrilege most vile
> To reave of life and eat the goodly limbs.
>
> All things were tame, and gentle toward men,
> All beasts and birds, and friendship's flame blew fair.

Speaking as a believer in the transmigration of souls, ("That the soul of our grandam might haply inhabit a bird", as Malvolio defines the doctrine when asked for the opinion of Pythagoras concerning wild fowl) Empedocles continues:

> Will ye not cease from this great din of slaughter?
> Will ye not see, unthinking as ye are
> How ye reave one another unbeknown?
>
> The father lifteth for the stroke of death
> His own dear son within a changéd form,
> And slits his throat for sacrifice with prayers—
> A blinded fool! But the poor victims press,
> Imploring their destroyers. Yet not one
> But still is deaf to piteous moan and wail.
> Each slits the throat and in his halls prepares
> A horrible repast. Thus too the son
> Seizes the father, children the mother seize,
> And reave of life and eat their own dear flesh.
>
> . . . . .
>
> Ah woe is me! that never a pitiless day
> Destroyed me long ago, ere yet my lips
> Did meditate this feeding's monstrous crime!

No stronger sanction against flesh-eating can be imagined than this identification of it with cannibalism, and it must have been a powerful influence on the Mediterranean peoples, whose minds were vaguely troubled with memories of sacrificial customs in which their own ancestors had slaughtered and devoured both animals and men.

This chapter began with a tribute to Orpheus from Pindar, who spent ten years in Sicily not long before Empedocles was writing these poems there, and was, "we may suppose, brought into contact with the Orphic cult in Sicily, where, along with the Pythagorean discipline, it had found a congenial home". W. K. C. Guthrie thinks it unlikely that Pindar was himself a wholehearted supporter of these beliefs; rather was he a staunch defender of the traditional Olympian religion of the Greeks. "The second Olympian ode, which is our chief Pindaric source for transmigration and the life of the blessed", Guthrie writes, "was written for recital before a Sicilian audience, who might be supposed to be more interested than others in Orphico-Pythagorean beliefs, and for a king who was nearing the end of his own earthly life." This was the magnificent Sicilian prince, Theron of Agrigentum, to whom the ode was dedicated. But J. A. Stewart considers Plato's reverence for the genius of Pindar largely derived from the genuine Orphic content of his poems, which Plato in turn adopted. The circumstance of Pindar's death in his eightieth year, of which there are other instances later in this tradition, adds colour to the belief that Pindar's Orphico-Pythagoreanism was more than skin deep. "His departure from life was gentle", we are told, "for it took place while he was sitting in a public assembly, and, till the spectators retired, he was thought to be slumbering." In the Golden Age, his countryman Hesiod had sung, "Death as a slumber pressed their eyelids down".

Some of the mythological genealogies in the second *Olympian Ode* derive from Hesiod's *Theogony*, and the description of the Isles of the Blessed has been called the "one great theological passage" in Pindar. Those islands too were known to Hesiod, as the Elysian plains beyond the seas were known to Homer and, if Morris interpreted the tradition aright, the Hesperides were known to Orpheus and the Argonauts. The view of Pindar as a primeval sports-commentator with a flair for opportunist mythological digression

becomes hard to sustain. When events of the Heroic Age are described, D. W. Turner observes, Pindar finds means to make his
myths didactic and pertinent to the victor whose triumph he is
celebrating. After the crucial description of the Isles of the Blessed
Pindar openly claims:

> On my quiver'd arm I bear
> Many an arrow swift and rare;
> Dealt to the wise delight they bring,
> To vulgar ears unmeaning ring.

He is deliberately claiming inner significances for his myth. "The
original conception, in Greek as in Celtic mythology," writes
J. A. Stewart, citing the *Voyage of Bran*, i, 329, for the Celtic comparison, "of Islands of the Blessed was that of an Elysium or Paradise,
somewhere on the surface of the Earth, inhabited by gods, in which
also certain elect heroes, who have been translated thither, enjoy
in the flesh eternal felicity. This is the conception which meets us in
Homer, Hesiod, Pindar, and the Hymn to Harmodius and Aris-
togeiton. But in course of time this original conception was modified
in the interest of morality and religion, especially the religion of the
Orphic cult, and the Islands of the Blessed came to be regarded as
the abode of the *souls* of the virtuous generally."

> O'er the Good soft suns the while
>   Through the mild day, the night serene,
> Alike with cloudless lustre smile,
>   Tempering all the tranquil scene,
> Theirs is leisure; vex not they
> Stubborn soil or watery way,
> To wring from toil want's worthless bread:
> No ills they know, no tears they shed,
> But with the glorious Gods below
> Ages of peace contented share.
>   Meanwhile the Bad with bitterest woe
> Eye-startling tasks, and endless tortures wear.

> All, whose steadfast virtue thrice
>   Each side the grave unchanged hath stood
> Still unseduced, unstain'd with vice,
>   They by Jove's mysterious road

> Pass to Saturn's realms of rest,
> Happy isle that holds the blest;
> Where sea-born breezes gently blow
> O'er blooms of gold that round them glow
> Which Nature boon from stream and strand
> Or goodly tree profusely pours;
> Whence pluck they many a fragrant band,
> And braid their locks with never-fading flowers.

Papyri discovered as recently as 1900 give many specimens of Pindar's poems other than Odes, but Myers (1892) quotes a fragment, here given in full, that appears to be another Pindaric description of the Isles of the Blessed. At any rate the emphasis on "bodily feats" seems to agree with Stewart's reading, that in the Pindaric Isles eternal felicity is still supposed to be enjoyed in the flesh:

. . . For them shineth below the strength of the sun while in our world it is night, and the space of crimson-flowered meadows before their city is full of the shade of frankincense-trees, and of fruits of gold. And some in horses, and in bodily feats, and some in dice, and some in harp-playing have delight; and among them thriveth all fair-flowering bliss: and fragrance streameth ever through the lovely land, as they mingle incense of every kind upon the altars of the gods. . . .

Orpheus himself might be imagined among the harp-players in such a place, for the Orphic paradise is a place of wholly human joy, rather than of mere asceticism. Pindar, in the fourth *Pythian Ode*, mentions Orpheus among the Argonauts who went in quest of the Golden Fleece, but—like the Argonautic island of Lemnos—the terrestrial paradises discovered by Pindar's heroic voyagers in other poems are of a more sensual kind, preoccupied with felicity in the flesh.

We noticed that Hesiod's description of the slain heroes of the Brass Age descending into freezing darkness agrees with the hypothesis that a historical Golden Age was in fact terminated by a glacial period when, with vegetation prisoned beneath ice, the human survivors were forced to kill and eat domesticated and other animals. Pindar, too, includes among the ancient traditions of the human race a post-glacial or cold period in the Peloponnesus, with snowstorms on the plains of Pisa and icebergs in the Pontus, at the time of Zeus (who overthrew the Cronus or Saturn of the Golden Age) and Pindar's translator F. A. Paley considered there was strong geological and other evidence of the historicity of such a period.

This possibility throws an interesting light on Pindar's account, in the tenth *Pythian Ode*, of the journey of Perseus to the Hyperboreans. The term was used by Vergil, Horace and later poets to mean only "most northerly" but the Hyperboreans were supposed by the Greeks to live in a land of perpetual sunshine beyond the north wind—an eloquent indication of climatic conditions among themselves. The character of the perfected earthly life envisaged is a Golden Age adulterated with the animal sacrifice and copulation of the more brutal Age of Brass, which are said to "scare not the Muse" who still discovers some of the true joys of the Golden Age— music, blissful feasts, health, longevity, peace, simplicity and freedom from toil:

> 'Tis not for man to climb the brazen heaven:
> They on the farthest fairest beach
> The bark of mortal life can reach
> Through dangers braved their sails display.
> But who with venturous course through wave or waste
> To Hyperborean haunts and wilds untraced
> E'er found his wondrous way?

> There Perseus press'd amain,
> And midst the feast enter'd their strange abode;
> Where hecatombs of asses slain
> To soothe the radiant god
> Astounded he beheld. Their rude solemnities,
> Their barbarous shouts Apollo's heart delight:
> Laughing the rampant brutes he sees
> Insult the solemn rite.

> Still their sights, their customs strange
> Scare not the Muse; while all around
> The dancing virgins range,
> And melting lyres and piercing pipes resound.
> With braids of golden bays entwined
> Their soft resplendent locks they bind,

> And feast in bliss the genial hour:
> Nor foul disease, nor wasting age,
> Visit the sacred race; nor wars they wage,
> Nor toil for wealth or power.

Perseus is the son of Danae by Zeus, who descended to her in a golden shower. Zeus was also involved in the elevation of the island of Rhodes from the sea and, as Homer and Pindar variously relate, that too received a shower of gold. In the *Iliad*, Homer describes the nine vessels of Tlepolemus "from Rhodes, with everlasting sunshine bright" and describes how formerly—

> A fleet he built, and with a numerous train
> Of willing exiles wanders o'er the main;
> Where, many seas and many sufferings past,
> On happy Rhodes the chief arrived at last:
> There in three tribes divides his native band,
> And rules them peaceful in a foreign land;
> Increased and prosper'd in their new abodes
> By mighty Jove, the sire of men and gods;
> With joy they saw the growing empire rise,
> And showers of wealth descending from the skies.

In the seventh *Olympian Ode*, Pindar relates how:

> Their high-built shrine the Rhodians sought,
> With unburnt offerings heap'd; yet showers of gold
> Jove pour'd upon them from the cloud.

He then reverts to the creation of this golden island as the special dominion of the Sun (which Pindar, following Hesiod and contrary to Homer, describes as the offspring of Hyperion) by consent of Saturnian Jove (that is, Zeus, son of the Golden Age god Cronus).

> Yet once, as stories say,
> When Jove Earth's ample field to part
> 'Mongst all the gods decreed, the Lord of Day
> Above the waves saw not the Rhodian steep,
> By fate still bound within the dungeon of the deep.
> Absent on function high the lot
> Of the bright Sun his peers forgot;
> And he the purest of the skies
> Shared not the rich terrestrial prize.

Warn'd of the wrong, high Jove again
The partial lots proposed, in vain;
"For that mine eye discerns", the Sun replied,
"A region gathering from the ground,
For man's delight all planted round
With fruits and pastures fair beneath the foaming tide."

Forthwith commanded he to rise
The golden-vested Lachesis,
With lifted hand and fatal nod
To give the sanction of a god,
Join'd with Saturnian Jove, and swear,
When time that shoal to heav'n should rear,
Its realm his boon should be. The pledge divine
On truth's unfailing pinion flew;
Promise to Consummation grew;
Up sprung the beauteous isle and budded from the brine.

But here too, as among the Hyperboreans, attributes are conflicting.
The sweet atonement appointed to Tlepolemus in Rhodes begins
with "the steaming sacrifice of sheep" and continues with a list of
victories in which are prominent "the brazen shield in Argos" and
memorials of brass in Arcadia.

In the first *Olympian Ode*, dedicated to Hiero of Syracuse, Pindar
finds it relevant to his Sicilian audience to repudiate the accusation
of cannibalism as expressed in the legend that Tantalus dismembered
his son and cooked the flesh for the gods who condescended to dine
with him. On the contrary, says Pindar, the gods took the purest
repast and the boy was carried back to heaven in a radiant car with
steeds of gold, rather than in a divine digestive tract.

Forthwith some envious foe was found
Whispering th' unseemly slander round,
"How all into the bubbling cauldron cast
Thy mangled limbs were seethed and shred
In fragments on the table spread,
While circling Gods looked on and shared th' abhorr'd repast."

Far be from me and mine the thought profane,
That in foul feast celestials could delight!
Blasphemous tale!

37

The crime for which Tantalus was punished, Pindar explains, was presumption and abuse, culminating in theft of the food of the gods:

> He from th' Immortals their ambrosial fare,
>   The nectarous flood that crown'd their bowl,
>   To feast his earth-born comrades, stole;
> Food that, by their celestial grace,
>   Eternal youth to him had given.

In Pindar's poetry, then, the Orphico-Pythagorean tradition strongly survives; but the dietary virtues are apparently reserved for the gods alone, and the "heroic" habits of blood-sacrifice and flesh-eating are regarded as normal features in the Hyperborean paradise beyond the icy north and in the equally sunny elysium on the island of Rhodes; the Islands of the Blessed preserve something of the Hesiodic purity. In Pindar's paradises gold is alloyed with brass. But the full rigour of the Birth of Iron was known in a north that had no Hyperborean oases, the bitter, wounding north of the Finnish traditions that survived to become the *Kalewala*.

Yet the Orphic tradition, with elaborate doctrines of pre-existence, penance, reincarnation and final purification, and even a sacramental tasting of blood, a survival of the sanguinary Dionysian orgies it had reformed, was growing in power and influence in these later times. There is no doubt that ancient tradition made Orpheus the foe of Dionysus and a victim of his worshippers. At Eleusis, on the coast north-west of Athens, the pure Orphism had strongly influenced the rites which are the subject of a poem by Schiller quoted in our final chapter. At these harvest festivals, says Jane Harrison, omophagia was wholly absent—as it continued to be among the Orphics except on sacramental occasions—and the ceremonies consisted of elaborate purifications and fasting followed by the removal of the taboo on first-fruits. It is impossible to over-look the resemblance of these practices to the symbolic communion through the flesh and blood of the god and the bloodless harvest festival of Christianity.

We get glimpses of Orphism through the eyes of three great Greek playwrights, Aeschylus, Aristophanes and, especially, Euripides and then it rises to its highest expression in the myths of Plato and on the lips of the Platonic Socrates.

Aeschylus died in the south of Sicily a few years after Pindar, having also been a conspicuous figure at the magnificent court of Hiero of Syracuse. He was, says W. K. C. Guthrie, keenly interested in the legends of Orpheus himself and portrayed the early conflict between Dionysiac and Apolline religion in a tragedy on Orpheus which has not survived. In Sicily Aeschylus must also have known the leading Pythagoreans, and a comment by Cicero implies that he himself was of their number, although there is no other evidence on the point.

Euripides was a young man in his early twenties when Aeschylus died, and Guthrie judges on the evidence of his plays that he too was at least sympathetic to Orphism. A fragment of a lost play by Euripides is strongly reminiscent of the simplicity of that tradition:

> Since what need mortals, save twain things alone,
> Crush'd grain (heaven's gift), and streaming water-draught?
> Food nigh at hand, and nature's aliment—
> Of which no glut contents us. Pampered taste
> Hunts out device of other eatables.

Elsewhere, Euripides put these lines into the mouth of an Orphic priest:

> Robed in pure white I have born me clean
>   From man's vile birth and coffined clay,
>   And exiled from my lip alway
> Touch of all meat where life hath been.[1]

Guthrie, who considers Euripides in the main an eclectic, also remarks that when Theseus taunts Hippolytus, in the play of that name, with the Orphic ideals he has adopted, it is Hippolytus who is the hero, and Theseus who is to be proved in the wrong:

> Now is thy day! Now vaunt thee; thou so pure
> No flesh of life may pass thy lips! Now lure
> Fools after thee; call Orpheus King and Lord;
> Make ecstasies and wonders! Thumb thine hoard
> Of ancient scrolls and ghostly mysteries—

The crime of which he is wrongly accused is sexual.

An earlier Chorus in the same play expresses the longing for the

---

[1] "The most interesting literary document extant on Orphic ceremonial is a fragment of the *Cretans* of Euripides, preserved for us by Porphyry in his treatise on 'Abstinence from Animal Food'."—Jane Harrison, *Prolegomena to the Study of Greek Religion*, p. 478.

Hesperides that Orpheus and the Argonauts saw, where such a life
was not mistaken for ascetic eccentricity or hypocrisy:

> To the strand of the Daughters of the Sunset,
> The Apple-Tree, the singing and the gold;
> Where the mariner must stay him from his onset,
> Yea, beyond that Pillar of the End
> That Atlas guardeth, would I wend:
> Where a voice of living waters never ceaseth
> In God's quiet garden by the sea,
> And Earth, the ancient life-giver, increaseth
> Joy among the meadows, like a tree.

One of Euripides' final plays, *The Bacchae*, written some twenty
years later, goes behind Orphism to describe the earlier Dionysian
orgies of frenzied women:

> Thereat, for fear they tear us, all we fled
> Amazed; and on, with hands unweaponéd
> They swept towards our herds that browsed the green
> Hill grass. Great uddered kine then hadst thou seen
> Bellowing in sword-like hands that cleave and tear,
> A live steer riven asunder, and the air
> Tossed with rent ribs or limbs of cloven tread.
> And flesh upon the branches, and a red
> Rain from the deep green pines. Yea, bulls of pride,
> Horns swift to rage, were fronted and aside
> Flung stumbling, by those multitudinous hands
> Dragged pitilessly. And swifter were the bands
> Of garb'ed flesh and bone unbound withal
> Than on thy royal eyes the lids may fall.

At the climax of the play, King Pentheus is torn to pieces—as
Orpheus was—by demented Maenads, led by his own mother, and
the poetry seems deliberately to recapitulate the earlier outrage:

> and the torn flesh cried,
> And on Autonoe pressed, and all the crowd
> Of ravening arms. Yea, all the air was loud
> With groans that faded into sobbing breath,
> Dim shrieks, and joys and triumph-cries of death.
> And here was borne a severed arm, and there
> A hunter's booted foot; white bones lay bare

With rending; and swift hands ensanguinéd
Tossed as in sport the flesh of Pentheus dead.
    His body lies afar. The precipice
Hath part, and parts in many an interstice
Lurk of the tangled woodland—no light quest
    To find.

In the play's final judgment, Dionysus, son of Zeus—and it was from the worship of Dionysus that Greek drama arose—spares only Pentheus' grandfather Cadmus, and his wife, to survive wars and tribulations and be saved alive "to the Islands of the Blest". Earlier the Chorus of Maidens invoked the god:

    Oh, where art thou? In thine own
    Nysa, thou our help alone?
    O'er fierce beasts in orient lands
      Doth thy throning thyrsus wave,
      By the high Corycian Cave,
    Or where stern Olympus stands;
    In the elm woods and the oaken,
      There where Orpheus harped of old,
      And the trees awoke and knew him,
      And the wild things gathered to him,
    As he sang amid the broken
      Glens his music manifold?

In Aristophanes' comedy *The Frogs*, written immediately after the death of Euripides, there is a discussion between Aeschylus, Euripides and Bacchus, who mocks at the choice of a story about a king long dead and buried as theme for a tragedy and the lamentation of a Chorus. Aeschylus answers with a vindication of the poet's high vocation:

    Such is the duty, the task of a poet,
    Fulfilling in honour his office and trust.
    Look to traditional history—look
    To antiquity, primitive, early, remote:
    See there, what a blessing illustrious poets
    Conferr'd on mankind, in the centuries past,
    Orpheus instructed mankind in religion,
    Reclaim'd them from bloodshed and barbarous rites:
    Musaeus delivered the doctrine of medicine,

And warnings prophetic for ages to come:
Next came old Hesiod, teaching us husbandry,
Ploughing, and sowing, and rural affairs,
Rural economy, rural astronomy,
Homely morality, labour, and thrift:
Homer himself, our adorable Homer,
What was his title to praise and renown?
What, but the worth of the lessons he taught us,
Discipline, arms, and equipment of war?

"According to the words which Aristophanes puts into the mouth of Aeschylus in *The Frogs*", Guthrie remarks, "Orpheus was famous for two things—he revealed the ways of initiations, and he taught men to abstain from killing. This then must certainly have been to contemporaries the most striking feature of Orphic life . . . the two things necessary for salvation were initiation and an Orphic life, we might have said simply initiation and a meatless diet." It is possibly significant—especially in the author of the *Lysistrata*, in which women "go on strike" until men stop war—that Homer is displaced in the historical recital and Hesiod is put next to Orpheus and the semi-mythological Musaeus. In reclaiming mankind from bloodshed, Orpheus must be credited with repudiating human as well as animal slaughter, and the lessons of adorable Homer were therefore flatly contradicted, an example of dissent among poets that brings to mind Plato's discussion of what poetry should and should not be tolerated in an ideal society.

But before turning to Plato we must not overlook the fact that other poets of the Old Comedy delighted to write about an orgiastic Utopia usually described by classical commentators as a Land of Cockaigne and certainly, like the passage quoted from Petronius in the next chapter, a forerunner of that mediaeval antithesis of the Golden Feast. The fragments survive in an obese work of the third century A.D., the fifteen books of the *Deipnosphistae*, or Sophists at Dinner, of Athenaeus, "the oldest cookery book that has come down to us" as its Loeb translator, C. B. Gulick remarks, and an epitome of plain thinking and high living.

One of the characters at these marathon banquets, Democritus quotes the description of the comic writer Crates in which it is literally unnecessary for the diner to raise his hand to his mouth

The table moves itself, the pot is self-emptied, self-cooked food walks into the mouth. Democritus then cites a whole string of other authors. Telecleides, for instance, who adds "a river of broth, whirling hot slices of meat" flowing by the couches, while roast thrushes fly into the gullet. "Men were fat in those days and every bit mighty giants." Pherecrates is quoted as giving the same particulars but also as placing the whole scene where one feels it to belong, in Hell, where "Rivers full of porridge and black broth flowed babbling through the channels spoons and all, and lumps of cheese-cakes too. Hence the morsel could slip easily and oilily of its own accord down the throats of the dead. Blood puddings there were, and hot slices of sausage lay scattered by the river-banks like oysters. Yes, and there were roasted fillets nicely dressed with all sorts of spiced sauces. Close at hand, too, on platters were whole hams with shin and all, most tender, and trotters well boiled which gave forth a pleasant steam; ox-guts and pork-ribs most daintily browned", the usual flying roast thrushes, girls in silk shawls with the hair shorn from their bodies, and other amenities. "Oh, you'll be the death of me if you dally any longer here", cries the enraptured hearer, "when the whole pack of you should dive at once into Tartary." No wonder the Orphics felt it necessary to advise their dead to keep to the right side of the road. Perhaps the most ghastly sight of all is that attributed to Pherecrates in yet another of these nightmares where "The trees on the mountains will put forth leaves of roast kids' guts, tender cuttle fish, and boiled thrushes." And Democritus concludes his sickening recital with more instances, this time from Nicophon and Metagoras whose "cutlets automatically stewed dart downwards into the mouth, others upwards at our very feet, while cakes of fine meal swim round us in a circle."

Plato was a younger contemporary of Aristophanes and outlived him by thirty years. Like Empedocles and Aeschylus, and the poet who so greatly influenced his own beliefs, Pindar, Plato was associated with the Sicilian princes, although his efforts to transfigure those opulent tyrants into something like the philosopher-kings of his own ideal were completely unsuccessful. More than a century before, the Orphic societies had appeared in Italy and Sicily, often closely associated with Pythagoreanism centred on the Sage's community at Crotona in Southern Italy. But, as J. A. Stewart says, "As Athens became more and more the centre of Greek life, the Orphic cult gravitated thither . . . and meeting the need of 'personal religion' felt especially during the tribulation caused by the Peloponesian War and the Great Plague, it had in Plato's day become firmly rooted in the city. . . . Now, what is Plato's attitude to this Orphic cult? This question can be answered, in part at least, without difficulty:—He derived the main doctrine, together with most of the details, of his Eschatological Myths . . . directly, and through Pindar, from Orphic sources", which lay at the foundation of Pindar's theology and later influenced Plutarch, Vergil and the Neoplatonic doctrines. Guthrie agrees that Plato was, "not only the greatest original genius of Greek religious thought, but also the one to whom the Orphic cycle of beliefs made the strongest appeal" and Bertrand Russell calls the Platonic Socrates, "the perfect Orphic saint". As mythologer, if not as dialectician, Plato was himself essentially a poet of the highest order, and Stewart finds in the Myths, "Orphic doctrine, refined by poetic genius for philosophic use".

Like Homer, Hesiod and Pindar, Plato visualised Isles of the Blessed to which the fortunate were translated after death. But where the earlier poets imagined them to be somewhere in a Western ocean, Plato's Isles, while physically connected with the region we inhabit, are on the True Surface of the Earth described in the *Phaedo* Myth, a place in the purer upper air or aether, which Stewart compares with the terrestrial paradise on the summit of the Purgatorial island-mountain in Dante's *Divine Comedy*. Dante's ascent from thence to the Celestial Paradise is also closely paralleled in the eschatology of the *Phaedo* Myth. "The ultimate destination of the virtuous soul is not any Terrestrial Paradise of sensual delights . . . but a Celestial Paradise, to which the Pure Intelligence rises by its own strenuous effort, recalling to memory more and more clearly the Eternal Truth which it ardently loves."

Plato's aetiological myths, describing the origin of mankind, include a description of the Golden Age of Cronus, a vision of metempsychosis, and a mystic chronology to explain the recurrent cycle of ages and phases that we detected in Hesiod. In the Golden Age, Plato says in the *Politicus* Myth, men were made from the Earth itself, which was kept in harmonious rotation by the God. When Cronus relinquished control the Earth began to turn of its own volition in the retrograde direction, and this continues in the present time, that of Zeus. Cronus will eventually resume control, and motion and the order of ages will be corrected, so that future Iron, Brass and Silver Ages will eventually give way to a new Golden Age. There is thus a future terrestrial paradise for the whole world as well as a paradise on the True Surface of the Earth for virtuous souls after death, and ultimately a Celestial Paradise.

The Eleatic Stranger, who relates the *Politicus* Myth, tells of the life when Cronus reigned: "The age when all things came forth spontaneous for the use of man congrueth not with this present motion, but with that which was before; for then did God control with His providence the whole revolution, and all the parts of the Universe everywhere were divided amongst gods appointed to rule over them, as now gods rule over certain places; and, moreover, living creatures, according to their kinds, were assigned unto angels,[1] as flocks unto divine shepherds, each angel being wholly sufficient in all things for his own flock, so that there was then no savagery, no devouring of one another, no war or sedition at all: nay, time would fail to tell of all the consequences of that dispensation. Now, therefore, hearken, and I will declare the truth that is in the old Tale of the time when all things came forth spontaneous. God himself was then the Overseer and Shepherd of men, even as now man, being as a god amongst the creatures which are beneath him, is the shepherd of their tribes. When God was our Shepherd there was no civil government, and men had not wives and children, but all came up again into life from the Earth, without remembrance of aught before. Instead of these things they had an abundance, from trees and other plants, fruits which the Earth without husbandry brought forth spontaneous. For the most part they lived without raiment and without couches, in the open air; for the seasons were tempered to do them no hurt; and soft beds had they in the grass which sprang abundantly from the Earth."[2]

---

[1] In the *Politicus* these divine beings are not deceased men of the Golden Age, as they are in Hesiod, and also elsewhere in Plato, e.g. *Republic*, V, 468.

[2] The *Protagoras* Myth gives an account inconsistent with the *Politicus* Myth here quoted and which anticipates Lucretius. In the *Protagoras* there is said to have been conflict between creatures and some carnivorism prior to the appearance of man, who first fed on fruits, but, himself menaced and sometimes devoured by wild animals, combined with his fellows to form cities for self-defence. In short, a Myth of hostile natural environment. Its status as a Platonic Myth has been disputed.

In the Myth of the Earth-born, in the *Republic*, the image here given to heighten identity with natural order (compare our "earth to earth" in the Burial Service) is given a twist to serve military propaganda: the earth-born must defend his "mother-land". Gold, silver, iron and copper are then only the distinctive qualities of rulers, soldiers, husbandmen and craftsman, a wide departure from the tradition.

The Stranger goes on to relate that the "nurslings of Cronus" had the faculty of conversing with beasts as well as men, and the implication of metempsychosis is confirmed in the Myth of Er in the *Republic*, where Orpheus himself is seen choosing a swan's life, while a swan chooses the life of a man, and other human souls choose the lives of a nightingale, an eagle, a lion and an ape. "Beasts likewise were changed into men and into one another, the unjust into those that were savage, and the just into those that were tame: yea in everywise were they mixed together." Metempsychosis here and elsewhere in Plato is a means of "Correction and Purification", says Stewart, ". . . its *raison d'être* also in the Orphic teaching and in Buddhism".

The fable in *The Laws* told by the Athenian is more strictly didactic than the Myths so far discussed. Only the state governed by a god can be truly ordered, he says. Long before the time of any existing cities there was a community under Saturn, of which the city now best administered is a sort of imitation. In the happy Saturnian time there was spontaneous production and everyone had sufficient. Saturn, knowing that man was not fit to rule other men, placed over them a race of Daemons, benevolent guardian spirits who imparted peace and modesty, good legislation and justice, and made mankind free from suspicion and happy. Such bliss is unattainable under any human government, however constituted, but "we ought, by every contrivance, to imitate the life said to have been under Saturn; and, as far as immortality is in us, by being obedient to it, to administer both publicly and privately our houses and cities, calling law the distribution of mind".[1]

[1] In the *Cratylus*, again, the Golden Age life as related in Hesiod is quoted as a precept for virtuous living:

SOCRATES: Know you then whom Hesiod says are daemons?
HERMOGENES: I do not understand.
S.: But know you not that he says, the golden race of men was first created?
H.: This I know.
S.: He says, then, concerning it,

> But when concealed had Destiny this race,
> Daemons there were, called holy, upon earth
> Good, ill-averters, and of man the guard.

H.: What then?
S.: I think he calls the race golden, not as being naturally of gold, but as being beautiful and good. And I infer this, from his calling us an iron race.
H.: You speak the truth.
S.: Do you not then think, that if any of those living now were good, Hesiod would say he was of that golden race?
H.: Probably . . .
S.: . . . Hence both he, and many other poets, say well, who say that when a good man shall have reached his end, he receives a mighty destiny and honour, and becomes a daemon. . . .
H.: And I, Socrates, seem to myself to give entirely the same vote with you on this point.

In this context it should be remembered that Socrates himself was credited with having a familiar spirit, and in Plato's *Phaedrus* Socrates rises to go away but is stopped by his familiar spirit who obliges him to stay and recant his blasphemous dispraise of Love.

In the sixth book of *The Laws*, the Athenian makes a direct appeal to a time free from the vices of the present, no longer fabulous but supposedly historical: "We see the custom remaining even now in many places of men sacrificing each other; and we hear, on the contrary, that in others we did not dare to taste the flesh even of oxen, and that the sacrifices to the gods were not animals, but cakes moistened with honey, and fruits, and other innocent offerings of a similar kind; and that we entirely abstained from flesh, as it was unholy to eat it, and to defile the altars of the gods with blood; and that there existed what is called the Orphic life amongst persons of that period, keeping fast to all things without life, but abstaining on the contrary from all that had life." Clinias concurs with the speaker that, "What you say is greatly bruited abroad, and is very easy to be believed". Why has this been mentioned? the Athenian asks himself, and answers that man is subject to a threefold want and desire. Virtue depends on the proper development of these appetites, which are full of "a mad feeling"—a blind urge and revulsion. On being born man is thus driven by ungoverned impulses of eating and drinking and later comes the sexual passion. "These three diseases it is meet to turn from what is called the most pleasant to the best, and to endeavour to keep them down by the three greatest [bonds], fear, and law, and truthful reasoning; and by making use moreover of the Muses, and the gods who preside over contests, to extinguish their increase and influx." A long discussion of discipline and education follows, leading to a vindication of common meals of first-fruits of the earth, an ideal vitiated by segregation and slavery. Similarly, when the subject of hunting is reached, fishing with hook or net, catching birds and snaring animals is condemned and associated with the vices of piracy and theft. But hunting with dogs, horses and hand weapons is approved as a sort of gymnastic, a exercise of skill and courage. The martial ideal is, in short, proving incompatible with the Orphic life, music and gymnastic in the military tempo cannot be harmonised.

In the tenth book of the *Republic*, where Homer is disadvantageously compared with Pythagoras, the Orphic music is for the moment triumphant. Homer has written about war and armies, civic constitutions and human education. But which states have been better constituted, which acknowledge him as lawgiver, what wars did he conduct or command? Not one. What then are his discoveries? None. "But if not in a public manner, has Homer the repute of having lived as a private instructor to any who delighted in his conversation, and to have delivered down to posterity a certain Homeric manner of life—just as Pythagoras was remarkably beloved on this account, and, as even to this day, such as denominate themselves Pythagoreans appear to be somehow eminent beyond others in their manner of life? Neither, said he, is there anything of this kind related about Homer"—and the conclusion is reached that "all the poets, beginning from Homer, are imitators of the images of virtue, and of other things about which they compose, but yet do not attain to the real truth". The argument may lack insight into the springs of creative composition and creative action, but is cited to reveal Plato's inclination towards Pythagoras as well as Orpheus, and against the Homeric cult, and to emphasise that the Pythagorean and Orphic ways of life were substantially the same and were alike contrary to the gory triumphs and orgies of Homer's "heroes".

Yet Homer was struggling with Orpheus in the bosom of Plato as in the heart of Greece. The ideal city of the *Republic* might be described as "a Dorian State and a Pythagorean Order" but, "of all Utopias, Plato's is the most militant", writes Stewart, ". . . Civilization, as its course is sketched in the Second Book of the *Republic*, begins with the formation of an Army. . . . The doctrine of the *Republic*, then, is that the leaders of civilization are men who have been trained for war. . . . Were war to cease in the world, what would become of the Platonic system of Education? Plato does not expect—and, more than that, does not wish—to see war cease. His ideal of earthly life is Hellas in arms against Barbarism." Stewart stresses the conflict of values: "The ideal, adumbrated in the *Republic* and the Atlantis Myth, of a Hellenic Empire, created and maintained by the joint forces of Athens and Delphi, is one between which and the ideal of personal salvation through union with God there is a very real opposition. The more men live for the ideal of national greatness the less does the ideal of personal salvation concern them. Plato's chief interest undoubtedly was in the ideal of personal salvation, which he derived mainly from the Orphic religion; and it was exactly this Orphic element in Platonism which constituted by far the most important part of its influence on subse quent philosophy, and, more especially, on the development of Christian doctrine and practice. The Heaven and Hell and Purgatory of Christian eschatology come not, to any large extent, from Jewish sources, or from the teaching of the Gospels and Epistles, but mainly from the Apocalypses, which are thoroughly Orphic in matter and spirit. It is not to be supposed, of course, that the Apocalypses got their Orphism or 'Sacramentalism'—to use a term which covers the ground better—from Plato. They got it from the teaching of the Orphic and similar sacramental societies which existed throughout the world. But the direction given, at the beginning, to Christian thought and feeling, and, it is safe to add, to Christian practice, by the influence of these societies, produced a condition of religious belief which afterwards lent itself easily to the influence of the refined Orphism of the Platonists."

This fundamental conflict in the *Republic* is reflected in a dialogue in Book II, between Socrates and Glaucon:

"Let us begin, then, with a picture of our citizens' manner of life, with the provision we have made for them. They will be producing corn and wine, and making clothes and shoes. When they have built their houses, they will mostly work without their coats or shoes in summer, and in winter be well shod and clothed. For their food, they will prepare flour and barley-meal for kneading and baking, and set out a grand spread of loaves and cakes on rushes or green leaves. Then they will lie on beds of myrtle-boughs and bryony and make merry with their children, drinking their wine after the feast with garlands on their heads and singing the praises of the gods. So they will live pleasantly together; and a prudent fear of poverty or war will keep them from begetting children beyond their means.

"Here Glaucon interrupted me: You seem to expect your citizens to feast on dry bread.

"True, I said; I forgot that they will have something to give it a relish, salt, no doubt, and olives, and cheese, and country stews of roots and vegetables. And for dessert we will give them figs and peas and beans; and they shall roast myrtle-berries and acorns at the fire, while they sip their wine. Leading such a healthy life in peace, they will naturally come to a good old age, and leave their children to live after them in the same manner.

"That is just the sort of provender you would supply, Socrates, if you were founding a community of pigs.

"Well, how are they to live, then, Glaucon?

"With the ordinary comforts. Let them lie on couches and dine off tables on such dishes and sweets as we have nowadays.

"Ah, I see, said I; we are to study the growth, not just of a state, but of a luxurious one. Well, there may be no harm in that; the consideration of luxury may help us to discover how justice and injustice take root in society. The community I have described seems to me the ideal one, in sound health as it were: but if you want to see one suffering from inflammation, there is nothing to hinder us. So some people, it seems, will not be satisfied to live in this simple way; they must have couches and tables and furniture of all sorts; and delicacies too, perfumes, unguents, courtesans, sweetmeats, all in plentiful variety. . . ." (Here follows a substantial catalogue of "luxuries"—including the arts.)

". . . And then swineherds—there was no need for them in our original state, but we shall want them now; and a great quantity of sheep and cattle too, if people are going to live on meat.

"Of course.

"And with this manner of life physicians will be in much greater request.

"No doubt.

"The country, too, which was large enough to support the original inhabitants, will now be too small. If we are to have enough pasture and plough land, we shall have to cut off a slice of our neighbours' territory; and if they too are not content with necessaries, but give themselves up to getting unlimited wealth, they will want a slice of ours.

"That is inevitable, Socrates.

"So the next thing will be, Glaucon, that we shall be at war.

"No doubt.

"We need not say yet whether war does good or harm, but only that we have discovered its origin in desires which are the most fruitful source of evils both to individuals and to states.

"Quite true."[1]

The Timaeus and *The Critias* continue the discussion begun in *The Republic*. The praise of the State militant is repeated in *The Timaeus* by a brief recital of the victory of a primordial Athens— later destroyed in a great flood that washed the fertile earth from

[1] Cornford, whose translation is quoted, seems to read his own opinion into the original when he comments that this passage is "partly a satire on a sentimental nostalgia for a supposed primitive state of nature, to which had it ever existed, there could, as Plato saw, be no return". For Cornford on "Plato and Orpheus" see *Classical Review*, December, 1903.
Plato's argument is urgently relevant to the present world food crisis, on the evidence of representative demographers, economists and nutritionists, quoted in my talk *Bread and Peace* (C. W. Daniel).
There are occasional references in later Utopian literature to the same theme. Sir Thomas More criticises a pastoral food economy and leaves slaughter to slaves. Samuel Butler satirises vegetarianism in *Erewhon* and misses the economic point. In H. G. Wells' *Modern Utopia* the slaughter of animals for food has ceased. For other Utopias see Marie Louise Berneri, *Journey through Utopia*, Kegan Paul, 1950.

the now rocky heights—over the aggressive armies of Atlantis, the island-continent fated to sink beneath the ocean. The full story of Atlantis is reserved for *The Critias*, where it is the main theme of the short fragment of a work thought to have been cut short by Plato's death.

The conflict in Plato's soul between the Orphic and Homeric traditions results in a very different emphasis in what he tells us of Atlantis in *The Critias*, which does not seem to be due to a common tendency to moralize about the militarism of former foes. In the centre of the island-continent of Atlantis was an island-mountain where dwelt one of the earth-born ancients of whom we learned in the *Politicus* Myth. His daughter was beloved of the god Poseidon who "with his divine power, agreeably adorned the centre of the island, causing two fountains of water to shoot upwards from beneath the earth, one cold and the other hot, and making every variety of food to spring abundantly from the ground. He also begat five twin-male children"—who became the ten kings whose descendants ruled Atlantis. This holy grove of Poseidon continued to have "all varieties of trees, reaching a wonderful height, owing to the excellence of the soil". There the Atlanteans erect a temple lined with silver but with pinnacles and statues of gold, and the Hesiodic echo of the four Ages is sustained in the facing of the concentric walls at varying distances from the island's circumference with orichalcum "which is now known only by name" by tin and by brass respectively.

Atlantis had the "fairest of all plains" and produced "an abundance of wood for builders, and furnished food also for tame and wild animals"—so plentifully as to sustain vast numbers of elephants, who are in the Myth only to contribute this ponderous image of vegetable plenty! The implication seems to be that wild and tame animals lived without preying on each other, and there was also everything that man could desire: "Besides these, whatever odorous plants the earth now bears, whether roots or grass, or woods or distilling gums, or flowers or fruits,—these it bore and produced them to perfection. And yet, further, it bore cultivated fruits, and dry edible fruits, such as we use for food;—all these kinds of food we call vegetables,—together with all that trees bear, as drinks, meats, and ointments; and those also, whose fruits, such as acorns, being used in sport and pleasure, are with difficulty hoarded up, together with certain dainty fruits for dessert that might provoke the satiated palate, or please the sick;—all these that once existing and warmly-acclimated island bore, sacred, beautiful, wonderful, and infinite in quantity."

The Atlanteans were at first fit inhabitants of this natural paradise, but as the spirit in them dwindled they fell to digging metals, making blood sacrifices, waging war, so that their history is a simulacrum of the history of mankind as told by Hesiod:

For many generations, as long as the natural power of the god sufficed them, they remained obedient to the laws and kindly affected towards the divine nature to which they were allied:—for they possessed true and altogether lofty ideas, and practised mildness united with wisdom, in reference to the casual occurrences of life and towards each other. Hence, looking above everything except virtue, they considered things present as of small importance, and contentedly bore, as a burden, the mass of gold and other property; nor were they deceived by the intoxication of luxury, or rendered intemperate through wealth;—but on the other hand being sober, they acutely perceived that all these things are increased through common friendship mingled with virtue, and that by too anxiously pursuing and honouring them, these goods themselves are corrupted, and with them [friendship] itself likewise perishes. To such a mode of reasoning then, and the abiding of such a nature, was it owing that they made all the progress that we before described. But when the divine portion within them became extinct through much and frequent admixture of the mortal nature, and the manners of men began to hold sway, then, through inability to bear present events, they began to exhibit unbecoming conduct and to the intelligent beholder appeared base, destroying the fairest among their most valuable possessions,—though all the while held by those who were unable to see a true life of happiness based on truth, to be in the highest degree worthy and blessed, though filled with avarice and unjust power. Zeus, however, the god of gods, who rules according to the laws, and is able to see into such things perceiving an honourable race in a condition of wretchedness, and wishing to inflict punishment on them, that they might become more diligent in the practice of temperance, collected all the gods into their own most ancient habitation, which indeed, being situated in the centre of the whole world, beholds all things that have had a share in generation: —and having assembled them, he said. . . .

There *The Critias* breaks off. If it is true that Plato died before he set down the speech of the god of gods, we must ourselves hear that divine judgment as best we can. Plato's world too was falling away from its purest inspiration, and incurring the wrath of the gods. Civilization was based on a war-making economy. Greece, and the West, had rejected the Socratic City of Pigs for the triumphant progress of the Gadarene swine.

Orpheus was to die again, the harmony lost. The Iron Age must fulfil its cataclysmic destiny with blood sacrifice, animal slaughter, inflamed passions and fratricidal war. A century before the Christian era, the poet Antipater of Sidon wrote a lament that found its way into the *Greek Anthology*:

> No longer, Orpheus, will thy soothing song,
> Oaks, rocks, and lawless monsters lead along:
> No longer lull the stormy winds to sleep;
> The hail, the drifting snow, the raging deep.
> Thou'rt gone; the Muses weep around thy bier,
> And most, Calliope, thy mother dear.
> Why mourn our children lost, when from the grave
> The gods themselves cannot their offspring save!

Orpheus had once braved Hell and returned again to the light. Some day the divine hand would turn the world back to its right motion and celestial harmonies would be heard again. So the old myth ran. Meanwhile jewels fell from the skies, fragments of the True Surface of the Earth where the Golden Age life was lived by the virtuous in the Islands of the Blessed; and sometimes a great poet heard singing in the air.

FROM TOWN TO TOWN OF THE ROMAN LANDS

"MANY peoples have been used to observe an annual period of license, when the customary restraints of law and morality are thrown aside, when the whole population give themselves up to extravagant mirth and jollity, and when the darker passions find a vent which would never be allowed them in the more staid and sober course of ordinary life. Such outbursts of the pent-up forces of human nature, too often degenerating into wild orgies of lust and crime, occur most frequently at the end of the year", writes Sir James Frazer in *The Golden Bough*. "Now of all these periods of license the one which is best known and which in modern language has given its name to the rest is the Saturnalia. This famous festival fell in December, the last month of the Roman year, and was popularly supposed to commemorate the merry reign of Saturn, the god of sowing and of husbandry, who lived on earth long ago as a righteous and beneficent king of Italy, drew the rude and scattered dwellers on the mountains together, taught them to till the ground, gave them laws and ruled in peace. His reign was the fabled Golden Age: the earth brought forth abundantly: no sound of war or discord troubled the happy world: no baleful love of lucre worked like poison in the blood of the industrious and contented peasantry. Slavery and private property were alike unknown: all men had all things in common. At last the good god, the kindly king, vanished suddenly; but his memory was cherished in distant ages, shrines were reared in his honour, and many hills and high places in Italy bore his name."

Saturn, god of sowing and husbandry, is a deity of the agricultural period of human development; the Greek Cronus represented an earlier phase of food-gathering. Otherwise the attributes of the Golden Age are substantially the same in both cases. Yet the

Roman Saturnalia was not a celebration of law and peace but an orgiastic mass indulgence that had more in common with the frenzied Maenads who tore to pieces and devoured wild animals and men. Frazer goes on to describe how the Saturnalia was celebrated among the Roman soldiery on the Danube. One of their number was chosen as Saturn. "Thus arrayed and attended by a multitude of soldiers he went about in public with full license to indulge his passions and to taste of every pleasure, however base and shameful. But if his reign was merry, it was short and ended tragically; for when the thirty days were up and the festival of Saturn had come, he cut his own throat on the altar of the god whom he personated." Early in the fourth century, the refusal of a Christian soldier to play the part of the god and indulge his last days with debauchery led to decapitation and subsequently to his canonization as a saint. Frazer concludes that in an earlier and more barbarous age it was the universal custom to celebrate the feast of Saturn in this fashion.

Rome itself staged gladiatorial games and mortal combats between human beings and wild animals as public entertainment, and if the capital celebrated the Saturnalia without a sacrificial human victim, the festival was otherwise bestial enough to disgust Seneca, whose own plays are hardly anaemic. "December is the month", he tells a correspondent, "when the city most especially gives itself up to riotous living. Free licence is allowed to the public luxury. Every place resounds with the gigantic preparations for eating and gorging, just as if the whole year were not a sort of *Saturnalia*." Frazer considers the Carnivals of modern Italy and other countries identical with the Saturnalia, though only a very pale reflection of it, and those festivities just before Lent[1] draw their name from the expressive Latin phrase *carnem levare*—"put away meat". Seneca's disgust at the Saturnalian excesses was Pythagorean, and his first-century contemporary Juvenal invoked the same name to reproach Roman gluttony: "What would not Pythagoras denounce, or whither would he not flee, could he see these monstrous sights—he who abstained from the flesh of all other animals as though they were human?" The idea of flight is a grim

[1] See Pieter Brueghel's picture of the "Battle of Carnival and Lent". Bosch had painted a picture on the same theme, and one by another Netherlands artist was in the possession of the Medici family in Florence in the fifteenth century.

reminiscence of the destruction of the sage's community at Crotona in Southern Italy and the massacre of his disciples by an infuriated mob some six hundred years before. Pythagoreanism could still be dangerous in Italy. Seneca explains why his father made him give it up: "Certain foreign religions became the object of the imperial suspicion, and, amongst the proofs of adherence to the foreign *cultus* or superstition, was that of abstinence from the flesh of animals."[1]

Yet still, as Plato had observed in his time, "even to this day such as denominate themselves Pythagoreans appear to be somehow eminent beyond others in their manner of life". For the most part these latter-day Pythagoreans were not Romans by birth, though they gravitated to Rome, much as Orphism migrated from Sicily to Athens. In the first century, Neopythagoreanism was a Graeco-Alexandrian school that combined something of Pythagorean ethics and Platonic mysticism with Orphic mysteries and Oriental philosophy, a combination less heterogeneous than it might seem. The Neopythagoreans profoundly influenced the Essenes who, Josephus records, "pursue the same kind of life as those whom the Greeks call Pythagoreans" and are sometimes believed to have imparted the same teaching to Jesus. But Neopythagoreanism also furnished Neoplatonism with the material for a stand against Christianity, although several leading Christians agreed in practice with the Pythagorean diet whilst carefully differing in principle from anything that smacked of metempsychosis.

Plutarch, who died early in the second century, was—like Hesiod—a Boeotian Greek. He was trained at Athens and became an initiate of the Dionysian mysteries. Despite the eminence to which he rose in Rome he returned to die in his native province, where he was archon and priest of the Pythian Apollo. Plutarch's *Essay on*

---

[1] History repeats itself. Notwithstanding that the monastic Rules of St. Basil and St. Benedict enjoined abstinence from flesh, a similar test was applied some fifteen hundred years later to those accused of Manicheism: "Under inquisitorial torture", according to Howard Williams (*The Ethics of Diet*, 1907 ed., p. 80), "and in the few recorded instances of reversion to the Catholic faith, to *eat flesh* was a chief outward sign of reconciliation with the Church."

Some twenty years ago, revolutionary Russia dissolved the Moscow Vegetarian Society, probably because the usual dietary habit was associated with Tolstoyan anarchism and pacifism, and the Society may also have given encouragement to the more bizarre diversionist activities of the surviving Russian Doukhobors. Russia, however, is not without the usual mythology. "The belief in a happy eastern region of perpetual warmth and light beyond the ocean in the place whence the sun came was widely current among the Slavs", wrote J. A. MacCulloch in the comprehensive article on *Blest, Abode of the*, in the *Encyclopaedia of Religion and Ethics*. "Such a belief is still found; and this region is sometimes thought to be tenanted by the Rakhmane, who abstained from flesh and led a holy life. The Rakhmane are obviously the Brahmans, and the traditions may be derived from apocryphal writings." This tradition surely throws a new light on the remarkable essay in which Tolstoy declared abstinence from flesh foods *The First Step* towards a truly ethical existence.

Flesh-eating explains "upon what grounds Pythagoras abstained from feeding on the flesh of animals" and in the *Parallel Lives* of the Spartan, Lycurgus, and Numa, the legendary second King of Rome, Plutarch begins the Life of Numa with the tradition that he was a disciple of Pythagoras—also assumed by Ovid in the last book of *Metamorphoses*—and in the final comparison prefers Numa: "Numa's muse was a gentle and loving inspiration, fitting him well to turn and soothe his people into peace and justice out of their violent and fiery tempers; whereas, if we must admit the treatment of the Helots to be a part of Lycurgus's legislation, a most cruel and iniquitous proceeding, we must own that Numa was by a great deal the more humane and Greek-like legislator, granting even to actual slaves a licence to sit at meat with their masters at the feast of Saturn, that they also might have some taste and relish of the sweets of liberty. For this custom, too, is ascribed to Numa, whose wish was, they conceive, to give a place in the enjoyment of the yearly fruits of the soil to those who had helped to produce them. Others will have it to be in remembrance of the age of Saturn, when there was no distinction between master and slave, but all lived as brothers and as equals in a condition of equality. In general, it seems that both aimed at the same design and intent, which was to bring their people to moderation and frugality; but of other virtues, the one set his affection most on fortitude, and the other on justice; unless we will attribute their different ways to the different habits and temperaments which they had to work upon by their enactments; for Numa did not out of cowardice or fear affect peace, but because he would not be guilty of injustice; nor did Lycurgus promote a spirit of war in his people that they might do injustice to others, but that they might protect themselves by it." It is Plato's common tables of first-fruits again, and the conflict between the Golden Age example of peace and natural plenty and the inevitability of war-preparation in a luxury state—as far as Sparta can be so called. It is not surprising that Plutarch, as he says, was suspected when dining out of "Orphic and Pythagorean notions" and besides his essay against flesh-eating and sympathetic account of the Saturnian Golden Age, he described the Fortunate Isles, in his life of Sertorius, in terms reminiscent of Hesiod and Pindar, as well as Homer, though said to be immediately imitated from Sallust: Sertorius is told of two Atlantic islands, ten thousand furlongs from the coast of Africa, "These are called the Islands of the Blest; rain falls there seldom, and in moderate showers, but for the most part they have gentle breezes, bringing along with them soft dews, which render the soil not only rich for ploughing and planting, but so abundantly fruitful that it produces spontaneously an abundance of delicate fruits, sufficient to feed the inhabitants, who may here enjoy all things without trouble or labour. The seasons of the year are temperate, and the transitions from one to another so moderate that the air is almost always serene and pleasant . . . so that the firm belief prevails, even among the barbarians, that this is the seat of the blessed, and that these are the Elysian Fields celebrated by Homer. When Sertorius heard this account, he was seized with a wonderful passion for these islands, and had an extreme desire to go and live there in peace and quietness, and safe from oppression and unending wars."

The leading Neoplatonists of the third and fourth centuries were also Pythagoreans. This can possibly be said of Plotinus himself, an Egyptian who went to Rome when he was forty and remained for the rest of his life. His importance in the history of thought and mysticism is hardly less than that of Plato, from whom much of his theoretical scheme was drawn. According to Porphyry, a Syrian who went to Rome at the age of thirty and wrote a biography of his mentor, Plotinus was of saintly character. Porphyry also wrote a *Life of Pythagoras*, or at least a fragment of one, and a Pythagorean treatise in four books, *Of Abstinence from the Flesh of Living Animals*, which ranks with Plutarch's essay on the same subject.

Iamblichus was in turn a student of Porphyry, and like him a Syrian. Iamblichus did not remain in Rome but returned to teach in his own country. His works include a surviving life of Pythagoras, and the fifth-century Neoplatonist, Proclus, who left several treatises on the Pythagorean system, mentions five books by Porphyry then extant, parts of a great work on the Pythagorean philosophy.

In his treatise *Of Abstinence*, Porphyry had described the similar practices of his own countrymen in former times, and the surviving observances of the Persian Magi. At the time when Porphyry was writing, Manicheism was rapidly gaining ground in Persia and enjoining strict abstinence from flesh foods. This synthesis of Buddhist, Zoroastrian and Christian elements later spread to

Europe and introduced similar dietary ethics to various heretical and persecuted sects.

The sixth-century Pythagorean Olympiodorus, who wrote a life of Plato, and six other Pythagoreans, left Athens and sought refuge with the Persian Magi, whose manner of living agreed with their own. But Platonism did not mix with the other Persian beliefs and the philosophers returned home after the Persian prince had magnanimously obtained from the Emperor Justinian an undertaking that they would be permitted to live out their lives in peace.

The tenth-century poet Firdausi describes the Golden Age of Yima, an essential element in Zoroastrian chronology, in terms almost identical with Hesiod's account of the Greek Golden Age:

> Beasts and men to be undying,
> Plants and waters never drying.
> Food invincible bestowing.
> In the reign of valiant Yima
> Neither cold nor heat was present,
> Neither envy, demon-founded.
> Fifteen years of age in figure
> Son and father walked together.

The demon of want does not rule their bodies, we are also told, and ten men are satisfied with one loaf. Humanity knew nothing of travail or ill in this Golden Age.

The eleventh-century Persian poet Omar Khayyam has been claimed for an ascetic and mystical tradition by a modern Asiatic authority, and as we shall see his nineteenth-century English translator, Edward FitzGerald, abstained from flesh fairly consistently for the last fifty years of his life and attached great importance to the principle. FitzGerald's reading list, found among his memoranda, included an article on Pythagoreanism and a life of Pythagoras, perhaps that by Iamblichus.

It seems probable that there was a direct line of influence from India, through Persia and the Syrian Neoplatonists to Rome and to Christianity.[1] The Manicheans, as has been mentioned, were

---

[1] Schopenhauer, writing on the Neoplatonists in his *Fragments of the History of Philosophy*, considers that the essential doctrines reached Plotinus and his followers from India mainly via Egypt:

"It is, namely, Indo-Egyptian wisdom, which they sought to embody in the Greek philosophy, and as a suitable connective tissue—a conduit or menstruum for this—they use the Platonic philosophy, especially those parts of it which branch off into the mystical. To the Indian origin, through Egypt, of the Neoplatonic dogmas, the All-One doctrine of Plotinos testifies directly and unmistakably, as we find it admirably presented in the fourth *Ennead*. . . . (*footnote continued on next page*)

regarded as heretical because of the Asian elements in their faith, although they included St. Augustine among their number for a time. The Syrian Neoplatonist philosophers too were at odds with Christianity, and Porphyry's treatise *Of Abstinence*—as Voltaire enjoyed reminding us—is addressed to one of his old disciples, named Firmus, who became a Christian, it is said, to recover his liberty to eat flesh and drink wine. Nevertheless, some outstanding Christian leaders were in agreement on the dietary issue, provided that the emphasis was on mortification of the rebellious flesh by austerity and not on any sense of kinship with animals or wish to restore a Golden Age or Eden diet for its own sake. The monastic Rule of St. Basil, who studied at Athens in the fourth century with Julian, later the ascetic and apostate Emperor, excluded flesh foods, like Tertullian and Clement of Alexandria a century before; and Basil's contemporary Chrysostom, as well as the Essenes, practised and preached the same abstinence. Of this tradition too there will be more to say anon.

These survivals of the Greek teaching of Pythagoras, and of ancient dietary traditions in Persia, and the similar practices of a few eminent Christian leaders and religious communities were events in the Roman Empire rather than in the Roman mind. The Romans had stained their own Saturnian tradition with the blood of animals and men, and in the first great aetiological poem of the age, Lucretius's *Of the Nature of Things*, written in the last century of the pre-Christian age, the golden aura is gone. As in the disputed *Protagoras* Myth in Plato, the first men, despite their reliance on the fruits of the earth, are both hunters and hunted.

The purpose of this philosophical poem, says J. D. Duff, is to convert the reader to the Epicurean system of philosophy. The universe of the poem is the illimitable inane, as Tennyson put it, the shower of atoms. Lucretius argues "against the immortality of

Footnote continued from page 59

"A further confirmation of the Indian origin is afforded us by Iamblichus in his exposition of the doctrine of Metempsychosis, where also may be found the doctrine of the finite liberation and salvation from the bonds of birth and death . . . in other words, the promise contained in all Indian religious books, which is designated in English by *final emancipation* or salvation. In addition to this there is, lastly, the account of an Egyptian symbol which represents a creative God sitting on the lotus; obviously the world-creating Brahma sitting on the lotus-flower. . . . This symbol is extremely important as a sure proof of the Hindu origin of the Egyptian religion, as, in the same respect, is the report also given by Porphyry *De Abstinentia,* lib. ii, that in Egypt the cow was holy, and might not be slaughtered. . . . Porphyry furnished a complete theory of Metempsychosis, which is conceived entirely in the Indian spirit, although impregnated with the Platonic Psychology."

Schopenhauer also found significance in Plotinus's project of going to Persia and India, doubtless to study the doctrines "more purely from their source".

The view that some elements of the Orphic religion reached Greece from, or at least via, Egypt has been mentioned in the first chapter.

the soul and denies the interference of the gods in human affairs".
In Book III, he shows that there is no transmigration of souls from
man to animals, or from one human body to another. In Empedocles' poetic fragments we observed that metempsychosis
could be a strong bond of kinship with animals, and its cannibalistic
implications powerfully persuasive. Lucretius, no narrow sectarian,
writes admiringly of Empedocles in the first book of his long poem,
and there allows that, while ultimate particles are identical—

> diverse things
> By diverse things are nourished. And, again,
> Often it matters vastly with *what* others,
> In *what* positions the primordial germs
> Are bound together, and *what* motions, too,
> They give and get among themselves; for these
> Same germs do put together sky, sea, lands,
> Rivers, and sun, grains, trees, and breathing things,
> But yet commixed they are in divers modes
> With divers things, forever as they move.

How little Lucretius had conceded appears in Book IV. The criteria
are as severely physiological as the scientific nutritionist could wish:

> Nor aught it matters with what food is fed
> The body, if only what thou take thou canst
> Distribute well digested to the frame
> And keep the stomach in a moist career.

It is the more remarkable that, in Book V, which describes the
origin of the world, of life, and of human society, Lucretius should
faithfully reproduce all the characteristics of the Golden Age. It is
not a world where man lives in harmony with nature. Yet Lucretius
cannot but confess that the advantage is not altogether with Rome.
If the food is a famine diet, Roman gluttony is more dangerous.
The horror of killing and eating flesh is skilfully retained, in the
description of man's "living flesh entombed within a living grave"
—the Pythagorean indictment of flesh-eating very similarly expressed in the last book of Ovid's *Metamorphoses*, "Where Bowels
are in other Bowels clos'd". And at least the savage men slaughter
not each other as the civilized do in legions. Lucretius is half in love
with the barbaric former age, half revolted by its crudities and

hardships. The following account of the earliest period of mankind
is from the translation by William Ellery Leonard who also rendered
the fragments of Empedocles:

> But mortal man
> Was then far hardier in the old champaign,
> As well he should be, since a hardier earth
> Had him begotten; builded too was he
> Of bigger and more solid bones within,
> And knit with stalwart sinews through the flesh,
> Nor easily seized by either heat or cold,
> Or alien food or any ail or irk.
> And whilst so many lustrums of the sun
> Rolled on across the sky, men led a life
> After the roving habit of wild beasts.
> Not then were sturdy guiders of curved ploughs,
> And none knew then to work the fields with iron,
> Or plant young shoots in holes of delvéd loam,
> Or lop with hookéd knives from off high trees
> The boughs of yester-year. What sun and rains
> To them had given, what earth of own accord
> Created then, was boon enough to glad
> Their simple hearts. Mid acorn-laden oaks
> Would they refresh their bodies for the nonce;
> And the wild berries of the arbute-tree,
> Which now thou seest to ripen purple-red
> In winter time, the old telluric soil
> Would bear then more abundant and more big.
> And many coarse foods, too, in long ago
> The blooming freshness of the rank young world
> Produced, enough for those poor wretches there.
> And rivers and springs would summon them of old
> To slake the thirst, as now from the great hills
> The water's down-rush calls aloud and far
> The thirsty generations of the wild.
> So, too, they sought the grottos of the Nymphs—
> The woodland haunts discovered as they ranged—
> From forth of which they knew that gliding rills
> With gush and splash abounding laved the rocks,
> The dripping rocks, and trickled from above
> Over the verdant moss; and here and there
> Welled up and burst across the open flats.

As yet they knew not to enkindle fire
Against the cold, nor hairy pelts to use
And clothe their bodies with the spoils of beasts;
But huddled in groves, and mountain-caves, and woods,
And 'mongst the thickets hid their squalid backs,
When driven to flee the lashings of the winds
And the big rains. Nor could they then regard
The general good, nor did they know to use
In common any customs, any laws:
Whatever of booty fortune unto each
Had proffered, each alone would bear away,
By instinct trained for self to thrive and live.
And Venus in the forests then would link
The lovers' bodies; for the woman yielded
Either from mutual flame, or from the man's
Impetuous fury and insatiate lust,
Or from a bribe—as acorn-nuts, choice pears,
Or the wild berries of the arbute-tree.
And trusting wondrous strength of hands and legs,
They'd chase the forest-wanderers, the beasts;
And many they'd conquer, but some few they fled,
A-skulk into their hiding-places. . . .

        And by the time of night
O'ertaken, they would throw, like bristly boars,
Their wildman's limbs naked upon the earth,
Rolling themselves in leaves and fronded boughs.
Nor would they call with lamentations loud
Around the fields for daylight and the sun,
Quaking and wand'ring in shadows of the night;
But, silent and buried in a sleep, they'd wait
Until the sun with rosy flambeau brought
The glory to the sky. From childhood wont
Ever to see the dark and day begot
In times alternate, never might they be
Wildered by wild misgiving, lest a night
Eternal should possess the lands, with light
Of sun withdrawn forever. But their care
Was rather that the clans of savage beasts
Would often make their sleep-time horrible
For those poor wretches; and, from home y-driven,

They'd flee their rocky shelters at approach
Of boar, the spumy-lipped, or lion strong,
And in the midnight yield with terror up
To those fierce guests their beds of out-spread leaves.
    And yet in those days not much more than now
Would generations of mortality
Leave the sweet light of fading life behind.
Indeed, in those days here and there a man,
More oftener snatched upon, and gulped by fangs,
Afforded the beasts a food that roared alive,
Echoing through groves and hills and forest-trees,
Even as he viewed his living flesh entombed
Within a living grave; whilst those whom flight
Had saved, with bone and body bitten, shrieked,
Pressing their quivering palms to loathsome sores,
With horrible voices for eternal death—
Until, forlorn of help, and witless what
Might medicine their wounds, the writhing pangs
Took them from life. But not in those far times
Would one lone day give over unto doom
A soldiery in thousands marching on
Beneath the battle-banners, nor would then
The ramping breakers of the main seas dash
Whole argosies and crews upon the rocks.
But ocean uprisen would often rave in vain,
Without all end or outcome, and give up
Its empty menacings as lightly too;
Nor soft seductions of a serene sea
Could lure by laughing billows any man
Out to disaster: for the science bold
Of ship-sailing lay dark in those far times.
Again, 'twas *then* that lack of food gave o'er
Men's fainting limbs to dissolution: now
'Tis plenty overwhelms. Unwary, they
Oft for themselves themselves would then outpour
The poison; now, with nicer art, themselves
They give the drafts to others.

Lucretius died of a love potion (or, as in Tennyson's poem, by
his own hand while drugged with it) when Vergil was abou
twenty-one, Horace a boy and Ovid yet unborn. The three chie

poets of the Augustan age all visited Athens and all wrote of Orpheus, so that it is not surprising to find that they all deal directly with the Greek tradition we have traced.

"The tradition to which the *Georgics* belong starts with Hesiod's *Works and Days*", writes W. F. Jackson Knight. "Vergil sometimes almost translates Hesiod. . . . Hesiod and Lucretius were in some sense primary for the *Georgics*." In the first *Georgic* there is an ingenious amalgam of Hesiod and Lucretius. Writing of an early but later stage of human development than Lucretius, Vergil depicts man fated to toil and poverty and to become a hunter. But this he contrasts with the primal Saturnian time, reconciling the two by the contention that Jove altered terrestrial conditions for the worse so that necessity might be mother to invention:

> No unlaborious path the Father willed:
> He first taught method as the means, and spurred
> The wits of men by cares, and suffered not
> His realms to slumber 'neath inveterate sloth.
> Before Jove's reign no farmers tilled the soil;
> No fence or boundary-stone to mark the fields
> Religion sanctioned: to the common store
> All labour tended, and the earth herself
> Gave all more freely for that no man asked.
> Then Jove endowed that cursed thing, the snake,
> With venom, and the wolf with thirst for blood,
> Lashed the still sea, shook honey off the trees,
> Robbed men of fire and emptied river-beds
> Which flowed apace with wine; to make men prove
> And hammer out by practice divers arts;
> Now slowly learning how to plough and sow,
> Now striking from flint-vein the lurking fire,
> Then rivers first the hallowed alder felt;
> Then sailors told the number of the stars
> And called them by their names, the brilliant Bear,
> Lycaon's child, Pleiad and Hyad too;
> Then came the wiles of trapping and the use
> Of birdlime, then too hounds were trained to watch
> Large covert-sides. And some with cast-net flog
> The river's breadth and try the deepest pools,
> While others scour the sea with dripping mesh,

Then strident saws were born of stubborn steel—
For logs were cleft with splintering wedge before—
Then divers arts ensued. Toil conquered all,
Unconquerable Toil, and Poverty,
The spur of hungry men. 'Twas Ceres first,
When arbute-berries failed and oaks denied
The wonted acorn in Dodona's woods,
Taught men the use and method of the plough.
Soon corn received its special plagues: the stalks
Were gnawed by mildew, and the thistle reared
Its head of sloth: death takes the crops, up comes
A mass of matted undergrowth, behold
Clivers[1] and caltrops; o'er the smiling tilth
Wild oat and darnel hold their barren sway!
So ply your hoes and give the weeds no peace,
Scare birds with noise, correct the leafy hedge
Too lavish with its shade, pray hard for rain.
Neglect these things, lo! 'neath your helpless gaze
Another's barns shall overflow, while you
From woodland oak shall shake a scanty meal.

In the second *Georgic*, Vergil himself says, "I sing my song like Hesiod's from town to town of the Roman lands" and at the end of it he summons a last glimpse of the Age of Gold:

Before the sceptred sway of Dicte's Jove,
Before men banqueted on slaughtered kine,
Whose blood be on them! golden Saturn lived
A life like this on earth. Not yet was heard
The blare of martial clarion, not yet
Upon hard anvil clanged the sounding sword.

Like Hesiod too is Vergil's adoption of the cyclic chronology which we found clearly developed in Plato's *Politicus* Myth. But the prophecy in the fourth *Eclogue* is that the Golden Age will return in the near future, which has inevitably aroused speculation as to whether it does not somehow foreshadow the birth of Christ.

The last age told by Cumae's seer is come,
A mighty roll of generations new
Is now arising. Justice now returns

[1] Burrs.

And Saturn's realm, and from high heaven descends
A worthier race of men. Only do thou
Smile, chaste Lucina, on the infant boy,
With whom the iron age will pass away.
The golden age in all the earth be born;
For thine Apollo reigns. Under thy rule,
Thine, Pollio, shall this glorious era spring,
And the great progress of the months begin,
Under thy rule all footprints of our guilt
Shall perish, and the peaceful earth be freed
From everlasting fear. Thou, child, shalt know
The life of gods, and see commingled choirs
Of gods and heroes, and be seen of them,
And rule a world by righteous father tamed.

 Then Earth shall haste to bring thee birthday gifts,
Uncultured Earth: the ivy's gadding curls
And cyclamen and arum lily twined
With laughing bear's-breech. Uncompelled thy goats
Shall bring their udders heavy-laden home,
And monstrous lions frighten herds no more.
Thy very cot shall bloom delightful flowers,
Serpents shall cease, the treacherous poison-plant
Shall fail, Assyrian balm o'erspread the land.
But when thou'lt read the praise of famous men
And thy sire's deeds, and know true excellence,
The plain shall softly teem with yellowing corn,
And grapes shall blush upon the unkempt briar,
And the hard oak-tree bole ooze honeydew.

 Nathless some taint of old iniquity
Shall stay, to bid men tempt with ships the sea
And build them city-walls and furrow earth
With ploughshares. A new Tiphys shall arise,
A second Argo fraught with chosen knights,
And other wars shall rage, and once again
Shall valorous Āchilles fare to Troy.

 And when strong time hath wrought thee into man,
The seafarer shall roam the wave no more,
Nor ships make merchandise: for all the earth
Shall be all-fruitful. Neither shall the vine
Suffer the pruning-hook, nor fields the hoe.
And lusty husbandmen from ox's neck

Shall loose the yoke; and wool with divers hues
Need not to cheat, for lo! the living ram
Shall softly blush with purple fleece, or glow
With saffron yellow; grazing lambs shall wear
Vestments of scarlet in the bounteous meads.
'So run, fair ages,' to their spindles sang
The Fates that weave the stedfast web of God.

Take thy great heritage, thine hour is come,
Blest offspring of the gods, great seed of Jove.
See how Creation bows her massy dome,
Oceans and continents and aery deeps:
All nature gladdens at the coming age.
O may a long life's evening then be mine,
And breath to tell thy deeds! Not Linus then
Nor Thracian Orpheus shall surpass my song,
E'en though the beautiful Apollo help
Linus, his son, and Orpheus call to aid
Calliope that bare him. Nay, though Pan
Before Arcadian judges with me strive,
Before Arcadia would he yield the palm.

Learn, babe, to laugh when mother calls thee now,
Thy mother weary with her ten long months.
Learn, baby, now: who answers not the smile
Of mother's eyes, he is not meet to share
Goddess's bed, or table of a god.[1]

It was partly under the inspiration of Vergil's fourth *Eclogue*, says Jackson Knight, that Horace wrote his remarkable sixteenth *Epode*, which in turn influenced Vergil's writing in the *Georgics*, "there is an exchange of thoughts on the Golden Age". Vergil had placed the Golden Age in the immediate future. Horace, who could likewise proclaim in the *Secular Hymn* that "Trust, Peace, Honour, ancient Modesty, And Virtue" together with the brimming horn of Plenty were now returning, could also, at the zenith of Augustan splendour, play the Pied Piper and call its heroes out of the doomed city, as though forewarned of the Empire's downfall. The sixteenth *Epode* brings the Isles of the Blessed close in space as Vergil's fourth *Eclogue* brings the Golden Age close in time.

---

[1] "A French scholar, Carcopino, gives good reason to believe that the poem contains allusions to Pythagorean doctrine."—T. S. Eliot, *Vergil and the Christian World*, in *The Listener*, 13th September, 1951.

The Isles are no longer reserved for the illustrious dead, no longer forbidden to the living Argonauts, no more removed to that Platonic True Surface of the Earth; they are quite simply a new place in the sun for intrepid Roman colonists, and in that bringing to earth of myth one may read the essential limitation of the characteristic Roman imagination.

> Already wastes away a second age
>   By civil wars fordone, and Rome
> Is falling by the might of Rome herself—
>   Rome, whom nor Marsi near our home
>
> E'er managed to destroy, nor Tuscan band
>   Of threatening Porsena, nor strength
> Of rival Capua, nor fierce Spartacus,
>   Nor the Allobroges, at length
>
> Faithless when revolution raised its head;
>   Rome, whom nor Germans blue-eyed, fierce,
> Nor Hannibal, by parents held detested,
>   Had ever managed once to pierce;
>
> Rome we, an impious age of blood accursed,
>   Are ruining; the land again
> Will fall to be possessed by beasts of prey.
>   The foreign victor is in train
>
> To trample on her ashes, and the City
>   With stamp of horses' hoofs will ring,
> And—shocking to behold!—in insolence
>   Quirinus' bones he'll careless fling
>
> To winds and suns they never yet have known.
>   Perhaps you all, the nobler part
> At least, would like to know what must be done
>   Such grave calamities to thwart:
>
> No better resolution can there be
>   Than this: as the Phocaeans, reft
> Of hope, took desperate oath and fled their fields,
>   Their firesides and their temples left

To boars and ravening wolves, so we should go
　　Where'er our feet the way may keep,
Where'er the south wind or the boisterous Afric
　　Shall summon us across the deep.

Is this agreed? Can any one suggest
　　A better course? . . . Why, then, delay,
When omens favour us, to go on board?
　　But this first let us swear and say:

That never may we dare again return
　　Till from the bottom of the sea
Rocks rise and float; nor may we sail for home
　　Till Po o'er Matine heights flow free;

Or till the Apennines plunge in the deep,
　　And passion strange new monsters join
In lust—so strange that tigers mate with deer
　　And doves their loves to kites confine,

Nor simple flocks fear tawny lions more,
　　And goats drop beards and love the sea.
Swear this, and swear what other oath may bar
　　The way to sweet return; and we—

Come, let us go, the city in a body,
　　Or else the part with better sense:
Those lacking nerve and hope may keep their beds
　　Uncheered by omens nor go hence;

But you with manhood, cease unmanly grief,
　　And fly along the Tuscan main.
The circling Ocean is awaiting us:
　　Haste let us make the fields to gain,

The happy fields, the islands of abundance,
　　Where yearly yields its fruits the earth
Untilled, and vines aye flourish though unpruned,
　　And olive blooms ne'er fail of birth,

Where purple figs adorn their native trees,
　　And honey from the oak distils,
And where with murmuring foot the water bright
　　Bounds lightly from the lofty hills.

And there the goats unbidden come to milking,
  The kindly flock with udders swelled,
Nor growls the bear at even around the fold,
  Nor heaves the ground with snakes unquelled.

And marvels more shall we in bliss behold:
  How nor will rainy Eurus scour
The fields with heavy showers, nor fertile seeds
  Be scorched by soils or dry or sour;

For Jove, the King of Gods, rules both extremes.
  Here never Argo landing made,
Here the lascivious Colchian ne'er set foot,
  Nor Sidon sailors came to trade,

Nor yet Ulysses' crew with hardships spent.
  With no disease are flocks infected;
From fiery violence of any star
  The herds are evermore protected.

When Jove debased the golden age with bronze,
  These shores for good folk he reserved;
With bronze he hardened the ages, then with iron;
  But for the good from all ills that environ
  A happy 'scape, believe me, is preserved.

In the *Ars Poetica*, Horace closely follows Aristophanes in singling out the greatest achievements of Orpheus:

Orpheus, the priest, the mouthpiece of the gods,
Deterred wild men from murders and foul foods,
And hence was said to tame the raging moods
Of tigers and of lions.

And in his *Ode on the Poet's Desire* Horace declared that while the sea-traders might carouse in golden tankards, "Olives and chicory and mallows Are good enough for me".

Horace takes up the same contrast between gluttony and frugality in *Ofellus; or the Simple Life*, the Second Satire in the second series:

Now hear from me what and how great the wealth
A frugal diet brings. Well, first, good health
You shall enjoy: what ills mixed foods effect
You may believe if you but recollect

How on your stomach once sat simple fare;
Whereas, so soon as you have mingled there
Boiled meat and roast, shell-fish and thrushes both,
The sweets will turn to bile, nor will be loth
The sluggish phlegm to cause stomachic stress.
You see how pale the guests rise from their seat
At banquets where they're puzzled what to eat.
Ay, and the body, laden with the excess
Of yesterday, the mind too doth depress,
And clamps to earth the deity in man.

Another, dining on another plan
Of quick dispatch, needs little time in bed,
And rises fresh his daily round to tread.

But Ofellus's admired régime is not Orphic, and the artistic contrast between the two diets is somewhat weakened by inclusion in the latter of ham, and on special occasions chicken and kid. This latent weakness becomes a considerable embarrassment to Alexander Pope, whose very free version of this poem on *The Simple Life* is discussed in Chapter 6.

The fullest Roman expression of the Golden Age theme is in Ovid, a poet who completed his education at Athens. The last and greatest book of the *Metamorphoses* is devoted to the Pythagorean philosophy, and bears that title. In Dryden's translation this final book is the starting point of our endeavour to trace this tradition through the eighteenth century, and although the poem is a Roman achievement we may defer consideration of it. Ovid's first book deals with the grandest metamorphosis of all, the transformation from the Chaos that preceded Nature's birth to the comparative order of Caesar's time. In that great change an empire greater than Caesar's is won and lost, a Golden Age of peace and plenty, lost to be found again by those who carry a vision of it through darkness and observe its precepts of peace and harmlessness to all that lives. This is the golden legend that has haunted the imagination of Europe's prophets, regardless of their own temperaments, habits or cultural environment. In essentials it is also the story of Genesis and its history is inevitably joined with that of the first book of the Bible.

Then sprang up first the golden age, which of itself maintained
  The truth and right of everything, unforced and unconstrained.
There was no fear of punishment, there was no threatening law
In brazen tables nailéd up, to keep the folk in awe.
There was no man would crouch or creep to judge with cap in hand;
They livéd safe without a judge in every realm and land.
The lofty pine-tree was not hewn from mountains where it stood,
In seeking strange and foreign lands to rove upon the flood.
Men knew none other countries yet than where themselves did keep:
There was no town encloséd yet with walls and ditches deep.
No horn nor trumpet was in use, no sword nor helmet worn.
The world was such that soldiers' help might easily be forborne.
The fertile earth as yet was free, untouched of spade or plough,
And yet it yielded of itself of every thing enow;
And men themselves contented well with plain and simple food
That on the earth by Nature's gift without their travail stood,
Did live by raspis, hips and haws, by cornels, plums and cherries,
By sloes and apples, nuts and pears, and loathsome bramble berries,
And by the acorns dropped on ground from Jove's broad tree in field.
The springtime lasted all the year, and Zephyr with his mild
And gentle blast did cherish things that grew of own accord.
The ground untilled all kind of fruits did plenteously afford.
No muck nor tillage was bestowed on lean and barren land
To make the corn of better head and ranker for to stand.
Then streams ran milk, then streams ran wine, and yellow honey flowed
From each green tree whereon the rays of fiery Phoebus glowed.

  But when that unto Limbo once Saturnus being thrust,
  The rule and charge of all the world was under Jove unjust,
And that the silver age came in, more somewhat base than gold,
More precious yet than freckled brass, immediately the old
And ancient springtime Jove abridged and made thereof anon
Four seasons: winter, summer, spring, and harvest off and on.
Then first of all began the air with fervent heat to swelt;
Then icicles hung roping down; then, for the cold was felt,
Men 'gan to shroud themselves in house; their houses were the thicks,
And bushy queaches, hollow caves, or hurdles made of sticks.
Then first of all were furrows drawn, and corn was cast in ground;
The simple ox with sorry sighs to heavy yoke was bound.

  Next after this succeeded straight the third and brazen age:
  More hard of nature, somewhat bent to cruel wars and rage,

73

But yet not wholly past all grace.
                                        Of iron is the last
In no part good and tractable as former ages past;
For when that of this wicked age once opened was the vein
Therein all mischief rushéd forth, the faith and truth were fain
And honest shame to hide their heads; for whom stepped stoutly in,
Craft, treason, violence, envy, pride, and wicked lust to win.
The shipman hoists his sails to wind, whose names he did not know;
And ships that erst in tops of hills and mountains high did grow,
Did leap and dance on uncouth waves; and men began to bound
With dowls and ditches drawn in length the free and fertile ground,
Which was as common as the air and light of sun before.
Not only corn and other fruits, for sustenance and for store,
Were now exacted of the earth, but eft they 'gan to dig
And in the bowels of the earth insatiably to rig
For riches couched and hidden deep in places near to hell,
The spurs and stirrers unto vice, and foes to doing well.
Then hurtful iron came abroad, then came forth yellow gold
More hurtful than the iron far, then came forth battle bold
That fights with both, and shakes his sword in cruel bloody hand.
Men live by ravin and by stealth; the wandering guest doth stand
In danger of his host; the host in danger of his guest;
And fathers of their sons-in-law; yea, seldom time doth rest
Between born brothers such accord and love as ought to be;
The goodman seeks the goodwife's death, and his again seeks she;
With grisly poison stepdames fell their husbands' sons assail;
The son inquires aforehand when his father's life shall fail;
All godliness lies under foot. And Lady Astrey,[1] last
Of heavenly virtues, from this earth in slaughter drownéd passed.

Ovid's lines recreate the vision of the Ages of Gold, Silver, Brass
and Iron, set down some seven hundred years before by Hesiod in
Works and Days. Captured Greece, as the candid Horace says, had
captured her rough conqueror.

In Hesiod's Golden Age, the first beatitude is the tranquil mind
which, rather than a high material standard of living, is the highest
good. Freedom from toil, next celebrated, expressed man's harmonious place in the natural order, in contrast to our civilization's
war on soil, animal and tree. Long life, free from violence and
disease, is as natural to the Golden Age as the abundance of fruits on

---

[1] Astraea, goddess of justice.

which mankind is nourished there. All things are shared. All men are free.

We have vestigial modern doctrines for all these qualities: pacifism, vegetarianism, communitarianism, anarchism, soil conservation, organic farming, "no digging", afforestation, nature cure, the decentralised village economy. At the golden touch of Hesiod's or Ovid's lines the clumsy polysyllables crack their seed cases and flower into the variegated life and colour of single vision. The vague association that many of these ideas have retained in their attenuated modern forms is not accidental.

Ovid has drawn into his Golden Age some other thoughts on the same theme for which there are precepts in *Works and Days*. There is remonstrance against laws and corrupt justices; a warning about seafaring, foreign trade may lead to a dependent economy and to war; and a list of natural foods of the Golden Age, which includes the acorn.

The oak is Jove's tree because he first taught mankind to feed upon it, as Ovid says in the *Elegy to Ceres*:

> On mast of oaks, first oracles, men fed,
> This was their meat, the soft grass was their bed,

and in *The Festivals* he expands the statement:

> Green herbs were first our hungry fathers' food,
> To them afforded from the earth unwooed.
> Sometimes young stalks they gathered here and there,
> And tender sprouts did make them goodly cheer.
> They thought them well when they had found out mast,
> The oak did yield them many a rich repast.
> First Ceres men with nobler meats did store,
> And into better food turned acorns poor.

The goddess herself meets an old countryman, trudging homewards:

> With mast and berries from the hedge for food.

Current authorities on acorns regard them simply as pig-food, and not food for a Socratic City of Pigs. Yet here again we are probably given accurate information by the poets. Edible acorns still grow in Elis on the west coast of the Peloponnesus, and ways of treating other kinds have long been known to uncivilized communities. "Along some lines", one expert writes, "primitive tribes have been more advanced in the processing of their foods than have more civilized peoples. Some of the aborigines of North America used acorns almost as a staple article of diet, they ground them to a pulp, placed it in the hollow of a heap of sand, and leached the acrid principles from it with hot water. The remaining mass of starch and protein was dried and stored for winter use." And Robert Graves writes from Mallorca, "Did you ever eat edible acorns like the Arcadians? Nourishing, tasty but indigestible. My children eat them here, like their playmates." An old Spanish custom, it seems. For when Don Quixote and Sancho Panza are at supper with the goatherds, eating acorns for dessert, it is "because the acorns they had given him put him in mind of the golden age" that the woeful Knight speaks of that age of innocence when "no one needed to take any other pains for his ordinary sustenance, than to lift up his hand and take it from the sturdy oaks, which stood inviting him liberally to taste of their sweet and relishing fruit". And this is from a witness whose diet "consisted more of beef than mutton; and with minced meat on most nights, lentiles on Fridays, and a pigeon extraordinary on Sundays consumed threequarters of his revenue!" Acorns remain a symbol of the Golden Age—for instance we shall find it later on in the Moral of Mandeville's *Fable of the Bees*.

But Rome was falling, as Horace had prophesied, by the might of Rome herself. Incredible as it seems, we may believe on the authority of Tacitus that the life of the author of that "supremely scandalous tale" the *Satyricon* was comparable in its excesses with the book itself. Petronius's appointment as organiser of the pleasures of Nero indeed necessitated such qualifications, and Tacitus makes him "a professor of voluptuousness". When Petronius was finally accused and placed under some sort of house arrest, he committed a slow suicide as comfortably as possible to the accompaniment of frivolous songs, the whipping of some of his servants and a luxurious dinner.

The *Satyricon,* which has at least literary merit, is mainly concerned with gluttony and lechery. Towards the end of the book two principal characters are put ashore at Crotona, "a town of great age, and once the first city in Italy". In Crotona now, they are told, "the pursuit of learning is not esteemed, eloquence has no place, economy and a pure life do not win their reward in honour . . ." and since purity is otherwise quite irrelevant to the *Satyricon* we must suppose the satyr is here grimacing at Pythagoras and the dedicated community he once founded at Crotona. "You will go into a town that is like a plague-stricken plain", their informant goes on, "where there is nothing but carcasses to be devoured, and crowds to devour them", a description doubtless meant literally as well as metaphorically.

The story ends at Crotona after "they grow fat on their pretension to be men of fortune, and disappear from sight, Encolpius after a disgraceful series of vain encounters with a woman named Circe, and Eumolpus after a scene where he bequeaths his body to be eaten by his heirs". That is as near as the disreputable tale approaches to morality—prolonged debauchery may result in the humiliations of sexual impotence, and a great eater of bodies may have his own corpse devoured by his successors. The main fragment of the story breaks off with examples of cannibalism, ending, "Some women were found with the half-eaten bodies of their children hidden in their bosoms".

A large part of the earlier portion of the *Satyricon* is occupied by an orgiastic banquet, "a merry Saturnalia indeed" given by one Trimalchio, and the details may well sicken the least finicky of readers. There is, for instance, the delicate fancy of the guests choosing one of three live pigs, which is brought back as it seems almost at once cooked but apparently not disembowelled. The cook is summoned and threatened with drastic punishment, and finally "seized a knife and carved the pig's belly in various places. . . . At once the slits widened under the pressure from within, and sausages and black puddings tumbled out."

Previously Petronius has introduced another reference to cooked pig that is important as revealing that there was a Roman source for the image that is prominent in the mediaeval folk-tale of Cockaigne, to be discussed in the next chapter. We may bear in mind the Saturnalian context of that besotted Fool's Paradise. "I engage you could not name a better country to call one's own, if only the men in it had sense. It has its troubles now like others. We must not be too particular when there is a sky above us all. If you were anywhere else, you would say that roast pig walked in the streets here.[1] Just think, we are soon to be given a superb spectacle lasting three days; not simply a troupe of professional gladiators, but a large number of them freedmen. And our good Titus has a big imagination and is hot-blooded: it will be one thing or another, something real anyway. I know him very well, and he is all against half-measures. He will give you the finest blades, no running away, butchery done in the middle, where the whole audience can see it."

Petronius was a man of learning and ability, and capable of more than one mood. Perhaps it was during a period of recuperation from his bacchanalian pleasures that he wrote in one of his short poems of a more natural order of things, although even this is alloyed with a leering allusion to licensed lechery. "Honest Heaven ordained that all things which can end our wretched complaints should be ready to hand. Common green herbs and the berries that grow on rough brambles allay the gnawing hunger of the belly. A fool is he who goes thirsty with a river close by. . . . The wealth of nature gives us enough for our fill: that which unbridled vanity teaches us to pursue has no end to it." In another short poem he describes the natural abundance of his lands and goes on, "Moreover, if my pleasure is to lay snares for birds, or if I choose rather to entrap the timid deer, or draw out the quivering fish on tender lines, so much deceit is all that is known to my humble fields. Go, then, and barter the hours of flying life for rich banquets. . . ." For his part may death find him thus innocently—or relatively so—employed. The sadistic sensuality of Petronius is something more than an individual perversion; it is as representative of the Roman harvest of dragon's teeth as was Petronius's own official position in the decadent Empire as pandar to the wicked voluptuary who murdered his wife and mother.

Even the sweet air of the Isle of the Blessed is drowsy with a sickening scent of opulence in decay in the work of the second-century writer Lucian. There is a whole city of gold, fountains of honey, oil, milk and wine: a glut for gluttons. For Rome *Metamorphoses* now meant not the metaphysical myths of Ovid but the salacious antics of that archetypal Bottom, *The Golden Ass*, a man turned beast who is, among other obscenities, seduced by a rich

---

[1] I owe this valuable reference to Herford and Simpson's edition of Jonson, where it is aptly cited in the note on Lubberland.

woman. Enormity and entertainment are now practically synony-
mous. Europa has herself leapt the bull.

Yet in these latter-day *Metamorphoses* the author and even the ass
are a queer mixture of the two elements of our tradition. The ass,
says Robert Graves, was identified with Cronus, Saturn's counterpart, but was also connected in folk-lore with the mid-winter
Saturnalia. Apuleius himself studied Platonic philosophy at Athens
and wrote about it: he claimed to be a descendant of Plutarch: and
he became a priest of Aesculapius as well as of Isis and Osiris. None
of this inhibited him from organising in later life the gladiatorial
and wild-beast shows for the whole province of Africa. *The Golden
Ass* owes its notoriety, like Rabelais, to its raciness rather than to
any didactic purpose, but ends with the sincere religious conversion
of its hero, which no doubt draws on the author's own initiations.
He conducts his ablutions "according to the divine philosopher
Pythagoras", prays to Ceres who "abolished the rude acorn diet of
our forefathers and gave them bread raised from the fertile soil of
Eleusis", is promised sight of the Elysian Fields after death and
enjoined to perfect chastity, and is instructed by the High Priest to
abstain, as the priests do, from forbidden foods. After a further vision
has been vouchsafed him, at the end of the book the hero says,
"Once more I fasted, this time voluntarily extending the usual period
of abstinence from meat. . . ." Perhaps we only see *The Golden Ass*
clearly in the perspective of the tradition we have been following.
In that focus the presence of these conflicting elements of orgy and
abstinence becomes intelligible, even inevitable. And in the conclusion of Apuleius's book we may read a sign that the old Saturnian
purity was not dead beneath the smother of Saturnalian debauchery.

Early in the sixth century, when the glory of Rome was gone, the
embers stirred to emit a spark that smouldered for a thousand years.
"The senator Boethius", says Edward Gibbon, "is the last of the
Romans who Cato or Tully could have acknowledged for their
countryman." "While Boethius, oppressed with fetters, expected
each moment the sentence or the stroke of death, he composed in
the tower of Pavia the *Consolation of Philosophy*, a golden volume
not unworthy the leisure of Plato or Tully, but which claims
incomparable merit from the barbarism of the times and the situation
of the author. The celestial guide, whom he had so long invoked at

Rome and Athens, now condescended to illuminate his dungeon, to revive his courage, and to pour into his wounds her salutary balm."

Each chapter of the *Consolation* is succeeded by verses on the same theme. The fifth chapter of Book II, The Vanity of Fortune's Gifts, praises the simple life: "Doubtless the fruits of the earth are given for the sustenance of living creatures." In the following verses, translated by Henry Vaughan, Boethius sings of the time when men lived so:

> Happy that first white age! when we
> Lived by the Earth's mere charity.
> No soft luxurious diet then
> Had effeminated men,
> No other meat, nor wine had any
> Than the coarse mast, or simple honey.
> And by the parents' care laid up
> Cheap berries did the children sup.
> No pompous wear was in those days
> Of gummy silks, or scarlet baize,
> Their beds were on some flow'ry brink,
> And clear spring-water was their drink.
> The shady pine in the sun's heat
> Was their cool and known retreat,
> For then 'twas not cut down, but stood
> The youth and glory of the wood.
> The daring sailor with his slaves
> Then had not cut the swelling waves,
> Nor for desire of foreign store
> Seen any but his native shore.
> No stirring drum had scarr'd that age,
> Nor the shrill trumpet's active rage,
> No wounds by bitter hatred made
> With warm blood soil'd the shining blade;
> For how could hostile madness arm
> An age of love, to public harm?
> When common justice none withstood
> Nor sought rewards for spilling blood.
> O that at length our age would raise
> Into the temper of those days!

> But—worse than Aetna's fires!—debate
> And avarice inflame our State.
> Alas! who was it that first found
> Gold, hid of purpose under ground,
> That sought out pearls, and div'd to find
> Such precious perils for mankind!

Boethius says he obeyed the Pythagorean command to **follow God**. And one of those last songs written in the death-cell was of Orpheus and Eurydice:

> Happy is he, that with fix'd eyes
> The fountain of all goodness spies!
> Happy is he that can break through
> Those bonds which tie him here below!
>   The Thracian poet long ago,
> Kind Orpheus, full of tears and woe,
> Did for his lov'd Eurydice
> In such sad numbers mourn, that he
> Made the trees run in to his moan,
> And streams stand still to hear him groan.
> The does came fearless in one throng
> With lions to his mournful song,
> And charmed by the harmonious sound,
> The hare stay'd by the quiet hound.
>   But when Love height'n'd by despair
> And deep reflections on his fair
> Had swell'd his heart, and made it rise
> And run in tears out at his eyes,
> And those sweet airs, which did appease
> Wild beasts, could give their lord no ease;
> Then, vex'd that so much grief and love
> Mov'd not at all the gods above,
> With desperate thoughts and bold intent,
> Towards the shades below he went;
> For thither his fair love was fled,
> And he must have her from the dead.
> There in such lines, as did well suit
> With sad airs and a lover's lute,
> And in the richest language dress'd
> That could be thought on or express'd,

H   81

Did he complain; whatever grief
Or art or love—which is the chief,
And all ennobles—could lay out,
In well-tun'd woes he dealt about.
And humbly bowing to the prince
Of ghosts begg'd some intelligence
Of his Eurydice, and where
His beauteous saint resided there.
Then to his lute's instructed groans
He sigh'd out new melodious moans;
And in a melting, charming strain
Begg'd his dear love to live again.
    The music flowing through the shade
And darkness did with ease invade
The silent and attentive ghosts;
And Cerberus, which guards those coasts
With his loud barkings, overcome
By the sweet notes, was now struck dumb.
The Furies, us'd to rave and howl
And prosecute each guilty soul,
Had lost their rage, and in a deep
Transport, did most profusely weep.
Ixion's wheel stopp'd, and the curs'd
Tantalus, almost kill'd with thirst,
Though the streams now did make no haste,
But wait'd for him, none would taste.
That vulture, which fed still upon
Tityus his liver, now was gone
To feed on air, and would not stay,
Though almost famish'd, with her prey.
    Won with these wonders, their fierce prince
At last cried out, "We yield! and since
Thy merits claim no less, take hence
Thy consort for thy recompense:
But Orpheus, to this law we bind
Our grant: you must not look behind.
Nor of your fair love have one sight,
Till out of our dominions quite."
    Alas! what laws can lovers awe?
Love is itself the greatest law!
Or who can such hard bondage brook
To be in love, and not to look?

Poor Orpheus almost in the light
Lost his dear love for one short sight;
And by those eyes, which Love did guide,
What he most lov'd unkindly died!
   This tale of Orpheus and his love
Was meant for you, who ever move
Upwards, and tend unto that light,
Which is not seen by mortal sight.
For if, while you strive to ascend,
You droop, and towards Earth once bend
Your seduc'd eyes, down you will fall
Ev'n while you look, and forfeit all.

III

PARADYS ERTHELY

BOETHIUS is a link between the classical and mediaeval worlds, and a link too between Pythagoreanism and Christianity, for he was subsequently numbered among the saints. We have already noted that although important questions of metaphysics might divide Neopythagoreans and Neoplatonists from the early Christian thinkers, on the dietary question some of the most outstanding Christians were at one with the pagan philosophers. It was therefore only a matter of time before Christian missionaries occupied the Graeco-Roman Earthly Paradise and identified the myth of the Golden Age with the Judaic Garden of Eden.

Alcimus Ecdicius Avitus was Bishop of Vienne from A.D. 470, a few years before Boethius was born. Some of his poems have been lately translated by Jack Lindsay in his *Song of a Falling World*, and as he says, "when Satan sees Adam and Eve, freshly created, in Paradise, his long outburst echoes on into a Miltonic world rather than looks back to the classical models on which its idiom is superficially founded". Yet the lines on life in the Earthly Paradise do carry forward into Christendom something that belongs not to the Book of Genesis but to *Works and Days*.

> Meanwhile, unguessing what's to come, their freedom
> tastes all things good in peace and fully enjoys
> the blessed plenty. Ready earth outstretches
> handfuls of food. Unceasing fruits are thick
> in splendid bushes of the yielding turf;
> and if the branch is burdened with its ripeness
> the tall tree bends and offers its mild apples.
>
> The empty shoot swells straight into a flower
> and brings a childing promise with new buds.
> If pleasant sleeps they seek to crop, they sleep:
> on gentle meadows, embroidered grass, they lie.

The sacred grove surrenders every sweetness
for joy, and teems, fulfilled, with powers renewed.
Thus still they feed and try new snacks of pleasure
though hunger cannot urge them.

They see their nakedness and know no shame,
seeing. Untaught, their goodness feels no evil.
For not man's nature causes shame, but sin.
Whatever members the good God created,
only bad use brings aftermath of shame.
But then the candid mind kept vision pure
as in the glory of high angelic life
which (as we're told) inhabits homes of stars.

Those lines belong to the dawn of mediaeval literature at the end of the fifth century. For the explicit identification of the Golden Age and the Christian Earthly Paradise we must turn to the sublime poem with which the long mediaeval day culminated at the beginning of the fourteenth century, *The Divine Comedy*. Although it is thought probable that the *Timaeus* was the only work of Plato's directly known to Dante, there is, as J. A. Stewart demonstrates, a close resemblance between the Platonic and Dantean cosmologies. The *Phaedo* Myth and *The Divine Comedy* stand alone among eschatological myths in making Tartarus or Hell a chasm bored right through the globe of the Earth. There is an equally close resemblance between the ascension of the purified soul into the presence of God in the *Paradiso* and in the *Phaedrus* Myth. But the comparison that concerns us here is between the True Surface of the Earth of the *Phaedo* Myth and Dante's Earthly Paradise on the summit of the purgatorial island-mountain. The upper parts of both are above the air, in the pure aether, and both are transitional places for souls that will be ultimately exalted to the celestial paradise. It is therefore anything but accidental or incidental to Dante's theme that the classical Golden Age should be blended with the Christian Earthly Paradise during the ascent of Purgatory.

Advancing from the fifth cornice where they have heard illustrious examples of voluntary poverty, Vergil and Dante are overtaken by the spirit of the Roman poet Statius on his way to Paradise, who tells them that—

> here from every change exempt,
> Other than that, which Heaven in itself
> Doth of itself receive, no influence
> Can reach us. Tempest none, shower, hail, or snow,
> Hoar frost, or dewy moistness, higher falls
> Than that brief scale of threefold steps: thick clouds,
> Nor scudding rack, are ever seen: swift glance
> Ne'er lightens; nor Thaumantian Iris gleams,[1]
> That yonder often shifts on each side Heaven.

The three advance together to the sixth cornice of the mountain, where the sin of gluttony is cleansed. "They find a tree hung with sweet-smelling fruit, and watered by a shower that issues from the rock. Voices are heard to proceed from among the leaves, recording examples of temperance." The canto closes with a voice crying:

> The women of old Rome were satisfied
> With water for their beverage. Daniel fed
> On pulse, and wisdom gain'd. The primal age
> Was beautiful as gold: and hunger then
> Made acorns tasteful; thirst, each rivulet
> Run nectar. Honey and locusts[2] were the food,
> Whereon the Baptist in the wilderness
> Fed, and that eminence of glory reach'd
> And greatness, which the Evangelist records.

The poets, proceeding onwards, are overtaken by spirits whom Dante compares with Erysicthon, who was punished with insatiable hunger for felling an oak which was sacred to Ceres, and driven to eat his own flesh, and with a Jewess who devoured her own child during the siege of Jerusalem. After hearing examples of gluttony, the three poets reach the seventh and last cornice, where the sin of incontinence is purged in fire, whence they are sent forward by an Angel to the Terrestrial Paradise on the summit. And just as in Plato's Myth, jewels fell from the True Surface of the Earth to our mundane world, so in Dante's poem the aether is impregnated with the seeds of the trees of the Earthly Paradise, which are carried to our hemisphere, says Stewart, where they germinate according as they find

---

[1] The rainbow.

[2] Probably not the winged edible insect but the fruit of the carob-tree or cassia pod, also called "locust" —*O.E.D.*

soils and climates suitable to their various virtues. Dante questions the lady whom he sees beyond a stream, and she answers:

> "They, whose verses of yore
> The golden age recorded, and its bliss,
> On the Parnassian mountain, of this place
> Perhaps had dream'd. Here was man guiltless; here
> Perpetual spring, and every fruit; and this
> The far-famed nectar." Turning to the bards,
> When she had ceased, I noted in their looks
> A smile at her conclusion.

"They recognise with delight", Cary notes, "that the poetic dreams of the Golden Age find their realization here."

Dante's younger contemporary, Petrarch, is chiefly famous for an interminable succession of sonnets to Laura, the object of his hopeless passion as Beatrice was of Dante's. But the occasion of Petrarch's retirement from the corrupt city of Avignon in Southern France, during his lifetime the residence of the Popes, to the beautiful and solitary valley of the Sorgue a few miles away seems to have been the birth of an illegitimate son by another mistress. "Here I make war upon my senses, and treat them as my enemies", he wrote in a letter soon after he settled in the cottage in Vaucluse, ". . . I keep silence from noon till night. There is no one to converse with; for the good people, employed in spreading their nets, or tending their vines and orchards, are no great adepts at conversation. I often content myself with the brown bread of the fisherman, and even eat it with pleasure. Nay, I almost prefer it to white bread. This old fisherman, who is as hard as iron, earnestly remonstrates against my manner of life; and assures me that I cannot long hold out. I am, on the contrary, convinced that it is easier to accustom one's self to a plain diet than to the luxuries of a feast. But still I have my luxuries —figs, raisins, nuts, and almonds. I am fond of the fish with which this stream abounds. . . ." Petrarch was then in his early thirties. Twenty years later we find him in the village of Garignano on the banks of the Adda, three miles from Milan, "more free than ever from the wearisomeness of the city. I have abundance of everything; the peasants vie with each other in bringing me fruit, fish, ducks, and all sorts of game." From this it appears that, like some monks, Petrarch abstained from the flesh of animals, but was not strict about fish or fowl. At any rate it has been definitely stated that reading Porphyry's essay, *Of Abstinence from the Flesh of Living Animals,* caused Petrarch to become a vegetarian. Perhaps this relates to the time ten years later still when Petrarch built himself a house on the high ground of the village of Arqua, where he went to recover his health. He planted a great number of fruit trees there, but three years later, in 1370, he was still ill, and the friend who was the only person from whom he would take medical advice, since he distrusted doctors, wrote to him that the true cause of his disease was eating fruits, drinking water and fasting frequently; he should abstain from all salted meats, and raw fruits, or herbs. Petrarch had no difficulty in dispensing with salted foods, "but, as to fruits, Nature must have been a very unnatural mother to give us such agreeable food with such delightful hues and fragrance, only to seduce her children with poison covered over with honey".

Plotinus, who displayed "dark Platonic truths in fuller light", and Porphyry, who is regarded only as a sophistical enemy of Christianity, are mentioned among many others in Petrarch's poem, *The Triumph of Fame.* But it is *The Triumph of Love* that reflects Petrarch's knowledge of the classical tradition of an island paradise, as it also expresses his own profound distrust of the pleasures of the senses:

> Far eastward, where the vext Aegean roars,
> A little isle projects its verdant shores:
> Soft is the clime, and fruitful is the ground,
> No fairer spot old ocean clips around;
> Nor Sol himself surveys from east to west
> A sweeter scene in summer livery drest.
> Full in the midst ascends a shady hill,
> Where down its bowery slopes a streaming rill
> In dulcet murmurs flows, and soft perfume
> The senses court from many a vernal bloom,
> Mingled with magic; which the senses steep
> In sloth, and drug the mind in Lethe's deep.
> Quenching the spark divine—the genuine boast
> Of man, in Circe's wave immersed and lost.
> This favour'd region of the Cyprian queen
> Received its freight—a heaven-abandon'd scene,

Where Falsehood fills the throne, while Truth retires,
And vainly mourns her half-extinguish'd fires.
Vile in its origin, and viler still
By all incentives that seduce the will,
It seems Elysium to the sons of Lust,
But a foul dungeon to the good and just.

It is a place of "Fantastic longings for unreal things, And fugitive delights, and lasting woes".

Outside the monasteries, or even within them, there must have been very few Renaissance Italians of wealth and breeding who reacted from the passionate exploration of the pleasures of the senses to such extreme asceticism; for Petrarch went as far beyond the golden mean in the direction of self-denial as most of his contemporaries ventured in self-indulgence. Yet he was not quite without illustrious successors. At the beginning of the sixteenth century, when he was already forty, the son of a leading Venetian family, Luigi Cornaro, found himself so debauched by the pleasures of the city that he placed himself under the most severe restraints and recovered his health. The treatises denouncing gluttony and kindred vices composed between the ages of eighty-five and ninety-five made his name famous in Europe, and his death was as painlessly natural as Pindar's. "After having passed his one hundredth year", Addison recorded in *The Spectator*, on the authority of the Venetian Ambassador, a relative of Cornaro, "he died without pain or agony, and like one who falls asleep".

But the most illustrious and interesting instance is that of Cornaro's great contemporary Leonardo da Vinci. "When he passed places where birds were sold", says Vasari, "he would frequently take them from their cages, and having paid the price demanded for them by the sellers, would then let them fly into the air, thus restoring to them the liberty they had lost." One of the lost pictures of Leonardo's youth was of Adam and Eve in the Garden of Eden which was remarkable for the infinite truth and elaboration of the foliage and animals as well as the beauty of the human figures, and Leonardo himself was full of tenderness to animals, a virtue, as one authority remarks, not common in Italy in spite of the example of St. Francis of Assisi. Leonardo's *Notebooks* contain a *Bestiary* and *Prophecies,* which are like nothing else in European literature. A Prophecy *Of Food which has been Alive* is followed by the forecast that "men will sleep and eat and make their dwelling among trees grown in the forests and the fields", a sort of new Golden Age, and the Platonic *Politicus* Myth in which the nurslings of Cronus talk with the beasts is echoed in Leonardo's Prophecy *Of Dreaming*, ". . . they shall hear creatures of every kind speaking human language . . . you shall hold converse with animals of every species, and they with you in human language". *Of the Mouth of Man which is a Tomb* prophesies that "there shall come forth loud noises out of the tombs of those who have died by an evil and violent death". "You have tried to make yourself a tomb for all animals", Leonardo writes, and he repeatedly mentions the young of animals, without that qualification, as "children" variously butchered and wronged. "That this horror of inflicting pain was such as to lead him to be a vegetarian", writes Edward MacCurdy, the editor of the *Notebooks,* in an earlier study of *The Mind of Leonardo Da Vinci,* "is to be inferred from the reference which occurs in a letter sent by Andrea Corsali to Guiliano de' Medici, in which, after telling him of an Indian race called Gujerats,[1] who neither eat anything that contains blood nor permit any injury to any living creature, he adds 'like our Leonardo da Vinci'." Leonardo was creative human genius in full sympathy and harmony with its total natural and sentient environment.

Such a harmony, prophetic perhaps of what man will become, or again become, is a miraculous equilibrium beyond the understanding of most human beings, at least during the brief span of European history. Leonardo must figure as a sort of eccentric neutral in a tug-of-war between self-denying hermits and self-centred ravishers, both of whom fail in opposite ways to achieve any sort of harmony with the good earth and its creatures. And in this tug-of-war, the instincts and senses have had an overwhelmingly heavier team, and have had no difficulty in convincing common humanity that practically unlimited indulgence of them is the fullest and highest consummation of natural behaviour.

In Greece we found the Orphic reformers purifying an ugly

[1] "Jainism was strong in Gujarat, and its influence was felt everywhere and on all occasions. The opposition to and abhorrence of meat-eating that existed in Gujarat among the Jains and Vaishnavas were to be seen nowhere else in India in such strength. These were the traditions in which I was born and bred."
—M. K. Gandhi, *The Story of my Experiments with Truth.*

orgiastic cult of bloodshed and bacchanal. In Rome Orphic and Pythagorean traditions exercised a strong influence on the greatest men and poets, without in the least inhibiting the excesses of the Saturnalia or the revolting crimes of the circus. For these debauches also there were Oriental precedents. J. C. Ferguson, writing on the prehistoric emperors in a volume of Chinese mythology, says that "At Sha-ch'iu, which is the modern district of P'ing-hsiang in the province of Chihli, there was still greater extravagance and dissipation. There was a pond of wine, and the trees were hung with human flesh; men and women chased each other about quite naked. In the palace there were places where large parties spent the whole night drinking and caressing." In the Indian epic *Mahabharata*, parts of which go back at least to the fourth century B.C., those who die in battle go to Swarga, where the "never-ending joys" are essentially joys of the senses. Thousands of Indra's girls cry out to them, "Be thou my husband." And the heaven of the *Atharva Veda* has a good larder: "Dykes of butter are there, with shores of honey, filled with brandy instead of water, full of milk, of water, of sour milk; such all the streams that flow, honey sweet, welling up in the heavenly land. Lotus groves shall surround thee on every side."

For the Greeks, as we have seen, there was an imaginative choice between the more or less Orphic paradise of the Islands of the Blessed and the orgy in Tartary, and for the Romans a choice between the Fortunate Isles and the gluttonous excesses chronicled by Petronius. In the Middle Ages, essentially the same antithesis was imaged as Eden and Cockaigne. From the sixth century, when the Irish monk St. Brendan was believed to have reached the Earthly Paradise, an island in the Western Ocean, to the fifteenth when Columbus and others went in search of it, the whereabouts of the other Eden was a burning question. But what the public wanted, they gradually discovered, was a paradise of sensual pleasures, embodying but monstrously magnifying the longings of ordinary people, and this was plainly recognised as the opposite of the ideal of Christendom and its contemporary monastic associations. Just where or when the legend of the Land or Island of Cockaigne began no one seems to know. But *The Land of Cockaygne*, dated at the beginning of the fourteenth century and bearing the strongest marks of being even then a translation, probably from the French, is described by F. J. Furnivall as "the airiest and cleverest piece of satire in the whole range of Early English, if not of English, poetry". It is a satire on monks and nuns. Cockaigne is explicitly contrasted with the Paradise of Genesis:

> Though Paradise be merry and bright,
> Cockaygne is of fairer sight;
> What is there in Paradise?
> Both grass and flower and green ris[1]
> Though there be joy and great dute[2]
> There is not meat, but fruit.
> There is not hall, bower nor bench,
> But water man's thirst to quench.

Whereas in Cockaigne:

> There both bowers and halls,
> All of pasties be the walls,
> Of flesh, and fish, and rich meat,
> The like fullest that man may eat.
> Flouren cakes beth the shingles[3] all
> Of church, cloister, bowers, and hall.
> The pinnes[4] beth fat puddings,
> Rich meat to princes and kings.

Other attractions include wells of treacle and spiced wine, and naked nuns in rivers of sweet milk. To come to this super Coney Island one must wade up to the chin in swine's dirt for seven years.

This grosser earthly paradise is folk-lore not poet-lore, and Sir Edmund Chambers gives an example of it in *The English Folk Play*. Beelzebub comes in with a dripping-pan in his hand and tells a tale on which another traditional character, John Finney, comments: "We've come to the land of plenty, rost stones, plum puddings, houses thatched with pancakes, and little pigs running about with knives and forks stuck in their backs crying, 'Who'll eat me, who'll eat me?'" "A great many of our poets in the sixteenth century allude to this story of Cockaygne, but they change its name without much improving it", remarks George Ellis, "they call it Lubberland. In France and Italy the original expression is become proverbial." And it may be added that there is something very similar in Spain in the legend of El Dorado. Ben Jonson certainly knew the tradition,

---

[1] Boughs.   Pleasure.   [3] Tiles.   [4] Pinnacles.

for Littlewit, in the third act of *Bartholomew Fair*, cries, "Good mother, how shall we find a pig, if we do not look about for 't! will it run o' the spit, into our mouths, think you, as in Lubberland, and cry *wee, wee!*" And the pig-wife at this Smithfield saturnalia is a gross, sweating procuress.

The folk-play description of Cockaigne is identical with the scene painted by Pieter Brueghel the Elder in 1567, *The Land of Cockaigne* or Fool's Paradise, where the house thatched with pancakes and the pig with the knife stuck in his back are shown, while in the foreground the symbolic figures of the scholar, the soldier and the peasant lie in bloated torpor, their true vocations neglected. This picture may owe something also to Hieronymus Bosch's nightmarish *Garden of Delights*, a tale of Beelzebub if ever there was one. Both Bosch and Brueghel are, in fact, counter-attacking the popular paradise. "It is possible", writes Anthony Bertram, "simply to share the sensual joy of all these pretty creatures on their primrose path between Paradise and Hell; but that is not what Bosch meant us to do." "The main didactic pattern seems clear enough."

The monk François Rabelais, who died a few years before Brueghel painted his picture of Cockaigne, also had his didactic purpose, although that is hardly what takes most readers to his book. The Rabelaisian Abbey of Theleme, "our earthly paradise" with its motto "Do What Thou Wilt", must be considered along with the island on which Pantagruel goes ashore in Book IV. "We found the Top of the Mountain so fertile, healthful and pleasant, that I thought I was then in the true Garden of Eden, or Earthly Paradise, about whose Situation our good Theologues are in such a quandary, and keep such a pother. . . . The Ruler of the Place was one Master Gaster. . . . In short, he is so unruly, that in his Rage he devours all Men and Beasts."

As for the Gastrolaters, they stuck close to one another in Knots and Gangs. Some of them merry, wanton, and soft as so many Milksops; others lowring, grim, dogged, demure and crabbed, all idle, mortal Foes to Business, spending half their Time in sleeping, and the rest in doing nothing, a Rent-charge and dead unnecessary Weight on the Earth, as Hesiod saith; afraid (as we judg'd) of offending or lessening their Paunch. . . . They all own'd Gaster for their Supreme God, ador'd him as a God, offer'd him Sacrifices as to their Omnipotent Deity, own'd

93

no other God, serv'd, lov'd and honour'd him above all things. You would have thought that the Holy Apostle spoke of those, when he said, Phil. Chap. 3. Many walk of whom I have told you often, and now tell you even weeping, that they are Enemies of the Cross of Christ: whose End is Destruction, whose God is their Belly. Pantagruel compar'd them to the Cyclops Polyphemus, whom Euripides brings in speaking thus, I only Sacrifice to my self (not to the Gods) and to this Belly of mine, the greatest of all the Gods.

The temptations of the flesh need not, of course, be quite so grossly portrayed as they are in the vulgar myth of Cockaigne or by Rabelais. But even in a rather more glamorous form, the contradiction between duty and debauch, a problem whose literary history goes back at least to the Argonauts and the *Odyssey*, is inescapable, and sooner or later the clash was bound to find adequate expression in the work of a Christian poet. In Tasso's *Gerusalemme Liberata*, published towards the end of the sixteenth century, the golden allurements of the Fortunate Isles are deadly peril to the Crusaders, although at the end there is a significant reconciliation between the knight, Rinaldo, and the enchantress, Armida.

Earlier, when Rinaldo is helpless under the amorous spell of Armida, as Ulysses with Calypso, two knights set out in search of him and come presently to the insidious earthly paradise:

> The Isles Fortunate these elder time did call,
> To which high Heaven they feigned so kind and good,
> And of his blessings rich so liberal,
> That without tillage earth gives corn for food,
>   And grapes that swell with sweet and precious wine
>   There without pruning yields the fertile vine.
>
> The olive fat there ever buds and flowers,
> The honey-drops from hollow oaks distil,
> The falling brook her silver streams downpours
> With gentle murmur from their native hill,
> The western blast tempereth with dews and showers
> The sunny rays, lest heat the blossoms kill,
>   The fields Elysian, as fond heathen sain,
>   Were there, where souls of men in bliss remain.

It is "everlasting spring". The whole setting, as C. M. Bowra says, is a triumph of enchantment. "It is Tasso's myth of a complete

94

sensuous joy. It alone could keep Rinaldo from his normal activities, and it does so with entire success. It is, of course, wrong, and must come to an end, but, in the interval, it overwhelms the senses and creates an unbroken illusion of happiness. It is Tasso's strongest and most alluring magic." The rescuers also are subjected to temptation:

> There on a table was all dainty food
> That sea, that earth, or liquid air could give,
> And in the crystal of the laughing flood
> They saw two naked virgins bathe and dive,
> That sometimes toying, sometimes wrestling stood,
> Sometimes for speed and skill in swimming strive,
>   Now underneath they dived, now rose above,
>   And ticing baits laid forth of lust and love.

. . . . . .

> This is the place wherein you may assuage
> Your sorrows past, here is that joy and bliss
> That flourished in the antique golden age,
> Here needs no law, here none doth aught amiss:
> Put off those arms and fear not Mars his rage,
> Your sword, your shield, your helmet needless is;
>   Then consecrate them here to endless rest,
>   You shall love's champions be, and soldiers blest.

The banquet of "all dainty food That sea, that earth or liquid air could give" is not the golden feast, but the treacherous entertainment to which Armida lured other knights:

> A banquet rich and costly furnished was,
>   All beasts, all birds beguiled by fowler's trade,
> All fish were there in floods or seas that pass,
>   All dainties made by art, and at the table
>   An hundred virgins served, for husbands able.

After which Armida turns them into fishes, as Circe turned Ulysses' companions into swine. The association of animal food with transformation into animal form suggests a metempsychosis fantasy, and is at least significant of degradation from full spiritual manhood. We shall find the same purposive use of flesh food imagery in *Comus*, and—as a temptation not to a Crusader but to Christ fasting in the wilderness—in *Paradise Regained*. Before that, Spenser, borrowing from Tasso, must struggle with the same difficult distinction between spiritual and sensual delight, in *The Faerie Queene*. Half a century after Spenser, the Reverend Robert Herrick will keep the piety of *Noble Numbers* and the songs of love and mixed diet in separate compartments of his own Devonshire *Hesperides*.

In his own account of the allegory of the epic, Torquato Tasso insists that Armida is a servant of the devil, and "The flowers, the fountains, the rivers, the musical instruments, the nymphs, are the deceitful enticements, which do here set down before us the pleasures and delights of the Sense, under the show of good". He was obsessed with anxiety about the orthodoxy of his poem and feared it might be pronounced heretical by the Inquisition. Had he not once written a Chorus, in *Aminta*, where constraint upon such pleasures was denounced as unnatural tyranny?[1] Leigh Hunt, translating it nearly three hundred years later, felt obliged to preface the poem with a warning: "It is to be borne in mind, that the opinions expressed in this famous ode of Tasso's, are only so expressed on the supposition of their compatibility with a state of innocence." They are far more compatible with a state of indulgence. Honour is an "idle name of Wind" not only to the preternaturally innocent shepherds but still more to plump Jack: "What is that word, honour? Air!" For, "thou knowest in the state of innocency Adam fell; and what should poor Jack Falstaff do in the days of villany? Thou seest I have more flesh than another man, and therefore more frailty." But if Tasso's Chorus also echoes the Renaissance rebellion of sentient human nature against traditional restraints, it has none of the instinctive vitality that contributes an essential lusty health to Rabelais and Shakespeare. Indeed, notwithstanding the nominal sentiments of this Chorus, W. W. Greg considers that "We are, indeed, justified in regarding what I may term the degeneration of sexual feeling in the *Aminta* as to a great extent the negation of chivalrous love, for, even apart from the allegorising mysticism of Dante, that love contained its ennobling elements". The following version of the Shepherds

---

[1] William Blake's early works, *The Garden of Love* and *A Little Girl Lost* are greater poems on the same theme. It is now fashionable to quote Blake as the apostle of unlimited indulgence. "But later in life", say his editors, D. J. Sloss and J. P. R. Wallis (O.U.P., 1926, II, pp. 3, 26), "though he would doubtless still have defended his earlier position against a challenge, he moves to higher ground in his claim for liberty. "Blake gives here" (in the *Memorable Fancy*, M.H.H., p. 13), "what apparently satisfied him as a basis of harmony between the ascetic life and the life of free expression of the passions. Mortification is not practised in obedience to an external law; for asceticism and enjoyment are equally the results of the prompting of the Genius or Spirit, the True Man."

Chorus is by the poet whom Edmund Spenser much admired,
Samuel Daniel:

> O Happy, Golden Age!
> Not for that Rivers ran
> With Streams of Milk, and Honey dropt from Trees:
> Not that the Earth did gage
> Unto the Husbandman
> Her voluntary Fruits, free without Fees.
> Not for no Cold did freeze,
> Nor any Cloud beguile
> Th' Eternal flow'ring Spring,
> Wherein liv'd ev'ry Thing;
> And whereon th' Heavens perpetually did smile:
> Not for no Ship had brought
> From foreign Shores, or Wars or Wares ill sought
> But only for that Name,
> That idle Name of Wind;
> That Idol of Deceit, that empty Sound
> Call'd HONOUR: which became
> The Tyrant of the Mind,
> And so torments our Nature without Ground,
> Was not yet vainly found:
> Nor yet sad Grief imparts
> Amidst the sweet Delights
> Of joyful, am'rous Wights.
> Nor were his hard Laws known to free-born Hearts;
> But Golden Laws, like these
> Which Nature wrote . . . *That's Lawful, which doth please.*
> Then amongst Flow'rs and Springs,
> Making Delightful Sport,
> Sat Lovers without Conflict, without Flame;
> And Nymphs and Shepherds Sings
> Mixing in wanton sort
> Whisp'rings with Songs, then kisses with the same,
> Which from Affection came.
> The naked Virgin then
> Her Roses fresh reveals,
> Which now her Veil conceals.
> The tender Apples in her Bosom seen;
> And oft in Rivers clear,
> The Lovers with their Loves consorting were.

HONOUR, thou first did'st close
  The Spring of all Delight;
  Denying Water to the am'rous Thirst,
  Thou taught'st fair Eyes to lose
  The Glory of their Light:
  Restrain'd from Men, and on themselves reverst.
  Thou in a Lawn did'st first
  Those Golden Hairs incase,
  Late spread unto the Wind:
  Thou mad'st loose Grace unkind;
  Gav'st Bridle to their Words, Art to their Pace.
  O Honour, it is thou
  That mak'st that Stealth, which Love doth free allow,
It is thy Work that brings
  Our Griefs and Torments thus.
  But thou fierce Lord of Nature and of Love,
  The Qualifier of Kings;
  What does thou here with us,
  That are below thy Pow'r, shut from above?
  Go, and from us remove;
  Trouble the Mighties Sleep;
  Let us neglected base
  Live still without thy Grace,
  And th' Use of th' Ancient Happy Ages keep.
  Let's Love—This Life of ours
  Can make no Truce with Time that all devours.
    Let's Love—The Sun doth set, and rise again;
    But when as our short Light
    Comes once to set, it makes Eternal Night.

So far we have seen the rise of our theme among the poets and philosophers of Greece, and considered the possibility that it may have still more ancient Oriental prototypes. We have followed it through the rise and fall of the Roman Empire, where its fortunes were linked with Neopythagorean and Neoplatonist thought, and with certain eminent Christian Fathers. In the present chapter we have observed the marriage of the classical and Christian traditions on the summit of Dante's purgatorial mountain, and the emergence of a Dionysiac or Saturnalian earthly paradise of the senses in the fabulous Cockaigne which completes a vulgarisation of the Isles of the Blessed implicit in the Homeric dream of a perfect home for heroes who, even after death, were—like the Vedic warriors—to be happy "in the flesh".

With some such sense of a long development in European culture, and of the basic dreams and counter-dreams that persisted through the permutation from Greek to Graeco-Roman, from Roman to mediaeval Christian times and on into the high Renaissance, we may now turn to the British Isles, and first to such traces as we may find of comparable Celtic, Anglo-Saxon and mediaeval beginnings. As we should suppose, the history of our theme in England is integral with what has gone before in Europe. Indeed it is in these fortunate isles, in this other Eden, that something whose value we do not ourselves well understand has been preserved by incomparable poets, something precious that otherwise was lost to Europe. It is not, therefore, a restriction but rather a true perspective that concentrates our attention throughout the three following chapters on the poets of the English Renaissance, the Puritan interregnum and the Augustan eighteenth century. Then, as the story broadens out into the very lives of the nineteenth-century Romantic poets, the focus must widen to reveal glimpses of kindred developments in France, Germany, Italy and the Americas, which are essential to such understanding as we may attain of a creative unfolding that is not yet come to full harvest.

In discussing Pindar we mentioned J. A. Stewart's comparison between the Greek and Celtic Islands of the Blessed, as the latter are known to us through the eighth-century *Voyage of Bran*, which is probably the record of a myth of very much earlier date. Indeed it is the general conclusion of the commentator, Alfred Nutt, that similarities between Celtic, Greek and Indian myths of this kind are due not to any transmission of Asiatic or Mediterranean traditions to these islands but to some archetypal tale that originated in a remote period before the separation of the main branches of the Aryan race. In the ninth to eleventh centuries there was, however, a romantic and didactic development of the Irish Elysium and Christian modification.

The earlier *Voyage of Bran*, as translated by Kuno Meyer, consists of two narrative poems, with introductory, intermediate and concluding narrative passages in prose. The story begins when Bran hears music which soothes him to sleep, and awakes to find a silver

99

branch with white blossoms, which he takes to his royal house where a stranger-woman sings to him, declaring that she has brought this branch of the apple-tree from Emain. There is a distant isle, a delight to the eyes, lovely throughout the world's age, on which the many blossoms drop:

> Unknown is wailing or treachery
> In the familiar cultivated land,
> There is nothing rough or harsh,
> But sweet music striking on the ear.
>
> Without grief, without sorrow, without death,
> Without any sickness, without debility,
> That is the sign of Emain—
> Uncommon is an equal marvel.

She goes on to sing of golden and silver chariots on the Plain of Sports, and of bronze without blemish, yellow and crimson steeds and others with sky-blue wool upon them.[1] A host will come across the sea—as Horace essayed to lead the Romans in the sixteenth *Epode*—and Bran is exhorted not to fall on a bed of sloth or let intoxication overcome him, but to voyage across the sea to reach "the Land of Women".

The conclusion of her song strikes an unexpected note, and she then departs, taking the branch which springs from Bran's hand to her own. On the morrow he embarks and after two days and two nights at sea, he sees coming towards him over the waves a man in a chariot who sings the second song. The singer himself is able to see in the promised place "Red-headed flowers without fault"—the phrase is overwhelmingly reminiscent of the crimson-flowered meadows of the Pindar fragment—rivers pour forth a stream of honey, there are men and women under a bush without sin or crime and a wood of acorn-trees; and there is a puzzling and obscure allusion to calves (apparently salmon!) as "coloured lambs, With friendliness, without mutual slaughter".

> A wood with blossom and fruit,
> On which is the vine's veritable fragrance,
> A wood without decay, without defect,
> On which are leaves of golden hue.

[1] cf. Vergil's fourth *Eclogue* quoted on p. 69.

We are from the beginning of creation
Without old age, without consummation of earth,
Hence we expect not that there should be frailty,
The sin has not come to us.

The next verse is evidently a Christian gloss, lamenting the advent of the Serpent who "has perverted the times in this world, So that there came decay which was not original. By greed and lust he has slain us." But the song ends with exhortation to Bran to row steadily, he is not far from the Land of Women.

The *Voyage* then reverts for the last time to prose, and makes a most interesting distinction between *two* places that the voyagers reach. First there is the Island of Joy on which one man only is put ashore. Not long afterwards they reach the Land of Women, and as with the Argonauts at Lesbos, "There was a bed for every couple. The food that was put on every dish vanished not from them. It seemed a year to them that they were there—it chanced to be many years. No savour was wanting to them." This situation is common to other Irish myths, for instance the later *Voyage of Maelduin* includes a similar episode on the Island of the Amorous Queen. In the *Voyage of Bran*, homesickness seizes one man, eventually, and all depart after being reminded that they should pick up the one man whom they had left on the Island of Joy. There is nothing to indicate they do so, for the three concluding paragraphs tell of the return to Ireland, where the nostalgic sailor is turned to dust and ashes as he lands, and of Bran's narration of their adventures.

The impression left on the inexpert reader is that two myths have been unskilfully combined, so that an "Eden" paradise and a "Cockaigne" paradise have become partially confused, though some trace of the two quite different places—and no doubt of the preference of the majority—has survived. Robert Graves refers me to his book *The White Goddess* for evidence that "Cronos-Saturn, the hero of the pre-agricultural Golden Age, is mythologically identical with the Irish hero, Bran. Bran's 'Islands of the Blessed' are true Golden Age places—but 'the Golden Age' and 'Paradise' are concepts that get mixed up inextricably with a common element of Repose; as 'arcady' in England gets mixed up with the 'May Dream' of the starved Northern chimney-corner." The Falstaffian shadow of Cockaigne has fallen across the picture.

But, as J. A. MacCulloch records, "the Irish could also look back to a golden age" of peace and friendship, plenty and prosperity, and "the result is that which everywhere marked the golden age." In his unique *Studies in Early Celtic Nature Poetry*, Kenneth Jackson is struck by the apparently disproportionate emphasis on particular natural foods: "Another peculiarity is the interest in woodland foods. It was shown that it is typical of the earlier hagiological literature and hermit poems to describe the holy man's frugal diet as one of his ascetic virtues, and perhaps later Irish poetry was influenced by this to develop a similar convention for itself. The treatment is different, however, for in this instance the foods are not catalogued to show the frugality of the Fiana but are treated with the joy of the woodsman in the varied and delicious eatables which he lives on in the wilds. This has had its reaction upon hermit poetry in the comparatively late *King and Hermit*, where the interest in food is expanded out of all proportion to such a poem and in a somewhat unascetic manner; and perhaps too upon the Wild Man theme in poem XIII, though there also a certain interest in foods, a complaint about their meagre nature, is natural. The variety of plants and animals found in the countryside and eaten by the early Irish on the testimony of the poems is quite astonishing to a twentieth-century town-dweller, to whom 'living on berries and nuts' seems such an improbable kind of existence."

It would not, we may surmise, have seemed improbable to Thoreau in the nineteenth century, or to Shelley and Keats. Jackson follows the foregoing remarks with a catalogue of foods mentioned in the poems, mainly fruits. In the poem cited, the seventh-century King of Connaught comes to the Christian hermit who is his own brother and asks why he has left the world. When he has heard the reply, mostly detailing the natural foods on which the hermit lives, the King envies him. One feels that this might be a Hindu tale of Brahmin and ruler, or another instance in the examples of hermit-saints related to Dante on the purgatorial mountain, while the joy of the woodsman in his delicious eatables looks backwards to the Eden myth and forward to the English hermit poetry of the eighteenth century, discussed in Chapter 6.

Here we may quote a shorter poem from the same source consisting of nothing but a series of references to natural food:

This my nightly sustenance,
ever the gleanings of my hands,
what I pluck in dark oak groves
of herbs and abundant fruits.

Splendid blaeberries are my delight,
they are sweeter than soft shoots;
brooklime, seaweed, they are delightful to me,
the herbage and the watercress.

Apples, berries, nuts of the goodly hazel,
blackberries, acorns from the oak-tree,
raspberries, the due of generosity,
haws of the prickly sharp hawthorn.

Wood-sorrel, sorrel, fine wild garlic,
and clean-topped watercress,
together they drive starvation from me,
berries of the moor, root of the wild onion.

This list may be compared with the "home-grown food of the
English New Eden" consisting solely of herbs, fruits, nuts and honey
—no cereals or animal foods—of the Christian Contemplatives'
Charity that has existed for the last thirty years at Burton Bradstock
in Dorset.

The anthology of poetry given to the Library of Exeter by
Leofric, who was first Bishop of Exeter in the middle of the eleventh
century, generally known as the *Exeter Book*, is the Anglo-Saxon
source for the poem of *The Phoenix* which—like others in the same
collection, but less certainly—has sometimes been attributed to
Cynewulf, who flourished in the middle of the eighth century.
The Phoenix is, however, based on a Latin poem ascribed by the
sixth-century Gregory of Tours to Lactantius, while Claudian has
an idyll on the Phoenix that makes the Earthly Paradise an island.
The island and its fruits are not, however, in the fourth-century
Latin poem. The Phoenix legend itself is said to be of Egyptian
origin and first appears in Herodotus and is developed in the final
book of Ovid's *Metamorphoses* that deals with the Pythagorean
philosophy. The subsequent history of the theme includes a poem
published over Shakespeare's name and a number of indubitable

allusions in his sonnets and plays. Poetically, at least, the Phoenix has justified its reputation for regeneration.

The Anglo-Saxon poem, quoted in the version by Israel Gollancz, opens with a description of the paradisal island-plateau where the door of Heaven's realm is ofttimes opened, and which is twelve fathoms higher than any mountain. It therefore escaped the flood— the Christian element is intrusive—and will abide perennially bloom- ing until the Day of Judgment.

> I have heard tell that there is far hence,
> in eastern parts, a land most noble,
> famed 'mong folk. That tract of earth is not
> accessible to many o'er mid-earth,
> to many chieftains; but it is far-removed,
> through might of the Creator, from evil-doers.
>
> Beauteous is all the plain, blissful with delights
> with all the fairest fragrances of earth;
> that island is incomparable; noble the Maker,
> lofty and in power abounding who founded that land.
> There the door of Heaven's realm is ofttimes opened
> in sight of the happy, and the joy of its harmonies is revealed.

We are reminded not only of Plato's True Surface of the Earth, but much more of the Terrestrial Paradise on the summit of Dante's Purgatorial Mountain.

> In that land there is not hateful enmity,
> nor wail, nor vengeance, nor any sign of woe,
> nor old age, nor misery, nor narrow death,
> nor loss of life, nor harm's approach,
> nor sin, nor strife, nor sorry exile,
> nor poverty's toil, nor lack of wealth,
> nor care, nor sleep, nor grievous sickness,
> nor winter's darts, nor tempest's tossing
> rough 'neath heaven, nor doth hard frost
> with cold chill icicles, crush any creature there.
> Nor hail nor rime descendeth thence to earth,
> nor windy cloud; nor falleth water there
> driven by the wind, but limpid streams,
> wondrous rare, spring freely forth;

With fair bubblings, from the forest's midst,
winsome waters irrigate the soil;
each month from the turf of the mould
sea-cold they burst, and traverse all the grove
at times full mightily. 'Tis the Lord's behest,
that twelve times o'er that glorious land
the joyous water-floods should sport.
The groves are all behung with blossoms,
with beauteous growths; the holt's adornments,
holy 'neath heaven, fade never there,
nor do fallow blossoms, the beauty of the forest trees,
fall then to earth; but there, in wondrous wise,
the boughs upon the trees are ever laden,
the fruit is aye renewed, through all eternity.
On that grassy plain there standeth green,
decked gloriously, through power of the Holy One,
the fairest of all groves. The wood knoweth no breach
in all its beauty; holy fragrance resteth there
throughout that land; ne'er shall it be changed,
in all eternity, until He who first created it
shall end His ancient work of former days.

In this wondrous place where the fruit eternally renews itself the fabulous bird also rises immortal in successive incarnations.

The eighth-century Anglo-Saxon poet elaborated and Christianised his Roman model, as the Celtic myths were being Christianised if not Latinised from that time onwards. Boethius, who had spoken of following the Pythagorean rather than the Christian command to follow God, but had been conscripted by general consent rather than ecclesiastical authority into the company of the saints a century or two after his death, underwent a similar embellishment in the ninth century at the hands of Alfred the Great of Wessex, whose version of *The Consolation of Philosophy* is fairly described as a paraphrase rather than a translation, and was one of Alfred's most important and accomplished literary performances. Into his adaptation of the verses on *The Former Age*, with which—in a more accurate translation—our last chapter concluded, Alfred introduces not only the Christian God but Christ and Hell-Fire also. Orpheus, we may note here, seems to have arrived in England with the Romans who pictured him in a mosaic found in the Isle of

Wight, and—after an unpromising start in the first circle of Dante's Hell, with the souls of others "who although they have lived virtuously and have not to suffer for great sins, nevertheless, through lack of baptism, merit not the bliss of Paradise", including Adam, Abel, Noah, Vergil, Socrates, Plato, Empedocles and other distinguished company—survived in Christian art, where he is finally metamorphosed into the Good Shepherd and his sheep.

It was, however, some measure of the influence of Boethius's work that he should be handled at all by one of the greatest British kings, the greatest British queen—for Elizabeth herself Englished Boethius, as we shall see—and by Britain's first great poet, Geoffrey Chaucer. Chaucer does not repeat the Christian allusions in his own expansion of *The Former Age*, made some five hundred years after Alfred's, although he characterises the golden times as those when no Nimrod sought for power—a reference to Nimrod, the mighty hunter of Genesis.

> A blisful lyf, a paisible and a swete
> Ledden the peples in the former age;
> They helde hem payed of fruites, that they ete,
> Which that the feldes yave hem by usage;
> They ne were nat forpampred with outrage;
> Unknowen was the quern and eek the melle;
> They eten mast, hawes, and swich pounage,
> And dronken water of the colde welle.
> Yit was the ground nat wounded with the plough,
> But corn up-sprong, unsowe of mannes hond,
> The which they gniden, and eete nat half y-nough.
>
> No man yit knew the forwes of his lond;
> Ne man the fyr out of the flint yit fond;
> Un-korven and un-grobbed lay the vyne;
> No man yit in the morter spyces grond
> To clarre, ne to sause of galantyne.

Glossary:
helde hem payed: thought themselves satisfied.
forpampred with outrage: spoilt by pampering and excess.
quern and eek the melle: hand-mill and also the (?wind) mill.
eten mast, hawes, and swich pounage: ate acorns, haws and such pannage (swine's food).
gniden: kneaded, rubbed. *forwes:* furrows.
un-korven and un-grobbed: unpruned and not digged round.
clarre: wine mixed with honey and spices and afterwards strained clear.
galantyne: sauce or galantine.

No mader, welde, or wood no litestere
Ne knew; the flees was of his former hewe;
No flesh ne wiste offence of egge or spere;
No coyn ne knew man which was fals or trewe;
No ship yit karf the wawes grene and blewe;
No marchaunt yit ne fette outlandish ware;
No trompes for the werres folk ne knewe,
No toures heye, and walles rounde or square.

What sholde it han avayled to werreye?
Ther lay no profit, ther was no richesse,
But cursed was the tyme, I dar wel seye,
That men first dide hir swety bysinesse
To grobbe up metal, lurkinge in darknesse,
And in the riveres first gemmes soghte.
Allas! than sprong up al the cursednesse
Of covetyse, that first our sorwe broghte!

Thise tyraunts putte hem gladly nat in pres,
No wildnesse, ne no busshes for to winne
Ther poverte is, as seith Diogenes,
Ther as vitaile is eek so skars and thinne
That noght but mast er apples is therinne.
But, ther as bagges been and fat vitaile,
Ther wol they gon, and spare for no sinne
With al hir ost the cite for t'assaile.

Yit were no paleis-chaumbres, ne non halles;
In caves and [in] wodes softe and swete
Slepten this blissed folk with-oute walles,
On gras or leves in parfit quite.
No doun of fetheres, ne no bleched shete
Was kid to hem, but in seurtee they slepte;
Hir hertes were al oon, with-oute galles,
Everich of hem his feith to other kepte.

Unforged was the hauberk and the plate;
The lambish peple, voyd of alle vyce,
Hadden no fantasye to debate,
But ech of hem wolde other wal cheryce;

Glossary:
mader, welde, or wood no litestere: madder, weld, or woad (plants used for dyeing yellow and blue) nor dyer.
egge: edge, sword. *werreye:* make war. *sorwe:* sorrow.
pres: ? forced labour. *wildnesse:* wilderness. *ost:* host, army.
kid: known. *everich:* each. *fantasye:* imaginary good.
debate: quarrel over. *cheryce:* cherish.

107

No pryde, non envye, non avaryce,
No lord, no taylage by no tyrannye;
Humblesse and pees, good feith, the emperice,
(Fulfilled erthe of elde curtesye.)

Yit was not Jupiter the likerous,
That first was fader of delicacye,
Come in this world; ne Nembrot, desirous
To reynen, had nat maad his toures hye.
Allas, allas! now may men wepe and crye!
For in our dayes nis but covetyse
(And) doublenesse, and tresoun and envye,
Poysoun, manslauhtre, and merdre in sondry wyse.

Chaucer's elaboration of *The Former Age* is the more justifiable in that he also offers a prose translation of the original in his complete version of *The Consolation of Philosophy*. If his rehandling of the material makes *The Former Age* an English poem it is one that does not depart at all in spirit from the "metre" by Boethius.

The Chaucerian fragment of *The Romaunt of the Rose*, translated or imitated from the French, conjures up an Earthly Paradise very different from the early fourteenth-century *Land of Cockaygne*. Chaucer's enchanted Garden, wherein is the Lady Beauty, fairer than any in the world, adored like Dante's Beatrice with a love transcending the senses, is not on the mediaeval map, or conceived in the likeness of the pleasures of his own day magnified into monstrosity. It is, as the poet tells us, a dream, a vision which only the foolish will dismiss as meaningless.

And whan I was [there]in, y-wis,
Myn herte was ful glad of this.
For wel wende I ful sikerly
Have been in paradys erth[e]ly;
So far it was, that, trusteth wel,
It semed a place espiritual.
For certes, as at my devys,
Ther is no place in paradys
So good in for to dwelle or be
As in that Gardin, thoughte me.

Glossary:
taylage: taxation. *emperice:* ? empress. *likerous:* lecherous. *delicacye:* wantonness.
sikerly: certainly. *syke:* sick, ill.

Presently he describes the trees of the Garden:

> Of fruyt hadde every tree his charge,
> But it were any hidous tree
> Of which ther were two or three.
> Ther were, and that wot I ful wel,
> Of pomgarnettes a ful gret del;
> That is a fruyt ful wel to lyke,
> Namely to folk whan they ben syke.
> And trees ther were, greet foisoun,
> That baren notes in hir sesoun,
> Such as men notemigges calle,
> That swote of savour been withalle.
> And alemandres greet plentee,
> Figes, and many a date-tree
> Ther weren, if men hadde nede,
> Through the yerd in length and brede.
> Ther was eek wexing many a spyce,
> As clow-gelofre, and licoryce,
> Gingere, and greyn de paradys,
> Canelle, and setewale of prys,
> And many a spyce delitable,
> To eten when men ryse from table.
> And many hoomly trees there were,
> That peches, coynes, and apples bere,
> Medlers, ploumes, peres, chesteynes,
> Cheryse, of which many on fayn is,
> Notes, aleys, and bolas,
> That for to seen it was solas;
> With many high lorer and pyn
> Was renged clene al that gardyn;
> With cipres, and with oliveres,
> Of which that nigh no plente here is.
> Ther were elmes grete and stronge,
> Maples, asshe, ook, ash, planges longe,
> Fyn ew, popler, and lindes faire,
> And other trees ful many a payre.

Glossary:
baren notes in hir sesoun: bear nuts in their season.
notemigges: nutmegs. *swote:* sweet.
greyn de paradys: grains of paradise (African plant used as spice).
cannelle, and setewale of prys: cinnamon and zedoary (Indian aromatic plant) of price (value).
coynes: quinces. *chesteynes:* chestnuts.
notes, aleys and bolas: nuts, service-berries and bullace-plums.
solas: solace, comfort, pleasure. *lorer and pyn:* laurel and pine.
asshe, ook, ash, planges longe: ash-trees, oaks, ash and plane-trees.
lindes: lindens, lime-trees.

> What sholde I tell you more of it?
> Ther were so many trees yit,
> That I sholde al encombred be
> Er I had rekened every tree.

In the following century, in Sir Thomas Malory's *Le Morte d'Arthur*, there is another visionary Earthly Paradise, as much beyond time and space as the Garden of Chaucer's dream. "The book belongs to no age and no condition of normal life", it has been said, "and this 'bodiless creation' is an element in its immortality." When the dying King Arthur's great sword is at last thrown into the water and has vanished, his soul is free to go to the apple-orchard paradise; "I will into the vale of Avilion". Tennyson expanded the passage from Malory as Chaucer had enlarged Boethius:

> The old order changeth, yielding place to new,
> And God fulfils himself in many ways,
> Lest one good custom should corrupt the world.
> Comfort thyself: what comfort is in me?
> I have lived my life, and that which I have done
> May He within himself make pure! but thou,
> If thou shouldst never see my face again,
> Pray for my soul. More things are wrought by prayer
> Than this world dreams of. Wherefore, let thy voice
> Rise like a fountain for me night and day.
> For what are men better than sheep or goats
> That nourish a blind life within the brain,
> If, knowing God, they lift not hands of prayer
> Both for themselves and those who call them friend?
> For so the whole round earth is every way
> Bound by gold chains about the feet of God.
> But now farewell. I am going a long way
> With these thou seest—if indeed I go
> (For all my mind is clouded with a doubt)—
> To the island-valley of Avilion;
> Where falls not hail, or rain, or any snow,
> Nor ever wind blows loudly; but it lies
> Deep meadow'd, happy, fair with orchard lawns
> And bowery hollows crown'd with summer sea,
> Where I will heal me of my grievous wound.

IV

THIS OTHER EDEN

S U C H manner time there was (what time I n'ot)
When all this earth, this dam or mould of ours,
Was only wonned with such as beasts begot.
Unknown as then were they that builded towers.
The cattle wild or tame, in Nature's bowers
Might freely roam, or rest, as seemed them;
Man was not made their dwellings in to hem.

The beasts had sure some beastly policy—
For nothing can endure where order n'is—
For once the lion by the lamb did lie,
The fearful hind the leopard did kiss,
Hurtless was tiger's paw and serpent's hiss:
This think I well, the beasts with courage clad,
Like senators a harmless empire had:

At which whether the others did repine
(For envy harboureth most in feeblest hearts),
Or that they all to changing did incline
(As even in beasts their dams love changing parts),
The multitude to Jove a suit imparts,
With neighing, blaying, braying, and barking,
Roaring and howling for to have a king.

A king, in language theirs, they said they would,
For then their language was a perfect speech;
The birds likewise with chirps and pewing could,
Cackling and chattering, that of Jove beseech.
Only the owl still warn'd them not to seech
So hastily that which they would repent:
But saw they would, and he to deserts went.

Jove wisely said (for wisdom wisely says),
O beasts, take heed what you of me desire:

Rulers will think all things made them to please,
And soon forget the swink due to their hire;
But, since you will, part of my heavenly fire
I will you lend; the rest yourselves must give,
That it both seen and felt may with you live.

. . . . .

Thus Man was made, thus Man their lord became:
Who at the first, wanting or hiding pride,
He did to beasts best use his cunning frame,
With water drink, herbs meat, and naked hide,
And fellow-like, let his dominion slide,
Not in his sayings saying *I*, but *we*,
As if he meant his lordship common be.

But when his seat so rooted he had found
That they now skill'd not how from him to wend,
Then gan in guiltless earth full many a wound,
Iron to seek, which gainst itself should bend,
To tear the bowels that good corn should send:
But yet the common dam none did bemoan,
Because, though hurt, they never heard her groan.

Then gan he factions in the beasts to breed;
Where helping weaker sort, the nobler beasts,
As tigers, leopards, bears, and lion's seed,
Disdain'd with this, in deserts sought their rests,
Where famine ravine taught their hungry chests.
Thus craftily he forced them to do ill,
Which being done, he afterwards would kill.

For murther done—which never erst was seen—
By those great beasts, as for the weakers' good,
He chose themselves his guarders for to been
Gainst those of might, of whom in fear they stood,
As horse and dog, not great, but gentle blood:
Blithe were the common cattle of the field,
The when they saw their foen of greatness kill'd.

But they or spent, or made of slender might,
Then quickly did the meaner cattle find
The great beams gone, the house on shoulders light.
For by and by the horse fair bits did bind;

112

The dog was in a collar taught his kind;
As for the gentle birds, like case may rue,
When falcon they and goshawk saw in mew.

Worst fell to smallest birds and meanest herd,
Whom now his own, full like his own he used.
Yet first but wool or feathers off he tear'd:
And when they were well used to be abused,
For hungry teeth their flesh with teeth he bruised.
At length for glutton taste he did them kill:
At last for sport their silly lives did spill.

But yet, O man, rage not beyond thy need;
Deem it no glory to swell in tyranny.
Thou art of blood: joy not to see things bleed.
Thou fearest death: think they are loth to die.
A plaint of guiltless hurt doth pierce the sky:
And you, poor beasts, in patience bide your hell,
Or know your strengths, and then you shall do well.

Sidney's song of a Golden Age of the creatures is sung by the old shepherd, Lanquet, in "oak's true shade", and sung again by the young shepherd to his sheep in the starless night. The viewpoint is almost that of the animals themselves, and the description—most of which is here omitted—of the emergence of man[1] almost foreshadows later evolutionary doctrines. Something of the urgent humanism of the Renaissance has been imparted to mankind's dealings with earth's other living inhabitants. It is man who sets dissension among the creatures, and his own decline from harmlessness to wanton butchery is imaged as a fall from water and herbs to flesh foods and blood sports, the *Arcadia* has its arcana.

Bishop Joseph Hall paints a similar picture of human depredation, but allows that there was a Golden Age, probably because the

---

[1] The idea seems to have been in the air of the age. Without searching for instances I have come across allusions in Spenser, Shakespeare and Donne, as well as Sidney.

In "The ancient chronicles of Britain and Fairyland" in the Legend of Temperance, Spenser makes Sir Guyon read a book that told "how first Prometheus did create A man, of many parts from beasts derived, and then stole fire from heaven to animate His work".

Shakespeare's Ferdinand in *The Tempest* (III. i) admires his Miranda as "created Of every creature's best".

John Donne opens his poem *To Sir Edward Herbert at Juliers* with the lines: "Man is a lump, where all beasts kneaded be, Wisdom makes him an Ark where all agree".

The Pythagorean doctrine that man comprehended within himself all the degrees of creation, and was the focus point of the great chain of being, has never been more strongly held than it was in the age of Elizabeth, according to E. M. W. Tillyard, *The Elizabethan World Picture*, pp. 60–2.

In another poem, *The Progress of the Soul*, Donne incidentally satirises the Pythagorean doctrine of metempsychosis, as Ben Jonson did in *Volpone*. We are returning to *The Golden Ass* phase of the cycle, with all that that implies of *fin de siècle*.

contrast drives home his satirical point. It also echoes the Spenserian contrast of Mammon and the antique age, which we shall next consider. Where the mediaeval emphasis fell upon a present, if remote, Earthly Paradise, visionary or gross, the Renaissance poetry is, surprisingly to the modern reader who is habituated to regarding that period as a glorious emergence from the Dark Ages, much occupied with nostalgia for the good old days. This is how Hall sees it.

> Time was, and that was termed the time of gold,
> When world and time were young, that now are old,
> When quiet Saturn swayed the mace of lead,
> And pride was yet unborn, and yet unbred.
> Time was, that while the autumn fall did last,
> Our hungry sires gaped for the falling mast.
> Could no unhuskéd acorn leave the tree,
> But there was challenge made whose it might be.
> And if some nice and lickerous appetite
> Desired more dainty dish of rare delight,
> They scaled the storéd crab with claspéd knee,
> Till they had sated their delicious eye;
> Or searched the hopeful thicks of hedgy-rows,
> For briary berries, or haws, or sourer sloes;
> Or when they meant to fare the finest of all,
> The licked oak-leaves besprent with honey fall.
> As for the thrice three-angled beech-nut shell,
> Or chestnut's arméd husk, and hid kernel,
> No squire durst touch; the law would not afford,
> Kept for the court, and for the king's own board.
> Their royal plate was clay, or wood, or stone;
> The vulgar, save his hand, else had he none.
> Their only cellar was the neighbour brook;
> None did for better care, for better look.
> Was then no plaining of the brewer's scape,
> Nor greedy vintner mixed the strained grape.
> The king's pavilion was the grassy green,
> Under safe shelter of the shady treen.
> Under each bank men laid their limbs along,
> Not wishing any ease, not fearing wrong;
> Clad with their own, as they were made of old,
> Not fearing shame, not feeling any cold.

But when, by Ceres' housewifery and pain,
Men learned to bury the reviving grain,
And father Janus taught the new-found vine
Rise on the elm, with many a friendly twine,
And base desire bade men to delven low,
For needless metals, then 'gan mischief grow.
Then farewell, fairest age, the world's best days,
Thriving in ill as it in age decays.
Then crept in pride, and peevish covetise,
And men grew greedy, discordous, and nice.
Now man, that erst hail-fellow was with beast,
Wox on to ween himself a god at least.
No airy fowl can take so high a flight,
Though she her daring wings in clouds have dight;
Nor fish can dive so deep in yielding sea,
Though Thetis' self should swear her safety;
Nor fearful beast can dig his cave so low,
All could he further than Earth's centre go;
As that the air, the earth, or ocean,
Should shield them from the gorge of greedy man.
Hath utmost Ind aught better than his own?
Then utmost Ind is near, and rife to gon.
O Nature! was the world ordained for nought,
But fill man's maw, and feed man's idle thought?
Thy grandsire's words savoured of thrifty leeks,
Or manly garlic; but thy furnace reeks
Hot steams of wine; and can aloof descry
The drunken draughts of sweet autumnity.
They naked went, or clad in ruder hide,
Or home-spun russet, void of foreign pride;
But thou canst mask in garish gaudery,
To suite a fool's far-fetchéd livery.
A French head joined to neck Italian;
Thy thighs from Germany, and breast fro Spain;
An Englishman in none, a fool in all;
Many in one, and one in severall.
Then men were men; but now the greater part
Beasts are in life, and women are in heart.
Good Saturn self, that homely emperor,
In proudest pomp was not so clad of yore,

115

As is the under-groom of the ostlery,
Husbanding it in work-day yeomanry.
Lo! the long date of those expired days,
Which the inspiréd Merlin's word foresays:
'When dunghill peasants shall be digt as kings,
Then one confusion another brings.'
Then farewell, fairest age, the world's best days,
Thriving in ill, as it in age decays.

Hall's poem of *The Olden Days* appeared in 1597. The previous poem, by Sir Philip Sidney, was published in his *Arcadia* in 1590, four years after his death at Zutphen, and in the same year Edmund Spenser published the first three books of *The Faerie Queene*. Faery Land is the mind, inner experience, and in Spenser's poem man, beast and nature are all such stuff as dreams are made on, and dreams meant to be interpreted. There, too is a Golden Age:

The antique world, in his first flowering youth,
Fownd no defect in his Creators grace;
But with glad thankes, and unreprovéd truth,
The guifts of soveraine bounty did embrace:
Like Angels life was then mens happy cace;
But later ages pride, like corn-fed steed,
Abusd her plenty and fat swoln encreace
To all licentious lust, and gan exceed
The measure of her meane and naturall first need.

Then gan a cursed hand the quiet wombe
Of his great Grandmother with steale to wound,
And the hid treasures in her sacred tombe
With Sacriledge to dig. Therein he fownd
Fountaines of gold and silver to abownd,
Of which the matter of his huge desire
And pompous pride eftsoones he did compownd;
Then āvārīce gan through his veines inspire
His greedy flames, and kindled life-devouring fire.

The verses are from the second book of *The Faerie Queene*, which tells *The Legend of Sir Guyon, or of Temperaunce*. Sir Guyon encounters Mammon and answers his persuasions with this description of the antique world of happy innocence. Mammon's advice is to engage his life for gold, "And leave the rudenesse of that antique age To them that liv'd therin in state forlorne". He leads the knight through the chambers of his palace, where Guyon is exposed to more searching temptations. When he refuses to wed Mammon's daughter:

> Mammon emmoved was with inward wrath;
> Yet, forcing it to fayne, him forth thence ledd,
> Through griesly shadowes by a beaten path,
> Into a gardin goodly garnished
> With hearbs and fruits, whose kinds mote not be redd:
> Not such as earth out of her fruitful woomb
> Throwes forth to men, sweet and well savoréd,
> But direfull deadly black, both leafe and bloom,
> Fitt to adorne the dead, and deck the dreary toombe.

This Garden of Proserpina is an inverted picture of the sovereign bounty of the "antique world". Its golden apples are natural fruits poisoned with Mammon's gold.[1] Had Sir Guyon, weak for want of food, tasted these tainted fruits, he would have been torn into a thousand pieces by the fiend that follows him. Refusing this last temptation, he is free to return "into the world".

The contrasting food symbolism is fairly clear but lacks the vital opposition of fruit and flesh which has been a main characteristic of the theme in the hands of earlier poets. It might be considered that Spenser used such symbolism purposefully at the beginning and end of the first book of *The Faerie Queene*[2] and we shall see immediately that the distinction is finally made in the last books of the poem. But in this book dealing with temperance, where such precision is most to be expected, Spenser's symbolic technique, as Wilson Knight observes, is faulty. "There is a certain want of imaginative common sense, and perhaps insincerity: as though ethical principles were not, in the wider issues of this work, perfectly integrated with esthetic associations into his imaginative scheme."

Imprecisions of symbolism are symptomatic of deeper confusions

---

[1] Spenser surely owes something here to Sir John Mandeville's Fable of *A Rich Man, that made a Marvel-us Castle, and cleped it Paradise; and of His Subtlety*, in tempting "any good knight" with "trees bearing manner of fruits" and "fairest damosels".

[2] The first contest of the Red Cross Knight (Holiness) is with Error (half woman, half serpent), whose pulsiveness is partially rendered through revolting flesh and blood food images, I, xx. His final combat with the terrible Dragon, described in closely similar terms (XI, xiii), and he triumphs through the living influence of the pure stream that flows from the Tree of Life. This is the tree, laden with fruit of rosy apples, planted by God, the source of great virtues and happy life. (XI, xlvi-xlviii.) The Knight is restored liberates Eden.

more evident elsewhere in the poem. "Spenser's moulds are themselves undisciplined and variable", because ". . . the poem is concerned heavily with man's erotic and sensuous nature, the problem of good and bad love." In the last canto of Book II, Spenser makes the Knight of Temperance surprise and overthrow the Bower of Bliss, representing the crude temptation of the flesh, and taken in part from Tasso's description of Armida's Island. The Bower of Bliss is sweeter than Eden itself, Spenser says explicitly, courteously adding: "if ought with Eden mote compaire". The opposition between knightly duty and amorous dereliction is not vitally rendered, and in the later descriptions of the Garden of Adonis and the Temple of Venus, Spenser tries to reconcile the virtues of the "antique world" and of Christendom with the pleasures of Armida and the Earthly Paradise, a synthesis that comes nearest to success not in *The Faerie Queene*, but in the triumphant marriage-music of *Epithalamion*. In all this he faithfully mirrors the urgencies of the late Renaissance. But in Spenser, for all the richness and delight of his poetry, "It is a dream-world, a 'faery' world, perilously near decadence". The Renaissance attempt to see as Ideal all embodied life on earth is vital, but cannot completely transmute all the iron into gold.

Spenser himself is aware of the unresolved tension, though he claims to inculcate the "antique use". In the verses that introduce the fifth of the six completed books of *The Faerie Queene*, The Legend of Justice, he reverts to the greater glories of remote antiquity:

> For from the golden age, that first was named,
> It's now at erst become a stony one.

And in this stony age all is awry. On the parallel planes of soul, society and the stars there are corresponding changes for the worse:

> But most is Mars amiss of all the rest;
> And next to him old Saturn, that was wont be best.
>
> For during Saturn's ancient reign it's said
> That all the world with goodness did abound;
> All lovéd virtue, no man was afraid
> Of force, ne fraud in wight was to be found;
> No war was known, no dreadful trumpet's sound;

> Peace universal reign'd 'mongst men and beasts:
> And all things freely grew out of the ground:
> Justice sat high adored with solemn feasts,
> And to all people did divide her dread beheasts.

In the seventh canto, Britomart comes to the Temple of Isis, antique embodiment of Justice. And here Spenser reacts towards a Puritan and monastic extreme that still half repels him, and which in less personal terms may be seen as an omen of the coming Puritan revolution, a false antithesis of promiscuity and austerity in which the golden mean is lost, as it always is when over-emphasis on one extreme appears to be the only corrective for over-development of the other. The priests of the Temple of Isis have no beds:

> But on their mother Earth's dear lap did lie,
> And bake their sides upon the cold hard stone,
> T' inure themselves to sufferance thereby,
> And proud rebellious flesh to mortify:
> For, by the vow of their religion,
> They tiéd were to steadfast chastity
> And continence of life; that, all forgone,
> They might the better tend to their devotion.

> Therefore they might not taste of fleshly food,
> Ne feed on aught the which doth blood contain,
> Ne drink of wine; for wine they say is blood

—the blood of slain Titans, sucked from earth by the vine and striving to infuriate men's minds to new war against the gods.

Spenser's synthesis has collapsed. Here again is the mediaeval dilemma, Eden or Cockaigne? Yet not Eden, with joy and great pleasure, as the nameless singer of the superior satisfactions of Cockaigne saw it, only a monastic discipline of chastity, abstinence and plain fare. The priest of Isis may interpret dreams aright, but Spenser interprets himself to us as not of that company.

Nevertheless, it is precisely this cloistered abnegation that gets loose in the world in the sixth book of *The Faerie Queene*. The noble Savage (VI, iv.) who rescues beauty in distress "ne knew the use of warlike instruments", sleeps on "The bare ground, with heavy moss bestrew'd" and his hospitality is a sort of refrigerated survival of the Golden Age:

> And the fruits of the forest was their feast:
> For their bad steward neither plough'd not sow'd,
> Ne fed on flesh, ne ever of wild beast
> Did taste the blood, obeying Nature's first beheast.

But "Nature's first beheast" does re-emerge in something of its primal glory in the final fragmentary Mutability Cantos. Spenser has found his way through the maze to the centre when he writes the lines with which the appeal to Nature herself begins:

> To thee, O greatest Goddess, only great,
> An humble suppliant lo! I lowly fly,
> Seeking for right, which I of thee entreat;
> Who right to all dost deal indifferently,
> Damning all wrong and tortious injury,
> Which any of thy creatures do to other,
> Oppressing them with power unequally,
> Sith of them all thou art the equal mother,
> And knittest each to each, as brother unto brother.

Thus Nature herself, "Nature's first beheast" and priestly holiness are merged at the end of Spenser's grand allegory, and the food imagery of priest and savage is exalted to its ultimate significance as an affirmation of the unity of all that lives.

A similar development might be traced in Shakespeare's works. From the first he felt the dangers, the sensuous intoxication of *Venus and Adonis*, the obsessional lust of *The Rape of Lucrece*. He begins by touching lightly the challenge of unbridled instinctive dynamism to the life of the spirit and the mind, laughing at the naïvety of the young noblemen of *Love's Labour's Lost* and the "little academe" where they are sworn for three years "Not to see ladies, study, fast, not sleep" and so quickly and so sweetly are forsworn. But the sky darkens later in *Troilus and Cressida*, *Hamlet*, the insane, jealous tragedy of *Othello*, the boiling cauldron of corruption that is Vienna in *Measure for Measure*, where chastity is the last threatened stronghold of any virtue whatsoever, (an apocalyptic vision of society with which only Proust can be compared), the bestial, unnatural adulteries of *Lear*, and finally the agonised and outraged revolt of *Timon* against the corruptions of gold and his Juvenalian vituperation against women. Only after that purgatorial crisis, that slow healing in the wilderness, is there joyful love again, for Ferdinand and Miranda in *The Tempest* after "full and holy rite". There must be the free consent of integrated manhood that—

> The most opportune place, the strong'st suggestion
> Our worser genius can, shall never melt
> Mine honour into lust, to take away
> The edge of that day's celebration.

This development may follow the contour of Shakespeare's own life experience, as many writers have supposed, and Ivor Brown has persuasively argued in a recent biography of the poet. But it also vindicated his high claim that poetic drama can "show the very age and body of the time his form and pressure". It is time to turn to the single aspect of some of these works which is the particular concern of this book.

Venus and Adonis is the Shakespearian equivalent of the Spenserian Bower of Bliss. Dowden called it "a glittering error of Shakespeare's earlier years . . . a somewhat laborious study of sensual passion, deliberately overwrought, rather than a poem of genuine youthful rapture". Modern critics hesitate to make such absolute moral judgments on poetry, often doubtful if any ethical criteria are relevant to criticism and aware that the moral foundations of their own age are shifting. Shakespeare drew this theme from Ovid's *Metamorphoses*, and five years later, in 1598, Francis Meres wrote in his *Palladis Tamia*, "As the soul of Euphorbus was thought to live in Pythagoras, so the sweet witty soul of Ovid lives in mellifluous and honey-tongued Shakespeare"—a comment whose original significance we may slightly extend by reference to *Timon of Athens*.

Timon is very different in temper from the early poem, but remains close to Ovid's *Metamorphoses*[1] in the Pythagorean echoes to which we now call attention. The play's earthquaking pattern gives us this theme in terms of harsh "realism", not unlike that of Lucretius describing the origins and savage period of mankind. Timon is also a significant development of Spenser's noble savage.

---

[1] The possibility, based on several apparent "echoes", that Shakespeare was drawing also on Chaucer's version of Boethius's poem, *The Former Age*, already quoted in the previous chapter, is worth consideration. Chaucer's version may have existed only in MS. at that time, but copies might have come into circulation f interest was aroused by the translation of Boethius made by Queen Elizabeth herself at Windsor in the winter of 1593. The MS. translation of *The Former Age* in Elizabeth's own handwriting is preserved in the Public Records Office and is reproduced in Caroline Pemberton's *Queen Elizabeth's Englishings*.

Incidentally, though perhaps accidentally, the Athenian Timon's views are even chronologically appropriate to a contemporary of Alcibiades, and therefore of Socrates, whose denunciation of the luxurious state, in Plato's *Republic*, already quoted, has many points in common with Timon's.

> Lord Timon will be left a naked gull,
> Which flashes now a phoenix

the crafty Senator foresees, and when Timon forsakes the corrupt city he is naked indeed in the wilderness, but not without the phoenix-quality that survives his own solitary death.

> There's nothing level in our cursed natures
> But direct villany. Therefore, be abhorr'd
> All feasts, societies, and throngs of men!
> His semblable, yea, himself, Timon disdains:
> Destruction fang mankind! Earth, yield me roots!
> Who seeks for better of thee, sauce his palate
> With thy most operant poison! What is here?
> Gold! yellow, glittering, precious gold! No, gods,
> I am no idle votarist. Roots, you clear heavens!

> That nature, being sick of man's unkindness,
> Should yet be hungry! Common mother, thou,
> Whose womb unmeasurable, and infinite breast,
> Teems, and feeds all; whose self-same mettle,
> Whereof thy proud child, arrogant man, is puff'd,
> Engenders the black toad and adder blue,
> The gilded newt and eyeless venom'd worm,
> With all the abhorréd births below crisp heaven
> Whereon Hyperion's quickening fire doth shine;
> Yield him, who all thy human sons doth hate,
> From forth thy plenteous bosom, one poor root!

> O! a root; dear thanks:
> Dry up thy marrows, vines and plough-torn leas;
> Whereof ingrateful man, with liquorish draughts
> And morsels unctuous, greases his pure mind,
> That from it all consideration slips!

Your greatest want is, you want much of meat.
Why should you want? Behold, the earth hath roots;
Within this mile break forth a hundred springs;
The oaks bear mast, the briers scarlet hips;
The bounteous housewife, nature, on each bush
Lays her full mess before you. Want! why want?

THIEF: We cannot live on grass, on berries, water,
As beasts, and birds, and fishes.

TIMON: Nor on the beasts themselves, the birds, and fishes;
You must eat men. Yet thanks I must you con
That you are thieves profess'd, that you work not
In holier shapes; for there is boundless theft
In limited professions. Rascal thieves,
Here's gold. Go, suck the subtle blood o' the grape,
Till the high fever seethe your blood to froth,
And so 'scape hanging; trust not the physician;
His antidotes are poison, and he slays
More than you rob; take wealth and lives together;
Do villany, do, since you protest to do't,
Like workmen.

Timon's demand that nature yield him roots, not gold, echoes Sir Guyon's defiance of Mammon. Gold in the wilderness must sleep there. The true Age of Gold has passed away and the new Golden Age is yet to come. "And nothing brings me all things."

Timon of Athens is the last of the tragedies of separation, in which one titanic figure after another—Hamlet, Othello, Lear, Macbeth—is torn asunder from society and within his own soul. But it is like a lightning flash of revelation on Lear's blasted heath, bringing a bare glimpse of the root from which will grow the golden world of Shakespeare's final plays. The universe of *Timon* does not dissolve between upper and nether millstones, City of Destruction and Temptation in the Wilderness. The man who broke away from the banquet of parasites senses indescribable harmonies and consolations in a life merged with Nature. There are plentiful intimations in *As You Like It* of what's to come, but rebirth can take place only after the spiritual ordeal of dying into life.

Timon is a parable of Shakespeare's pilgrimage. The break with worldly values is final. Waves sweep over Timon's lonely tomb, but from them drowned Marina arises to miraculous life in the next play, *Pericles*; they lap the sea-coast of Bohemia in *The Winter's Tale* of eternal spring, and bathe the shores of the Blessed Isle for which the Middle Ages sought in vain, in *The Tempest*, where a faithful and compassionate old nobleman sees a vision and is laughed at for it by a pair of traitors:

GONZALO: Had I plantation of this isle, my lord,—

ANTONIO: He'ld sow't with nettle-seed.

SEBASTIAN: Or docks, or mallows.

GONZALO: And were the king on't, what would I do?

SEBASTIAN: 'Scape being drunk for want of wine.

GONZALO: I' the commonwealth I would by contraries
Execute all things; for no kind of traffic
Would I admit; no name of magistrate;
Letters should not be known; riches, poverty,
And use of service, none; contract, succession,
Bourn, bound of land, tilth, vineyard, none;
No use of metal, corn, or wine, or oil;
No occupation; all men idle, all;
And women too, but innocent and pure;
No sovereignty:—

SEBASTIAN: Yet he would be king on't.

ANTONIO: The latter end of his commonwealth forgets the beginning.

GONZALO: All things in common nature should produce
Without sweat or endeavour: treason, felony,
Sword, pike, knife, gun, or need of any engine,
Would I not have; but nature should bring forth,
Of its own kind, all foison, all abundance,
To feed my innocent people.

SEBASTIAN: No marrying 'mong his subjects?

ANTONIO: None, man; all idle; whores and knaves.

GONZALO: I would with such perfection govern, sir,
To excel the golden age.

From the time of Warburton onwards there has been a disposition to treat Gonzalo's vision of the commonwealth as a Shakespearian satire on Utopian treatises and schemes, and the fact that it is largely transcribed from Montaigne has also rather obscured its significance in Shakespeare's play.[1] Only "innocent people" may feed on the feast that Nature brings forth:

Solemn and strange music: and PROSPER *on the top, invisible. . . . Enter several strange shapes, bringing in a banquet; and dance about it with gentle actions of salutation; and, inviting the King, etc., to eat, they depart.*

ALONSO: Give us kind keepers, heavens! What were these?

SEBASTIAN: A living drollery. Now I will believe
That there are unicorns, that in Arabia
There is one tree, the phoenix' throne, one phoenix[2]
At this hour reigning there.

ANTONIO: I'll believe both;
And what does else want credit, come to me,
And I'll be sworn 'tis true: travellers ne'er did lie,
Though fools at home condemn 'em.

GONZALO: If in Naples
I should report this now, would they believe me?
If I should say, I saw such islanders,—
For certes, these are people of the island,—
Who, though they are of monstrous shape, yet, note,
Their manners are more gentle-kind than of
Our human generation you shall find
Many, nay, almost any.

PROSPERO: Honest lord,
Thou hast said well: for some of you there present
Are worse than devils. . . .

[1] Furness quotes Holt (1749) as rejecting Warburton's opinion that Gonzalo's speech is "a fine satire on the Utopian treatises of government, and the impracticable, inconsistent schemes therein commended" —"It may with greater justice be regarded as a compliment to Sidney's *Arcadia* and Bacon's *New Atlantis*; the praises being put in the mouth of Gonzalo, a good and wise man, and the sneers in those of Sebastian and Antonio, two not very favourable characters." Holt is surely right as to Shakespeare's purpose—in discussing Montaigne's essay in Chapter 6, I point out the significance of Shakespeare's *selection* from the passage he adapted—but the Warburton view is still expressed, e.g. in Derek Traversi's interesting essay on the play, *Scrutiny*, Vol. XVI, No. 2, p. 141. Arthur Golding's translation of Ovid's description of the Golden Age, quoted in Chapter 2, probably gives a fair idea of the Elizabethan attitude towards Gonzalo's vision that we may suppose to have appealed to Shakespeare.
    I have ventured to suggest earlier that Cornford makes a similar mistake in commenting on the kindred passage from Plato. To the modern mind there is something intolerable about the idea of a State of Nature, and it is a short step from that to reluctance to believe that such notions could have been respectfully entertained by Plato and Shakespeare. Rousseau, who made it quite impossible for any critic to save him from his own folly, has been the subject of derision that usually seems quite ignorant of the fact that Rousseau was substantially repeating what many other men of genius had said before him. But that too is a subject for our sixth chapter.

[2] Shakespeare doubtless has in mind not the Anglo-Saxon *Phoenix*, but Golding's translation of Book XV of Ovid's *Metamorphoses*, *The Pythagorean Philosophy*: "One bird there is that doth renew itself and as it were Beget itself continually; the Syrians name it there A Phoenix. Neither corn nor herbs this Phoenix liveth by But by the juice of frankincense and gum of amomie." Dryden, like Shakespeare, has "Arabia".

ALONSO: I will stand to, and feed,
　　　　Although my last—no matter, since I feel
　　　　The best is past. Brother, my lord the duke,
　　　　Stand to, and do as we.

ALONSO, SEBASTIAN and ANTONIO seat themselves. Thunder and lightning. Enter ARIEL, like a harpy; claps his wings upon the table, and, with a quaint device, the banquet vanishes.

ARIEL: You are three men of sin. . . .

The three draw their swords . . . make to attack, but are charmed from moving.

　　　　　　You fools! I and my fellows
　　Are ministers of fate. The elements,
　　Of whom your swords are tempered, may as well
　　Wound the loud winds, or with bemocked-at stabs
　　Kill the still-closing waters, as diminish
　　One dowle that's in my plume: My fellow ministers
　　Are like invulnerable; if you could hurt,
　　Your swords are now too massy for your strengths,
　　And will not be uplifted.

But to the true lovers, Ferdinand and Miranda, Ceres promises:

　　　　Earth's increase, foison plenty,
　　　　Barns and garners never empty;
　　　　Vines with clustering bunches growing;
　　　　Plants with goodly burthen bowing;
　　　　Spring come to you at the farthest
　　　　In the very end of harvest!
　　　　Scarcity and want shall shun you;
　　　　Ceres' blessing so is on you.

Like Spenser, Shakespeare often sees his ideal embedded in the Nation. There is precise meaning in John of Gaunt's dying prophecy, in *Richard II*:

　　　　This other Eden, demi-paradise,
　　　　This fortress built by Nature for herself
　　　　Against infection and the hand of war,
　　　　This happy breed of men, this little world,
　　　　This precious stone set in a silver sea.

At the end of his writing days, Shakespeare can express his ideal through a vision of England's high destiny. Cranmer's speech over the infant Virgin Queen, which closes *Henry VIII* and the master dramatist's panorama of English history, opens a door on a golden future. Vergil's fourth *Eclogue* hailed the royal infant in whose time the Golden Age shall be reborn on earth, and so do Shakespeare's last words:

> In her days every man shall eat in safety
> Under his own vine what he plants; and sing
> The merry songs of peace to all his neighbours;
> God shall be truly known; and those about her
> From her shall read the perfect ways of honour,
> And by those claim their greatness, not by blood.
> Nor shall this peace sleep with her: but as when
> The bird of wonder dies, the maiden phoenix,
> Her ashes new create another heir,
> As great in admiration as herself;
> So shall she leave her blessedness to one,
> When heaven shall call her from this cloud of darkness,
> Who from the sacred ashes of her honour
> Shall star-like rise, as great in fame as she was,
> And so stand fix'd: peace, plenty, love, truth, terror,
> That were the servants to this chosen infant,
> Shall then be his, and like a vine grow to him:
> Wherever the bright sun of heaven shall shine,
> His honour and the greatness of his name
> Shall be, and make new nations: he shall flourish,
> And, like a mountain cedar, reach his branches
> To all the plains about him: our children's children
> Shall see this, and bless heaven.

As in the preceding play, *The Tempest*, Shakespeare uses the Ovidian Phoenix with full awareness of the paradisal environment it implies,[1] and it may be from Golding's translation of another book of the *Metamorphoses* that he drew the Orphic theme that the lute-player sings to the Queen, and which had been heard earlier in *The Two Gentlemen of Verona* and *The Merchant of Venice*:

> Orpheus with his lute made trees,
> And the mountain tops that freeze,

[1] The recurrence of the phoenix here and in *The Tempest* may be due also to the association with 'married chastity" in the earlier poems of Shakespeare's, *The Phoenix and the Turtle*.

> Bow themselves when he did sing:
> To his music plants and flowers
> Ever sprung; as sun and showers
> There had made a lasting spring.
>
> Every thing that heard him play,
> Even the billows of the sea,
> Hung their heads, and then lay by,
> In sweet music is such art,
> Killing care and grief of heart
> Fall asleep, or hearing die.

It is some such music in the air that Ferdinand heard upon the enchanted island, and from Ariel's lips.

Other Elizabethans danced to a different tune, and one that would have been more to Falstaff's taste. John Fletcher, reputed part author of *Henry VIII*, has this song in *The Spanish Curate*:

> Let the pig turn merrily, merrily, ah!
> And let the fat goose swim;
> For verily, verily, verily, ah!
> Our vicar this day shall be trim.
>
> The stewed cock shall crow, cock-aloodle-loo,
> A loud cock-a-loodle shall he crow;
> The duck and the drake shall swim in a lake
> Of onions and claret below.[1]

Sir Epicure Mammon, in Ben Jonson's *The Alchemist*, visualises for himself a more sumptuous Cockaigne:

> My meat shall all come in, in Indian shells,
> Dishes of agat set in gold, and studded
> With emeralds, sapphires, hyacinths, and rubies.
> The tongues of carps, dormice, and camels' heels,
> Boiled in the spirit of sol, and dissolved pearl,
> Apicius diet, 'gainst the epilepsy:
> And I will eat these broths with spoons of amber,
> Headed with diamond and carbuncle.
> My foot-boy shall eat pheasants, calvered salmons,
> Knots, godwits, lampreys: I myself will have
> The beards of barbels served, instead of salads;

[1] In Dekker's *The Shoemaker's Holiday* "meat marches in", etc., for the great feast.

> Oiled mushrooms; and the swelling unctuous paps
> Of a fat pregnant sow, newly cut off,
> Drest with an exquisite and poignant sauce;
> For which, I'll say unto my cook, *There's gold.*

Which last sickening refinement, if that is the right word, on the poor man's pig, in *Bartholomew Fair*, that would run off the spit into our mouths as in Lubberland, is also to be found in the nauseating orgy described by Petronius. Everything turns to dross not to gold at the touch of the lecherous, gluttonous and rapacious Sir Epicure Mammon. As he froths on about "gloves of fishes and birds' skins, perfumed with gums of paradise", he is reminded that the man for whom base metal becomes gold "must be *homo frugi*" much as Spenser's Knight of Temperance reminded Mammon of the true nature of wealth.

"If his dream last, he'll turn the age to gold", laughs Subtle, and in an earlier comedy Jonson puts a witty satire on the virtues of the Golden Age into the mouth of a brilliant charlatan who has—for a time—the Midas touch. Volpone greets the rising sun as one more golden guinea in the coffer and bids Mosca open the shrine wherein is hoarded his extorted golden treasure.

> Well did wise poets, by thy glorious name,
> Title that age which they would have the best

he gloats, and rejoices

> More in the cunning purchase of my wealth,
> Than in the glad possession, since I gain
> No common way; I use no trade, no venture;
> I wound no earth with plough-shares, fat no beasts
> To feed the shambles; have no mills for iron,
> Oil, corn, or men, to grind them into powder:
> I blow no subtle glass, expose no ships
> To threat'nings of the furrow-facéd sea;
> I turn no monies in the public bank,
> Nor usure private.

He proceeds to savour the entertainment of his three servants, figures whose physical deformities image Volpone's inner perversity. The dwarf, the eunuch and the hermaphrodite present a doggerel jest in which is "inclosed the soul of Pythagoras". It is a satire on metempsychosis, with allusions to "forbid meats", "the eating of beans" and "devouring flesh"—what the spirit repudiates in one incarnation, they declare, is forced upon it in another.

Jonson could exploit as well as satirise the tradition. In 1615 he presented at Court his masque of *The Golden Age Restored*, in which Astraea and the personification of the Golden Age descend and join with Pallas:

PALLAS: Already do not all things smile?

ASTRAEA: But when they have enjoyed a while
  The Age's quickening power:

GOLDEN AGE: That every thought a seed doth bring,
  And every look a plant doth spring,
  And every breath a flower:

PALLAS: Then earth unploughed shall yield her crop,
  Pure honey from the oak shall drop,
  The fountain shall run milk:
  The thistles shall the lily bear,
  And every bramble roses wear,
  And every worm make silk.

CHORUS: The very shrub shall balsam sweat,
  And nectar melt the rock with heat,
  Till earth have drunk her fill:
  That she no harmful weed may know,
  Nor barren fern, nor mandrake low,
  Nor mineral to kill.[1]

There is love in sweet simplicity, and the souls of the poets "went away from earth, as if but tamed with sleep". The Iron Age which is banished by the Golden Age has the usual attributes of War and Rapine, and "Corruption with the golden hands", a phrase irresistibly reminiscent of Volpone.

Like Shakespeare in a gentler vein, Jonson also put the ideal to national service, in the masque of *The Fortunate Isles, and Their Union*, given at Court on Twelfth-Night 1626. One of the principal Fortunate Isles, announces the airy spirit Jophiel, outdoing Shakespeare's Ariel,

---

[1] As the modern editors Herford and Simpson note, "Jonson borrows touches from the poetic description of the Golden Age in Hesiod, Ovid, and Vergil" in this masque.

> That hitherto hath floated, as uncertain
> Where she should fix her blessings, is tonight
> Instructed to adhere to your Britannia.

That it does so in no merely diplomatic sense is apparent from the Drury-Lane-like stage-direction, *By this time, the island having joined itself to the shore* . . . and Proteus, Portunus, Saron and Chorus combine to praise this latest accretion to the British Isles:

PROTEUS: Ay, now the heights of Neptune's honours shine,
           And all the glories of his greater style
           Are read reflected in this happiest isle.

PORTUNUS: How both the air, the soil, the seat combine
           To speak it blessed!

SARON: These are the true groves
           Where joys are born.

PROTEUS: Where longings,

PORTUNUS: And where loves!

SARON: That live!

PROTEUS: That last!

PORTUNUS: No intermitted wind
           Blows here, but what leaves flowers or fruit behind.

CHORUS: 'Tis odour all that comes!
           And every tree doth give his gums.

PROTEUS: There is no sickness, nor no old age known
           To man, nor any grief that he dares own.
           There is no hunger here, nor envy of state,
           Nor least ambition in the magistrate.
           But all are even-hearted, open, free,
               And what one is, another strives to be.

Portunus is explicit that "the trees be thick". The speech of Proteus quoted above is very reminiscent of Gonzalo's commonwealth in *The Tempest*.

But, like Tasso's identification of the Fortunate Isles and the Golden Age, the annexation of the Earthly Paradise by Britain was a conquest of the Golden Age simplicities by Cockaigne, not the renewal in Britain of the mythical Golden Feast. Twenty years before Jonson's masque moored the Fortunate Isles to the coast of Britain, and some five years before Shakespeare wrote of the Enchanted

Isle, Michael Drayton, a major poet of the age, published, in 1606, *Poems Lyrick and Pastorall*, including *To the Virginian Voyage*. "And ours to hold Virginia", he wrote, "Earth's only paradise:

> Where Nature hath in store
> Fowl, venison, and fish,
> And the fruitful'st soil,
>   Without your toil
>   Three harvests more
> All greater than your wish.
>
> And the ambitious vine
> Crowns with his purple mass,
> The cedar reaching high
>   To kiss the sky;
>   The cypress, pine,
> And useful sassafras.
>
> To whose, the golden age
> Still Nature's laws doth give,
> No other cares that tend,
>   But them to defend,
>   From winter's rage
> That long there doth not live."

When the British mariners see the shore they "Let cannons roar Frighting the wide heaven". The precise equivalence of Drayton's "Fowl, venison, and fish" with Tasso's "all dainty food That sea, that earth, or liquid air could give" neatly illustrates how completely Drayton had fallen hook, line and sinker for what Tasso called deceitful enticements. No wonder cannon frighted the wide heaven. That too, as Shakespeare knew in *Hamlet*, was an image of disaster. Here, in fact, is the extraordinary phenomenon of a major and representative poet writing what is meant to be a triumphal ode, in which images turn about as though by their own volition to become beacon lights, warning the heedless pilot away from such dangerous shores.

Until the Garden of Eden, in Milton's epic, and Pythagoras, in Golding's and Dryden's translations of Ovid, came to purify it once more, the Golden Age tradition in poetry became hopelessly confused with the pastoral. W. W. Greg observed the distinction. He writes of "an idea which comes perhaps as near being universal in pastoral as any—the idea, namely, of the 'golden age'. This embraces, indeed, a field not wholly coincident with that of pastoral, but the two are connected alike by a common spring in human emotion and constant literary association." Some excellent critics make no such distinction. G. Wilson Knight writes of the poets' paradise and pastoral as interchangeable terms. But if the writers of pastoral knew that the clue was in the countryside, they no longer knew what it was. Just how great is the distinction between pastoral and arboreal paradise we shall see in the last chapter when Byron sides with Cain against Abel, and is supported by a poet and a prophet of our own generation. For the present it is enough to note that the Golden Age theme meanders into pastoral water-meadows late in the Renaissance, just as it becomes attenuated from Platonic myth to Butlerian satire in the more intellectualised Utopias, or is popularly coarsened into the gross travesty of Cockaigne. The Ideal is lost in the idyll.

Here and there a thin vein of pure gold ran through a thick seam of baser matter. Thomas Heywood, who is said to have had a hand in more than two hundred plays of which only about a score survive, achieved some of his best poetry in his Ovidian plays of the four epochs, which together fill more than four hundred pages. The *Golden*, *Silver* and *Bronze* ages well illustrate the influence of masque on the drama, and were published in 1611 and 1613, a year or two before Ben Jonson produced *The Golden Age Restored*. The *Iron Age*, very suitably in two parts, did not appear until 1632. Even Heywood's *Golden Age* is a bloody business. In Act II there is a banquet of human flesh and later an interlude in which Satyrs with javelins, bows and quivers sing to Diana of chastity—and the chase. The last verse, however, also echoes the Ovidian theme:

> Our food is honie from the Bees,
> And mellow fruits that drop from trees,
> In chace we climb the high degrees
>   Of euerie fteepie mountaine,
> And when the wearie day is paft,
> We at the evening hie vs faft,
> And after this our field repaft,
>   We drinke the pleafant fountaine.

In *Britannia's Pastorals*, 1614, William Browne is quite carried away by the same theme:

> O! the golden age
> Met all contentment in no surplusage
> Of dainty viands, but (as we doe still)
> Dranke the pure water of the crystal rill,
> Fed on no other meats than those they fed,
> Labor the salads that their stomachs bred.

Most of the other traditional attributes of the Golden Age are there: "More golden slumbers then this age agen", "That time Physitians thriv'd not", "The bowels of our mother were not ripp'd", "Through the wide Seas no winged Pine did goe", "The word of Mine did no man then bewitch", and after seven pages on the theme, Browne recalls himself:

> O what a rapture have I gotten now
> That age of gold, this of the lovely brow
> Have drawne me from my Song!

Charming compliments to the ladies' faces, however, were an afterthought to placate fair readers who might well be outraged by an unexpected and vindictive attack on contemporary feminine lust, interpolated in a description of the less vicious joys of the Golden Age. Then sexual appetite was naturally moderate, men had no need to gorge flesh-meats to inflame their passions sufficiently to satisfy inordinate feminine desire, as now they must do. Moreover, then they produced legitimate and healthy heirs, which is no longer so. Browne recovers to write some amusing lines about diet and health. But the loathing with which he denounced woman's monstrous lust, so out of keeping with the mood and theme of his poem,[1] is as significant as Timon's equally irrelevant vilification of Phrynia and Timandra. The pretty pretences of pastoral are rudely violated. The blind Samson of instinct is loose, the pillars of society

---

[1] Cervantes makes Don Quixote, in an otherwise orthodox exposition of the Golden Age (I, xi) break out in much the same way about masculine concupiscence. Then, he says, "beauteous young shepherdesses trip it from dale to dale, and from hill to hill, their tresses sometimes plaited, sometimes loosely flowing, with no more clothing than was necessary modestly to conceal what modesty has always required to be covered. . . . Maidens and modesty, as I said before, went about alone, and mistress of themselves, without fear of any danger from the unbridled freedom and lewd designs of others; and if they were undone, it was entirely owing to their own natural inclination and will. But now, in these detestable ages of ours, no damsel is secure, though she were hidden and locked up in another labyrinth like that of Crete; for even there, through some cranny or through the air, by the zeal of cursed importunity, the amorous pestilence finds entrance, and they miscarry in spite of their closest retreat. For the security of whom, as times grew worse and wickedness increased, the order of knight-errantry was instituted to defend maidens . . ."—and produced such champions as Spenser's Knight of Temperance and the comical-tragical Knight of La Mancha himself.

crack. But a greater blind man, suffering through the ordeal of virility betrayed to woman, is even now growing to manhood to chain the giant in a dark Puritan cave so that the purified vision may live again. We may, if we choose to do so, see a premonition of what was to come in two lines from Henry Vaughan's poem *Corruption*, published some seventeen years before *Paradise Lost*:

> He sigh'd for Eden, and would often say
> "Ah! what bright days were those!"

And about ten years after Milton's epic appeared Vaughan affirms, in his lines on *Retirement*,

> If Eden be on earth at all,
> 'Tis that which we the country call.

The sentiment is elaborated in *The Bee*:

> To the wild woods I will be gone,
> And the coarse meals of great St. John.
>
> .   .   .   .   .
>
> Here something still like Eden looks;
> Honey in woods, juleps in brooks.

V

THE GARDEN AND THE
WILDERNESS

DANTE'S lifetime saw the completion of the synthesis that forms the fundament of European culture. The Greek philosophies of Pythagoras, Plato and others, mixed after Alexander's conquests with Oriental elements and working through Orphism, transformed the outlook of the Greek-speaking world, says Bertrand Russell, and ultimately of the Latin-speaking world also. "This influx of barbarian ideas and practices was synthesised with certain Hellenic elements in the Neoplatonic philosophy. In Orphism, Pythagore-anism, and some parts of Plato, the Greeks had developed points of view which were easy to combine with those of the Orient, perhaps because they had been borrowed from the East at a much earlier time. With Plotinus and Porphyry the development of pagan philosophy ends."

"The learning of the mediaeval Church had been Aristotelian; and the great Myth of the Church, the *Divina Commedia*, sprang into life out of the ashes of Aristotelianism", says J. A. Stewart. "Antagonism to the Roman Church had, doubtless, much to do with the Platonic revival, which spread from Italy. Ficino, the great Florentine Platonist, took the place of Thomas Aquinas, and is the authority the Cambridge Platonists were always found appealing to. Their Platonism, moreover, was that of Plato the mythologist, not that of Plato the dialectician." Milton's Latin poem, Englished by Cowper as *On the Platonic Idea as it was Understood by Aristotle,* complaining in effect that Aristotle misunderstood Plato and took his Myths as dogma, is one symptom of the Platonist reaction.

"In the seventeenth century", to quote yet a third authority, "Plato, seen chiefly through the medium of Plotinus, supplied the inspiration of a group of noble thinkers who were vindicating a more inward morality and religion against the unspiritual secularism and

136

Erastianism of Hobbes, the so-called 'Cambridge Platonists', Whichcote, Henry More, Cudworth, John Smith." Henry More, who is described as the outstanding and most memorable name among the Platonists, entered Christ's College Cambridge in 1631, where Cudworth was his contemporary, just before Milton left the same college, a year or two after Milton wrote the poem to his friend Deodati quoted later in this chapter. Henry More was also a poet of marked ability who wrote numerous philosophical poems as a disciple of Plato and Plotinus. One of them, the *Democritus Platonissans,* or an Essay upon the Infinity of Worlds, published in 1647 and given in A. B. Grosart's complete edition, magnifies the Phoenix myth into an allegory of the regeneration of the world, closely resembling the Platonic resumption of divine motion that will restore the Golden Age. These three verses appear towards the end of the poem which has more than a hundred stanzas:

> The burning bowels of this wasting ball,
> Shall gullop up great flakes of rolling fire,
> And belch out pitchie flames, till over all
> Having long rag'd, Vulcan himself shall tire
> And (th' earth an asheap made) shall then expire:
> Here Nature laid asleep in her own Urn
> With gentle rest right easly will respire,
> Till to her pristine task she do return
> As fresh as Phenix young under th' Arabian Morn.

> O happy they that then the first are born,
> While yet the world is in her vernall pride:
> For old corruption quite away is worn
> As Metall pure so is her mold well-tride.
> Sweet dews, cool breathing airs, and spaces wide
> Of precious spicery wafted with soft wind:
> Fair comely bodies, goodly beautifi'd,
> Snow-limb'd, rose-cheek'd, ruby-lipp'd, pearl-teeth'd, star-eyn'd:
> Their parts, each fair, in fit proportion all combin'd.

> For all the while her purged ashes rest,
> Those relicks dry suck in the heavenly dew,
> And roseid Manna rains upon her breast,
> And fills with sacred milk, sweet, fresh, and new,
> Where all take life, and doth the world renew;

And then renew'd with pleasure be yfed.
A green soft mantle doth her bosome strew
With fragrant herbs and flowers embellishéd,
Where without fault or shame all living creatures bed.

The interest of Milton's early and deep devotion to Plato, says E. M. W. Tillyard, is that it brought him into close relations with the Cambridge Platonists. "It can be said dogmatically that Milton's religious and ethical ideas, as gathered from the body of his prose works, are in their outlines close to those of the Cambridge Platonists. . . . Henry More was Milton's younger contemporary at Christ's, and Milton may have been loosely associated with the Cambridge Platonists for many years of his life." A passage in More's prose work, *Immortality of the Soul,* published five years before *Paradise Lost* and doubtless while that epic poem was in course of composition, seems to be the source of the very interesting reply made by Raphael to Adam, who supposes that the fruits of Eden are unfit for angels and not to be compared with Heaven's high feasts.

"The Bad Genii have execrable feasts, made up into dishes, but made of vaporous air, as is proved by the faintness and emptiness of those who have been entertained at such banquets", writes More. But the Superior Daemons which inhabit that part of the air that no storm or tempest can reach are regaled with whole Gardens and Orchards of most delectable fruits and flowers silently sent forth by the Spirit of Nature. They[1] "may taste of such Fruits as whose natural juice will vie with their noblest Extractions and Quintessences. For such certainly will they there find the blood of the Grape, the rubie-coloured Cherries, and Nectarines." They may also meet with Birds and Beasts of curious shapes and colours with musical and pleasing voices. That there may be Food and Feasting in those higher Aereal Regions is hardly doubted by Platonists.

So that the *Nectar* and *Ambrosia* of the Poets may not be a mere fable. For the *Spirit of Nature,* which is the immediate Instrument of God, may enrich the fruits of these *Aereal Paradises* with such liquours, as being received into the bodies of these purer *Daemons,* and diffusing itself through their Vehicles, may cause such grateful motions analogical to our *tast,* and excite such a more than ordinary quickness in their minds,

---

[1] I.e. "the *Chymists* . . . whenever they are admitted into those *higher regions* of the Aire".

and benign chearfulness, that it may far transcend the most delicate Reflection that the greatest Epicures could ever invent upon Earth; and that without all satiety, burdensomeness, it filling them with nothing but Divine Love, Joy, and Devotion.

The Cambridge Platonists, following Philo, believed moreover that the ultimate inspiration of their Greek mentors was Biblical. In the Preface to his *Conjectural Essay of Interpreting the Mind of Moses in the Three First Chapters of Genesis*, More wrote in the same year as the Myth just quoted that "Moses seems to have been aforehand, and prevented the subtilest and abstrusest inventions of the choicest philosophers that ever appeared after him to this very day. And further presumption of the truth of this *Philosophical Cabbala* is that the grand mysteries therein contained are most-what the same that those two eximious philosophers, Pythagoras and Plato, brought out of Egypt, and it is generally acknowledged by Christians that they both had their philosophy from Moses."

With this close and important influence of Neoplatonist poetry and myth, supposedly stemming from the author of the Book of Genesis, we may turn to the passage in Milton's *Paradise Lost* where Raphael—

> now is come
> Into the blissful field, through groves of myrrh,
> And flowering odours, cassia, nard, and balm,
> A wilderness of sweets; for Nature here
> Wantoned as in her prime, and played at will
> Her virgin fancies, pouring forth more sweet,
> Wild above rule or art, enormous bliss.
> Him, through the spicy forest onward come,
> Adam discerned, as in the door he sat
> Of his cool bower, while now the mounted Sun
> Shot down direct his fervid rays, to warm
> Earth's inmost womb, more warmth than Adam needs;
> And Eve, within, due at her hour prepared
> For dinner savoury fruits, of taste to please
> True appetite, and not disrelish thirst
> Of nectarous draughts between, from milky stream,
> Berry or grape: to whom thus Adam called:—
>   "Haste hither, Eve, and, worth thy sight, behold
> Eastward among those trees what glorious Shape

Comes this way moving; seems another morn
Risen on mid-noon. Some great behest from Heaven
To us perhaps he brings, and will voutsafe
This day to be our guest. But go with speed,
And what thy stores contain bring forth, and pour
Abundance fit to honour and receive
Our heavenly stranger; well we may afford
Our givers their own gifts, and large bestow
From large bestowed, where Nature multiplies
Her fertile growth, and by disburdening grows
More fruitful; which instructs us not to spare."

   To whom thus Eve:—"Adam, Earth's hallowed mould,
Of God inspired, small store will serve where store,
All seasons, ripe for use hangs on the stalk;
Save what, by frugal storing, firmness gains
To nourish, and superfluous moist consumes.
But I will haste, and from each bough and brake,
Each plant and juiciest gourd, will pluck such choice
To entertain our Angel-guest, as he
Beholding, shall confess that here on Earth
God hath dispensed his bounties as in Heaven."

   So saying, with dispatchful looks in haste
She turns, on hospitable thoughts intent
What choice to chose for delicacy best,
What order so contrived as not to mix
Tastes, not well joined, inelegant, but bring
Taste after taste upheld with kindliest change:
Bestirs her then, and from each tender stalk
Whatever Earth, all-bearing mother, yields
In India East or West, or middle shore
In Pontus or the Punic coast, or where
Alcinous reigned, fruit of all kinds, in coat
Rough or smooth rined, or bearded husk, or shell,
She gathers, tribute large, and on the board
Heaps with unsparing hand. For drink the grape
She crushes, inoffensive must, and meaths
From many a berry, and from sweet kernels pressed
She tempers dulcet creams—nor these to hold
Wants her fit vessels pure; then strews the ground
With rose and odours from the shrub unfumed.

     ·   ·   ·   ·

[Raphael]

"Hail! Mother of mankind, whose fruitful womb
Shall fill the world more numerous with thy sons
Than with these various fruits the trees of God
Have heaped this table!" Raised of grassy turf
Their table was, and mossy seats had round,
And on her ample square, from side to side,
All Autumn piled, though Spring and Autumn here
Danced hand-in-hand. A while discourse they hold—
No fear lest dinner cool—when thus began
Our Author:— "Heavenly Stranger, please to taste
These bounties, which our Nourisher, from whom
All perfect good, unmeasured-out, descends,
To us for food and for delight hath caused
The Earth to yield: unsavoury food, perhaps,
To Spiritual Natures; only this I know,
That one Celestial Father gives us all."

To whom the Angel:—"Therefore, what he gives
(Whose praise be ever sung) to Man, in part
Spiritual, may of purest Spirits be found
No ingrateful food: and food alike those pure
Intelligential substances require
As doth your Rational; and both contain
Within them every lower faculty
Of sense, whereby they hear, see, smell, touch, taste,
Tasting concoct, digest, assimilate,
And corporeal to incorporeal turn.
For know, whatever was created needs
To be sustained and fed. . . .

Though in Heaven the trees
Of life ambrosial fruitage bear, and vines
Yield nectar—though from off the boughs each morn
We brush mellifluous dews and find the ground
Covered with pearly grain—yet God hath here
Varied his bounty so with new delights
As may compare with Heaven; and to taste
Think not I shall be nice." So down they sat,
And to their viands fell; nor seemingly
The Angel, nor in mist—the common gloss
Of theologians—but with keen dispatch
Of real hunger, and concoctive heat

141

To transubstantiate: what redounds transpires
Through Spirits with ease; nor wonder, if by fire
Of sooty coal the empiric alchemist
Can turn, or holds it possible to turn,
Metals of drossiest ore to perfect gold,
As from the mine.

.   .   .   .   .

Thus when with meats and drinks they had sufficed,
Not burdened nature, sudden mind arose
In Adam not to let the occasion pass,
Given him by this great conference, to know,
Of things above his world, and of their being
Who dwell in Heaven, whose excellence he saw
Transcend his own so far, whose radiant forms,
Divine effulgence, whose high power so far
Exceeded human; and this wary speech
Thus to the empyreal minister he framed:
    "Inhabitant with God, now know I well
Thy favour, in his honour done to Man;
Under whose lowly roof thou hast voutsafed
To enter, and these earthly fruits to taste,
Food not of Angels, yet accepted so
As that more willingly thou could'st not seem
At Heaven's high feasts to have fed: yet what compare!"
    To whom the wingéd Hierarch replied:—
"O Adam, one Almighty is, from whom
All things proceed, and up to him return,
If not depraved from good, created all
Such to perfection; one first matter all,
Endued with various forms, various degrees
Of substance, and, in things that live, of life;
But more refined, more spirituous and pure,
As nearer to him placed or nearer tending
Each in their several active spheres assigned,
Till body up to spirit work, in bounds
Proportioned to each kind. So from the root
Springs lighter the green stalk, from thence the leaves
More aery, last the bright consummate flower
Spirits odorous breathes: flowers and their fruit,
Man's nourishment, by gradual scale sublimed,
To vital spirits aspire, to animal,

To intellectual; give both life and sense,
Fancy and understanding; whence the Soul
Reason receives, and Reason is her being,
Discursive, or Intuitive: Discourse
Is oftest yours, the latter most is ours,
Differing but in degree, of kind the same.
Wonder not, then, what God for you saw good
If I refuse not, but convert, as you,
To proper substance. Time may come when Men
With Angels may participate, and find
No inconvenient diet, nor too light fare;
And from these corporal nutriments, perhaps,
Your bodies may at last turn all to spirit,
Improved by tract of time, and wing'd ascend
Ethereal, as we, or may at choice
Here or in heavenly paradises dwell,
If ye be found obedient, and retain
Unalterably firm his love entire
Whose progeny you are. Meanwhile enjoy
Your fill, what happiness this happy state
Can comprehend, incapable of more."[1]

Before the end of the fifth century, Avitus, Bishop of Vienne, had anticipated the fusion of the Golden Age tradition with the vision of Eden in Genesis. Subsequently Alfred the Great and Dante, among others, were discovered to be Christianising the classical theme. Now we have passed from the Middle Ages and the Renaissance to the Puritan revolution, and the position is reversed; Milton is enriching a substantially Christian subject with neoclassical philosophy. "And God said, Behold, I have given you every herb bearing seed, which is upon the face of all the earth, and every tree, in the which is the fruit of a tree yielding seed: to you it shall be for meat." Milton's text was the first chapter of Genesis, the Eden of the Rubens-Brueghel picture which would be incomplete without the wild and tame animals that live there harmlessly together and in harmony with the human pair. Only after the Fall, when Adam and Eve are driven from the Garden, do they fall also to flesh foods. The first murder arises from the quarrel between Cain and Abel as

---

[1] Cf. the fourth-century Christian writer Chrysostom: "With this repast [of fruit and vegetables] even angels from Heaven, as they behold it, are delighted and pleased."—*Homilies*.

to whether sacrifice of fruits or of slaughtered flesh is more acceptable to God. That theme, however, awaited the coming of Byron
for its resurrection into the imaginative world of European
poetry.

The seeds of the fruit-trees of Dante's Earthly Paradise were
carried to our hemisphere to germinate according as they found
soils and climates suitable to their various virtues. To trace some of
the scattered seeds of Eden-practices in the world of fallen mankind
will help us to interpret the food imagery of *Paradise Regained*,
and perhaps to understand why that poem is considered so unortho-
dox. From Genesis, from such Biblical texts as "It is good neither to
eat flesh, nor to drink wine, nor any thing whereby thy brother
stumbleth," and from reports that John the Baptist, James brother
of Jesus, Matthew, Peter and Paul kept to bloodless food, a long
tradition descends, obscured from modern eyes through the later
association of such dietary practices with heretical Christian sects
often alloyed with Asiatic religions. Some believe that Jesus
himself followed the Eden rule, from Essene example, and the
Essenes, as we noted, were profoundly influenced by Neopythagoreanism.

Certainly, in the first centuries of the Christian era, Clement of
Alexandria, Tertullian and St. John Chrysostom followed the rule.
In the monastic orders of the Eastern and Western Churches
abstinence from flesh (although not usually from fish, which the
Gospels seemed to sanction) was common. The Rules of the fourth-
century St. Basil and of the early sixth-century St. Benedict expressly
forbid flesh food, and we shall find the same observance among
heretical sects. In St. Francis of Assisi, seven hundred years after
Benedict, joy, simplicity, and a wonderful sense of kinship with
bird and beast put a halo about the tradition that illuminated with
love the routine of uncomprehended austerities. Relations between
Francis and the hierarchy were not untroubled and in more recent
history it has usually been the rebel or the militant, a Wesley, a
Swedenborg, a Tolstoy, a General Booth, who has kept the Eden-
tradition alive, while the orthodox failure to do so alienated Shelley—
as is apparent from *A Refutation of Deism*—and perhaps not a few
other humanitarians, though the Churches retained an annual Harvest
Festival, as bloodless as the Eleusinian rites, as well as a more

frequent Communion in which the Christian, like the Dionysian, partook of the flesh and blood of the God.

How far dietary resolution may go is movingly brought home in the First Book of Maccabees in the Apocrypha: "And many in Israel were fully resolved and confirmed in themselves not to eat unclean things. And they chose to die, that they might not be defiled with the meats, and that they might not profane the holy covenant; and they died." Another apocryphal story relates that the Lost Ten Tribes of Israel "neither eat flesh nor drink wine" as in the text already quoted. The Israelites were not the only believers who died, or risked death, for their dietary faith. The Persian and partly Christian Manicheans, of whom St. Augustine for a time was one, joined Armenian Paulicians to form the Bulgarian Bogomiles, who in turn strengthened the Cathari or Albigenses, a sect embracing in the thirteenth century many in Northern Italy and the great majority of people in the South of France. The Cathari believed that after death sinful souls migrated into the bodies of animals and they consequently abstained from flesh and even from eggs, cheese and milk, but not from fish, though only an elite achieved full observance of the rule. All these sects suffered more or less severe persecution and, as previously noted, a test of reconciliation with the Church was to eat flesh-meat. Similar repressive measures in Tsarist times forced the strange Russian vegetarian sect of Doukhobors into exile overseas.

Some of the early Fathers were aware of the classical as well as Biblical sources: "Dicearchus", says St. Jerome, "relates in his book on Grecian antiquities, that, during the reign of Saturn, when the earth was as yet fertile of itself, no man ate flesh, but all lived upon the fruits and pulses which were naturally produced." In Britain, enforcement of the dietary rule slowly became difficult and then virtually impossible. "There can, indeed, be no doubt", writes Dom David Knowles, "that complete abstinence from flesh-meat, [in using this term the author does not include fish or the flesh of fowls] save in the case of definite illness, was the rule throughout the monasteries of England between 960 and 1216; there is not a single piece of trustworthy evidence to show that meat was ever allowed in the common refectory during that period. But before the Lateran Council certain relaxations had begun to come in outside the refectory." A writer on Wolsey mentions that his predecessors "had tried to force upon Northerners a discipline which was easy enough in Italy. Perpetual abstinence from flesh-meat was the crucial point. The result of this measure of discipline was always the same. The monks tried over and over again to undertake the perpetual abstinence and failed. In almost every case dispensations were bought from Rome." Another writer remarks: "It is not surprising that, after a time, it should be questioned whether St. Benedict, if legislating for a cold northern climate, would have laid down the same regulations as for Italy, even though he may have regarded his rule as applying, on the whole, to all countries. . . . In 1237 the papal legate congratulated the English abbots on having passed the rule for entire abstinence from flesh meat, but in 1300 a Provincial Chapter, held at Oxford, dispensed with this. . . . Later on a decree was passed allowing the eating of meat, 'for the reason that doctors and experience both teach that a total abstinence from flesh is contrary to nature and hurtful to the system: so were monks to be confined to such diet alone they would become weak and suffer, a thing the rule neither orders nor desires'." There seems to have been no positive conception behind the practice of the rule during most of this time. But undoubtedly the restricted diet was considered helpful in achieving continence.

As we have just observed, it was the doctors not of divinity but of medical orthodoxy who finally helped the dedicated faithful to steer a middle course between Eden and Cockaigne, by discovering a change of nature, which is given crude and revealing expression by Sir Thomas Elyot in *The Castel of Helth*, 1539, in terms that remind us of the diagnosis of Petrarch's doctor some two centuries before, and of that poet's reply to any suggestion that his illness was due to eating fruit, drinking water and fasting frequently. "Forasmoche as before that tyllage of corne was inuented, and that deuorying of flesh and fyshe was of mankynde vsed, men undoubtedly lyued by fruites, & Nature was therwith contented & satisfied", Elyot wrote, "but by chaunge of the diets of our progenitours, there is caused to be in our bodies such alteration from the nature, which was in man at the begynnyng, that nowe all fruites generally are noyfulle to man, and do ingender ylle humours, and be ofte-tymes the cause of putrified feuers, yf they be moche and contynually eaten." In this change of nature the British Medical Association seems still to believe.[1]

Theological argument recognised, however, that the change of nature was part of the Fall, and therefore deplored it. Much later, Bossuet writes that "before the time of the Deluge, the nourishment which without violence men derived from the fruits which fell from the trees of themselves, and from the herbs which also ripened with equal ease, was, without doubt, some relic of the first innocence and of the gentleness for which we were formed. Now to get food we have to shed blood in spite of the horror which it naturally inspires in us; and all the refinements of which we avail ourselves, in covering our tables, hardly suffice to disguise for us the bloody corpses which we have to devour to support life. But this is but the least part of our misery. Life, already shortened, is still further abridged by the savage violences which are introduced into the life of the human species. Man, whom in the first ages we have seen spare the life of other animals, is accustomed henceforward to spare the life not even of his fellow men. It is in vain that God forbade, immediately after the Deluge, the shedding of human blood; in vain, in order to save some vestige of the first mildness of our nature, while permitting the feeding on flesh did he prohibit consumption of the blood. Human murders multiplied beyond all calculation." Shelley was not the first to associate flesh-eating and war.

This digression was necessary to a full understanding of the food imagery of *Paradise Regained*. The poem is, among other things, the climax of the development in which Spenser's savage and Shakespeare's Timon are crucial stages, a profound study of Christ in the Wilderness.

> Full forty days he passed—whether on hill
> Sometimes, anon in shady vale, each night
> Under the covert of some ancient oak
> Or cedar to defend him from the dew,
> Or harboured in one cave, is not revealed;
> Nor tasted human food, nor hunger felt,
> Till those days ended; hungered then at last

---

[1] "Once, however, so much as the probability [that the physiological effects of the diet are satisfactory] conceded, the ethical argument becomes irresistible."—Article, "Vegetarianism" in the *Encyclopaedia Religion and Ethics.*

Among wild beasts. They at his sight grew mild,
Nor sleeping him nor waking harmed; his walk
The fiery serpent fled and noxious worm;
The lion and fierce tiger glared aloof.

There comes to him first an aged man in rustic weed who must,
like Timon, "live on tough roots and stubs, to thirst inured".

In the second book of the poem, Satan deliberates with the
Demonian Spirits how the Son of God may be tempted. The only
suggestion comes promptly from Belial:

Belial, the dissolutest Spirit that fell,
The sensualest, and, after Asmodai,
The fleshliest Incubus, and thus advised:—
    "Set women in his eye and in his walk,
Among daughters of men the fairest found.
Many are in each region passing fair
As the noon sky, more like to goddesses
Than mortal creatures, graceful and discreet,
Expert in amorous arts, enchanting tongues
Persuasive, virgin majesty, with mild
And sweet allayed, yet terrible to approach,
Skilled to retire, and in retiring draw
Hearts after them tangled in amorous nets.
Such object hath the power to soften and tame
Severest temper, smooth the rugged'st brow,
Enerve, and with voluptuous hope dissolve,
Draw out with credulous desire, and lead
At will the manliest, resolutest breast,
As the magnetic hardest iron draws.

Satan rejects this lure without hesitation as bound to fail.

                    For Beauty stands
In the admiration only of weak minds
Led captive; cease to admire, and all her plumes
Fall flat, and shrink into a trivial toy,
At every sudden slighting quite abashed.
Therefore with manlier objects we must try
His constancy—with such as have more show
Of worth, of honour, glory, and popular praise
(Rocks whereon greatest men have oftest wrecked);

Or that which only seems to satisfy
Lawful desires of nature, not beyond.
And now I know he hungers, where no food
Is to be found, in the wide Wilderness:
The rest commit to me; I shall let pass
No advantage, and his strength as oft assay."
    He ceased, and heard their grant in loud acclaim.

If not through sexual hunger, is there a way to corruption of divine manhood through his hunger for food? Satan will offer the deceitful enticement of the banquet that is the antithesis of the golden feast that nourished spiritual nature in the Garden of Eden.

"Tell me, if food were now before thee set,
Would'st thou not eat?" "Thereafter as I like
The giver," answered Jesus. "Why should that
Cause thy refusal?" said the subtle Fiend.
"Hast thou not right to all created things?
Owe not all creatures, by just right, to thee
Duty and service, nor to stay till bid,
But tender all their power? Nor mention I
Meats by the law unclean, or offered first
To idols—those young Daniel could refuse;
Nor proffered by an enemy—though who
Would scruple that, with want oppressed? Behold,
Nature, ashamed, or, better to express,
Troubled, that thou shouldst hunger, hath purveyed
From all the elements her choicest store,
To treat thee as beseems, and as her Lord
With honour. Only deign to sit and eat."
    He spake no dream; for, as his words had end,
Our Saviour, lifting up his eyes, beheld,
In ample space under the broadest shade,
A table richly spread in regal mode,
With dishes piled and meats of noblest sort
And savour—beasts of chase, or fowl of game,
In pastry built, or from the spit, or boiled,
Crisamber-steamed; all fish, from sea or shore,
Freshet or purling brook, of shell or fin,
And exquisitest name, for which was drained
Pontus, and Lucrine bay, and Afric coast.

> Alas! how simple, to these cates compared,
> Was that crude apple that diverted Eve!

And just in case the fleshliest Incubus might be right after all, beyond the stripling youths who attended on the sideboard laden with wine,

> distant more,
> Under the trees now tripped, now solemn stood,
> Nymphs of Diana's train, and Naiades
> With fruits and flowers from Amalthea's horn,
> And ladies of the Hesperides, that seemed
> Fairer than feigned of old, or fabled since
> Of faery damosels met in forests wide.

The Tempter now earnestly renews his invitation to Jesus to fall to:

> "What doubts the Son of God to sit and eat?
> These are not fruits forbidden; no interdict
> Defends the touching of these viands pure;
> Their taste no knowledge works, at least of evil,
> But life preserves, destroy's life's enemy,
> Hunger, with sweet restorative delight."

Christ answers that he might command all:

> "Why shouldst thou then, obtrude this diligence
> In vain, where no acceptance it can find?
> And with my hunger what hast thou to do?
> Thy pompous delicacies I contemn,
> And count thy specious gifts no gifts, but guiles."

Satan complains:

> "What I can do or offer is suspect,
> Of these things others quickly will dispose,
> Whose pains have earned the far-fet spoil." With that
> Both table and provision vanished quite,
> With sound of harpies' wings and talons heard.

Milton here inverts the image Shakespeare used in *The Tempest*: "*Enter* ARIEL, *like a harpy; claps his wings upon the table, and, with a quaint device, the banquet vanishes.*" Then it was the men "worse than devils" who might not partake of the golden feast. Now it is the man divine who will not sup with the devil. Satan reluctantly admits,

> "By hunger, that each other creature tames,
> Thou art not to be harmed, therefore not moved;
> Thy temperance, invincible besides,
> For no allurement yields to appetite;
> And all thy heart is set on high designs,
> High actions."

The flesh feast that Satan offered to seduce spiritual nature from high designs to animality is reminiscent of Armida's treacherous temptation of the crusaders in Tasso's epic, who are likewise offered a banquet of beasts, birds and fishes, with a hundred virgins standing by, "for husbands able".

In the fourth and final book of *Paradise Regained,* his other temptations rejected, Satan is defeated and Christ's victory is celebrated by the true feast:

> So, strook with dread and anguish, fell the Fiend,
> And to his crew, that sat consulting, brought
> Joyless triumphals of his hoped success,
> Ruin, and desperation, and dismay,
> Who durst so proudly tempt the Son of God.
> So Satan fell; and straight a fiery globe
> Of Angels on full sail of wing flew nigh,
> Who on their plumy vans received Him soft
> From his uneasy station, and upbore,
> As on a floating couch, through the blithe air;
> Then, in a flowery valley, set him down
> On a green bank, and set before him spread
> A table of celestial food, divine
> Ambrosial fruits fetched from the Tree of Life,
> And from the Fount of Life ambrosial drink,
> That soon refreshed him wearied, and repaired
> What hunger, if aught hunger, had impaired,
> Or thirst; and, as he fed, Angelic quires
> Sung heavenly anthems of his victory
> Over temptation and the Tempter proud.

With these anthems the poem closes. By vanquishing temptation Christ has "regained lost Paradise", "A fairer Paradise is founded now for Adam and his chosen sons". But historically, of course, the struggle is not over, though the emphasis is shifting back, as in this prophetic poem, from sexual lust to gluttony, from the Bower of Bliss to Cockaigne. Milton does not believe, like Vergil or Shakespeare's Cranmer, that the new Golden Age is just around the corner or that the Fortunate Isles can, as in Jonson's conceit, be securely moored to the British mainland.

The significant food imagery and other associations recur in *Comus*, where the Virtuous Lady who resists seduction provides a striking parallel to Christ in the wilderness rejecting the temptations of Satan. Comus, child of Bacchus and Circe, is gifted—like his mother, and also like Tasso's enchantress, Armida—with the power of metamorphosing his victims, at least partially:

> The express resemblance of the gods, is changed
> Into some brutish form of wolf or bear,
> Or ounce or tiger, hog, or bearded goat,
> All other parts remaining as they were.

In this poem, therefore, the repugnance to flesh-eating is supported by the fact that the body of a beast may contain the soul of a man, as in the metempsychosis verses of Empedocles. Comus and his rout of monsters are virtually identical with the rout of Dionysus in which the human or divine form is mixed with that of some animal, especially the horse or wild goat.

COMUS: O foolishness of men! that lend their ears
   To those budge doctors of the stoic fur,
   And fetch their precepts from the Cynic tub,
   Praising the lean and sallow Abstinence!
   Wherefore did Nature pour her bounties forth
   With such a full and unwithdrawing hand,
   Covering the earth with odours, fruits, and flocks,
   Thronging the seas with spawn innumerable,
   But all to please and sate the curious taste?
   And set to work millions of spinning worms,
   That in their green shops weave the smooth-haired silk,
   To deck her sons; and, that no corner might

Be vacant of her plenty, in her own loins
She hutched the all-worshipped ore and precious gems,
To store her children with. If all the world
Should, in a pet of temperance, feed on pulse,
Drink the clear stream, and nothing wear but frieze,
The All-giver would be unthanked, would be unpraised,
Not half his riches known, and yet despised;
And we should serve him as a grudging master,
As a penurious niggard of his wealth,
And live like Nature's bastards, not her sons,
Who would be quite surcharged with her own weight,
And strangled with her waste fertility;
The earth cumbered, and the winged air darked with plumes,
The herds would over-multitude their lords;
The sea o'erfraught would swell, and the unsought diamonds
Would so emblaze the forehead of the deep,
And so bestud with stars, that they below
Would grow inured to light, and come at last
To gaze upon the sun with shameless brows.
List, Lady; be not coy, and be not cozened
With that same vaunted name, Virginity.
Beauty is Nature's coin; must not be hoarded,
But must be current; and the good thereof
Consists in mutual and partaken bliss,
Unsavoury in the enjoyment of itself.

Poetically it is a far stronger plea than Satan made, but the Lady's
answer surpasses it and is decisive:

Impostor! do not charge most innocent Nature,
As if she would her children should be riotous
With her abundance. She, good cateress,
Means her provision only to the good,
That live according to her sober laws,
And holy dictate of spare Temperance.
If every just man that now pines with want
Had but a moderate and beseeming share
Of that which lewdly-pampered Luxury
Now heaps upon some few with vast excess,
Nature's full blessings would be well dispensed
In unsuperfluous even proportion,

And she no whit encumbered with her store;
And then the Giver would be better thanked
His praise due paid: for swinish gluttony
Ne'er looks to Heaven amidst his gorgeous feast,
But with besotted base ingratitude
Crams, and blasphemes his Feeder. Shall I go on?
Or have I said enow?

The Attendant Spirit repairs not to Heaven but to the Hesperides:

To the ocean now I fly,
And those happy climes that lie
Where day never shuts his eye,
Up in the broad fields of sky.
There I suck the liquid air,
All amidst the gardens fair
Of Hesperus, and his daughters three
That sing about the golden tree.
Along the crisp'éd shades and bowers
Revels the spruce and jocund Spring;
The Graces and the rosy-bosomed Hours
Thither all their bounties bring.
There eternal summer dwells,
And west winds with musky wing
About the cedarn alleys fling
Nard and cassia's balmy smells.

But we may remember that the "blissful field" of Eden visited by
the Archangel Raphael in *Paradise Lost* was fragrant with "flowering
odours, cassia, nard and balm".[1] Heaven and the Hesperides were
not far apart on John Milton's celestial globe.

The classical inspiration of Milton's food imagery is clear from
the *Sixth Latin Elegy*, here quoted in William Cowper's translation.
The poet's friend, Charles Deodati, had sent a poem, not so good as
usual because he had been much distracted by Christmas feasting
among friends.

With no rich viands overcharged, I send
Health, which perchance you want, my pamper'd friend

---

[1] Cf. Dryden's Ovid *Met.*, XV. 592: "Of *Casia, Cynamon,* and Stems of *Nard*". Golding has "cassis sweet and nardus soft".

Milton replies. It is not wine that offends against good verse, he continues. Excellent lyric poetry may carol from such festivity,

> But they who demigods and heroes praise,
> And feats perform'd in Jove's more youthful days,
> Who now the counsels of high heaven explore,
> Now shades that echo the Cerberean roar,
> Simply let these, like him of Samos, live,
> Let herbs to them a bloodless banquet give;
> In beechen goblets let their beverage shine,
> Their youth should pass in innocence secure
> From stain licentious, and in manners pure,
> Pure as the priest, when robed in white he stands,
> The fresh lustration ready in his hands.

It is the Orphic priest of Euripides' play, perhaps, who had always exiled from his lips the touch of meat where life had been. And "him of Samos"[1] is, of course, Pythagoras.

The *Elegy* was written when Milton was about twenty-one, and is contemporary with the ode *On the Morning of Christ's Nativity*. In the ode is prefigured that merging of the Greek and Judaic visions that matures in *Paradise Regained*:

> For, if such holy song
> Enwrap our fancy long,
> Time will run back and fetch the Age of Gold.

Andrew Marvell, in the Commendatory Verses prefixed to *Paradise Lost*, 1667, confessed that he, no more than other poets of the time, could attempt such high themes as Milton does: "I too transported by the mode offend." But in *The Garden*, Marvell, seeking the Quiet and Innocence that "Only among the plants will grow" finds his way into an orchard that is touched with the grace of Paradise, as well as with humour:

> What wondrous life is this I lead!
> Ripe apples drop about my head;
> The luscious clusters of the vine
> Upon my mouth do crush their wine;

---

[1] Samos is also mentioned—and the association of ideas is significant—in *Paradise Lost*, v. 265, in connection with Raphael's mission from Heaven to Eden, just prior to the long description of the feast of fruits already quoted.

> The nectarine, and curious peach,
> Into my hands themselves do reach;
> Stumbling on melons, as I pass,
> Insnared with flowers, I fall on grass.
>
> Meanwhile the mind, from pleasure less,
> Withdraws into its happiness;
> The mind, that ocean where each kind
> Does straight its own resemblance find;
> Yet it creates, transcending these,
> Far other worlds, and other seas,
> Annihilating all that's made
> To a green thought in a green shade.
>
> Here at the fountain's sliding foot,
> Or at some fruit-tree's mossy root,
> Casting the body's vest aside,
> My soul into the boughs does glide:
> There, like a bird, it sits and sings,
> Then whets and combs its silver wings,
> And, till prepared for longer flight,
> Waves in its plumes the various light.

There is here a mystical image, which Katharine Garvin has brilliantly identified, by reference to the thirteenth-century *Rule for Anchoresses*. "True anchoresses are indeed birds of heaven that fly on high, and sit singing merrily on the green boughs; that is, they meditate upwards, and upon the bliss of heaven that never withers, but is evergreen, and they sit in this green, singing exceedingly merrily; that is, they come to rest in such thoughts and have mirth of heart as do those who sing."[1] And the same commentator considers that Marvell's poem was probably written about the garden of Nun Appleton House which was a convent until 1542. Perhaps this helps us to follow the transition in the very next lines:

> Such was that happy garden state,
> While man there walked without a mate.

That jest was certainly an earnest in the womb of time, and we shall recall it in discussing the next epoch's mild epidemic of poetic misogyny. For, as we deduced from Milton's emphases, not concupiscence but gluttony is now becoming the issue by which man's higher nature must stand or fall.

[1] Marvell's lines also recall the ascent from terrestrial to celestial paradise, in Plato and Dante.

PYTHAGORAS IN BRITAIN

EPIC poetry is epiphenomenal, it sums up an age. Poetry more often anticipates history, creative vision can look into the seeds of time and say which grain will grow and which will not. The poetic crisis in the struggle to integrate sensuality into a fully human wisdom was endured by Shakespeare at the turn of the century, and resolved in the chaste marriage in *The Tempest*. Whatever Milton's personal perplexities might have been, as a poet also expressing the spirit of the age he no longer had the same battle to fight and can utter premonitions of what was to become a major preoccupation in the next century, the sin of gluttony. But historic-ally, of course, the end of the Puritan régime—part purification, part mere repression of instinctive forces—signalled an orgy of sexuality frankly regardless of the good life which was—as fore-shadowed in Herrick's mildly schizophrenic division of his poetry— quite another matter. There is a bee-line from the Bower of Bliss to the beaux in the boudoirs.

Restoration comedy was the principal, almost the only, literary offspring of this elegant saturnalia. "Vicious as the stage was", wrote the historian J. R. Green, "it only reflected the general vice of the time. The Comedy of the Restoration borrowed everything from the Comedy of France save the poetry, the delicacy, and good taste which veiled its grossness. Seduction, intrigue, brutality, cynicism, debauchery, found fitting expression in dialogue of a studied and deliberate foulness, which even its wit fails to redeem from disgust. Wycherley, the popular playwright of the time, remains the most brutal among all writers of the stage; and nothing gives so damning an impression of his day as the fact that he found actors to repeat his words and audiences to applaud them."

John Dryden too, who was always inclined to keep one eye on the muse and the other on the weathercock, "condemned his comedies to well-merited oblivion", writes W. H. Hudson, "by his shameless indulgence in the foulness and profanity unfortunately so characteristic of the Restoration stage." Dryden was arraigned for these faults by Jeremy Collier, whose main targets were Congreve and Vanbrugh, in his *Short View of the Immorality and Profaneness of the English Stage*, 1698. In the Preface to his *Fables*, published in 1700, after his adoption of Roman Catholicism, Dryden confessed the fault. "I shall say the less of Mr. Collier, because in many Things he has tax'd me justly; and I have pleaded Guilty to all Thoughts and Expressions of mine, which can be truly argu'd of Obscenity, Profaneness and Immorality; and retract them."

But Dryden had no need of Collier's reproaches to restore him to a sense of his higher poetic vocation. Several years before the *Short View* appeared he wrote, in the famous poem on the death of Anne Killigrew:

> O Gracious God! How far have we
> Prophan'd thy Heav'nly Gift of Poesy!
> Made prostitute and profligate the Muse,
> Debas'd to each obscene and impious use,
> Whose Harmony was first ordain'd *Above*,
> For Tongues of *Angels* and for *Hymns* of *Love*!
> O wretched We! why were we hurry'd down
> This lubrique and adult'rate age,
> (Nay added fat Pollutions of our own)
> T' increase the steaming Ordures of our Stage?
> What can we say t' excuse our *Second Fall*?
> Let this thy *Vestal*, Heav'n, atone for all:
> Her Arethusian Stream remains unsoil'd,
> Unmixt with Forreign Filth and undefil'd,
> Her Wit was more than Man, her Innocence a Child.

The victory of *Paradise Regained* practically coincided with this "*Second Fall*". Comus and his rout were unleashed and only the Virtuous Lady, it seemed to Dryden, remained undefiled. A decade earlier still, Dryden had begun in real earnest to devote the heavenly gift of poesy to heavenly ends, in such works as *Religio Laici* and later, *The Hind and the Panther*, to which Dr. Johnson objected, not unreasonably, that "A fable, which exhibits two beasts talking theology, appears at once full of absurdity; and it was accordingly ridiculed in the City Mouse and Country Mouse, a parody".

Dryden was the first and foremost of the Augustans. His most successful didactic poetry was inspired less by the Rome of the Catholic Church than by the Rome of Ovid. How the fifteenth and final book of Ovid's *Metamorphoses—Of the Pythagorean Philosophy—* cast its spell upon him he described in the Preface to the *Fables*, which are also translations, some of them from Ovid. "From translating the First of *Homer's Iliads* (which I intended as an essay to the whole Work) I proceeded to the Translation of the Twelfth Book of Ovid's *Metamorphoses*, because it contains, among other Things, the Causes, the Beginning, and Ending of the *Trojan* War: Here I ought in reason to have stopp'd; but the speeches of *Ajax* and *Ulysses* lying next in my way, I could not balk 'em. When I had compass'd them, I was so taken with the former Part of the Fifteenth Book (which is the Masterpiece of the whole *Metamorphoses*) that I enjoyn'd myself the pleasing Task of rendring it into *English*. And now I found by the Number of my Verses, that they began to swell into a little Volume; which gave me an Occasion of looking backward on some Beauties of my Author, in his former Books." The only other book of which Dryden made a complete translation was the first, which contains "the Causes, the Beginning" of the matter that leads the *Metamorphoses* to culminate in a discourse on Pythagorean philosophy, that Hesiodic account of the Golden and successive ages already quoted in an earlier chapter in the Elizabethan translation of Arthur Golding.

In "the Masterpiece of the whole *Metamorphoses*" it is not inordinate lust but unnatural gluttony that is chiefly condemned. Milton, as a young man, had told Deodati that an epic poet must live in Pythagorean purity. John Dryden reminded his age that Pythagorean restraint was the supreme title to temporal rule—the qualification of Numa, legendary second King of Rome, Plutarch's admiration of whom has been mentioned. In the fourth century Rome achieved an Emperor with at least this qualification. The Platonist and pagan Julian, educated with St. Basil at Athens, adopted "a light and sparing diet, which was usually of the vegetable kind", and which, according to his intimate friend, Libanius, "left his mind and body always free and active for the various and important business of an author, a pontiff, a magistrate, a general, and prince".

We begin Dryden's translation from the last book of Ovid's *Metamorphoses* with the account of the founding of the community at Crotona by Pythagoras and conclude where Numa brings the Pythagorean wisdom to Rome. That with the passing of the centuries this didactic poem had lost none of its power to influence human behaviour is evidenced by the young Lord Chesterfield some twenty years later. While still at the university, Chesterfield was "so much affected with that very pathetic speech which Ovid puts into the mouth of Pythagoras against the eating of the flesh of animals, that it was some time before I could bring myself to our college mutton again, with some inward doubt whether I was not making myself an accomplice to a murder".

Here, by the God's Command, he built and wall'd
The Place predicted; and Crotona call'd
Thus Fame, from time to time, delivers down
The sure Tradition of th' Italian Town.
Here dwelt the Man divine whom Samos bore,
But now Self-banish'd from his Native Shore,
Because he hated Tyrants, nor cou'd bear
The Chains which none but servile Souls will wear:
He, tho' from Heav'n remote, to Heav'n could move,
With Strength of Mind, and tread th' Abyss above;
And penetrate with his interiour Light
Those upper Depths, which Nature hid from Sight:
And what he had observ'd, and learnt from thence,
Lov'd in familiar Language to dispence.
    The Crowd with silent Admiration stand,
And heard him, as they heard their God's Command;
While he discours'd of Heav'ns mysterious Laws,
The World's Original, and Nature's Cause;
And what was God, and why the fleecy Snows
In silence fell, and rattling Winds arose;
What shook the stedfast Earth, and whence begun
The Dance of Planets round the radiant Sun;
If Thunder was the Voice of angry Jove,
Or Clouds with Nitre pregnant burst above:
Of these, and Things beyond the common Reach,
He spoke, and charm'd his Audience with his Speech.
    He first the tast of Flesh from Tables drove,
And argued well, if Arguments cou'd move.

O Mortals! from your Fellow's Blood abstain,
Nor taint your Bodies with a Food profane:
While Corn and Pulse by Nature are bestow'd,
And planted Orchards bend their willing Load;
While labour'd Gardens wholesom Herbs produce,
And teeming Vines afford their generous Juice:
Nor tardier Fruits of cruder Kind are lost,
But tam'd with Fire, or mellow'd by the Frost:
While Kine to Pails distended Udders bring,
And Bees their Hony redolent of Spring:
While Earth not only can your Needs supply,
But lavish of her Store, provides for Luxury;
A guiltless Feast administers with Ease,
And without Blood is prodigal to please.
Wild Beasts their Maws with their slain Brethren fill;
And yet not all, for some refuse to kill:
Sheep, Goats, and Oxen, and the nobler Steed,
On Browz and Corn, and flow'ry Meadows feed.
Bears, Tygers, Wolves, the Lion's angry Brood,
Whom Heaven endu'd with Principles of Blood,
He wisely sundred from the rest, to yell
In Forests, and in lonely Caves to dwell,
Where stronger Beasts oppress the weak by Might
And all in Prey, and Purple Feasts delight.
    O impious use! to Nature's Laws oppos'd,
Where Bowels are in other Bowels clos'd:
Where, fatten'd by their Fellow's Fat, they thrive;
Maintain'd by Murder, and by Death they live.
'Tis then for nought that Mother Earth provides
The Stores of all she shows, and all she hides,
If Men with fleshy Morsels must be fed,
And chaw with bloody Teeth the breathing Bread:
What else is this but to devour our Guests,
And barbarously renew Cyclopean Feasts!
We, by destroying Life, our Life sustain;
And gorge th' ungodly Maw with Meats obscene.
    Not so the Golden Age, who fed on Fruit,
Nor durst with bloody Meals their Mouths pollute.
Then Birds in airy space might safely move,
And timerous Hares on Heaths securely rove:

Nor needed Fish the guileful Hooks to fear,
For all was peaceful; and that Peace sincere.
Whoever was the Wretch (and curs'd be He)
That envy'd first our Food's simplicity;
Th' essay of bloody Feasts on Bruits began,
And after forg'd the Sword to murther Man.
Had he the sharpen'd Steel alone employ'd
On Beasts of Prey that other Beasts destroy'd,
Or Men invaded with their Fangs and Paws,
This had been justify'd by Nature's Laws,
And Self-defence: But who did Feasts begin
Of Flesh, he stretch'd Necessity to Sin.
To kill Man-killers, Man has lawful Pow'r,
But not th' extended License, to devour.

.   .   .   .

'Tis time my hard-mouth'd Coursers to controul,
Apt to run Riot, and transgress the Goal:
And therefore I conclude, whatever lies
In Earth, or flits in Air, or fills the Skies,
All suffer change, and we, that are of Soul
And Body mix'd, are Members of the whole.
Then, when our Sires, or Grandsires shall forsake
The Forms of Men, and brutal Figures take,
Thus hous'd, securely let their Spirits rest,
Nor violate thy Father in the Beast,
Thy Friend, thy Brother, any of thy Kin;
If none of these, yet there's a Man within:
O spare to make a Thyestæan Meal,
T' inclose his Body, and his Soul expel.
    Ill Customs by degrees to Habits rise,
Ill Habits soon become exalted Vice:
What more Advance can Mortals make in Sin
So near Perfection, who with Blood begin?
Deaf to the Calf that lies beneath the Knife,
Looks up, and from her Butcher begs her Life:
Deaf to the harmless Kid, that, e'er he dies,
All Methods to procure thy Mercy tries,
And imitates in vain thy Children's Cries.
Where will he stop, who feeds with Household Bread,
Then eats the Poultry which before he fed?

Let plough thy Steers; that when they lose their Breath,
To Nature, not to thee, they may impute their Death.
Let Goats for Food their loaded Udders lend,
And Sheep from Winter-cold thy Sides defend;
But neither Sprindges, Nets, nor Snares employ,
And be no more Ingenious to destroy.
Free as in Air, let Birds on Earth remain,
Nor let insidious Glue their wings constrain;
Nor opening Hounds the trembling Stag affright,
Nor purple Feathers intercept his Flight;
Nor Hooks conceal'd in Baits for Fish prepare,
Nor Lines to heave 'em twinkling up in Air.
　　Take not away the Life you cannot give:
For all Things have an equal right to live.
Kill noxious Creatures, where 'tis Sin to save;
This only just Prerogative we have;
But nourish Life with vegetable Food,
And shun the sacrilegious tast of Blood.
　　These Precepts by the Samian Sage were taught,
Which Godlike Numa to the Sabines brought,
And thence transferr'd to Rome, by Gift his own:
A willing People, and an offer'd Throne.
O happy Monarch, sent by Heav'n to bless
A Salvage Nation with soft Arts of Peace,
To teach Religion, Rapine to restrain,
Give Laws to Lust, and Sacrifice ordain:
Himself a Saint, a Goddess was his Bride,
And all the Muses o'er his Acts preside.

In one of his two last plays, *Don Sebastian* (1690), Dryden himself has a particularly interesting antithesis which we shall consider further in connection with a poem of Nahum Tate's. The climax of Dryden's play contrasts rebellious affirmation of unlimited sexual rights and "voluptuous" but monastic seclusion. Dryden's hero learns that he and his mistress are half-brother and sister; their love is incestuous. He rebels against the inevitable separation:

> One moment longer,
> And I should break through laws divine and human,
> And think them cobwebs spread for little man,
> Which all the bulky herd of nature breaks.

> The vigorous young world was ignorant
> Of these restrictions; 'tis decrepit now;
> Not more devout, but more decayed, and cold.
> All this is impious, therefore we must part. . . .

And in a single short sentence he embraces the merciful judgment conveyed to him by Dorax:

> Your fate has gratified you all she can;
> Gives easy misery, and makes exile pleasing. . . .
> A safe retreat, a gentle solitude,
> Unvexed with noise, and undisturbed with fears. . . .
> Under the ledge of Atlas lies a cave,
> Cut in the living rock by Nature's hands
> The venerable seat of holy hermits;
> Who there, secure in separated cells,
> Sacred even to the Moors, enjoy devotion;
> And from the purling streams, and savage fruits,
> Have wholesome beverage, and unbloody feasts.

> 'Tis penance too voluptuous for my crime.

This is a long way from Dryden's version of Shakespeare's *The Tempest*, which he wrote with Davenant more than twenty years earlier and which displaced Shakespeare's play on the English stage for two centuries. There Gonzalo's longing is for "a Heavenly Vision of Boyl'd, Bak'd and Roasted!" and the Spirits obligingly bring on a banquet "With all varieties of Meats and Fruits."

Dryden's classicism purifies the poetic tradition of the Golden Age that had become adulterated with a grosser kind of wishful thinking in Tasso and Spenser and had been Christianised by Milton in a way that escaped rather than solved the Renaissance problem. Dryden is herald and exemplar of the Augustan period of English poetry, and henceforward most poets who touch this particular subject are aware that their variations are played on a Pythagorean theme. The variations, of course, are often more significant than the sometimes conventional acceptance of classical material, and often include Don Sebastian's segregation from his mistress, which belongs to the monastic tradition of austerity rather than to the myth of the Golden Age. The Latin models themselves, moreover, were usually virtuoso performances on Grecian themes, feats of skill and taste rather than direct revelations, although Arthur Golding, the first English translator of the *Metamorphoses*, was not far wrong in asserting that Ovid was a disciple of Pythagoras. But in outward form at least the eighteenth-century Augustans were steeped in the classics.[1]

Nahum Tate, who shared with Dryden the work of translating the *Metamorphoses* and wrote most of the second part of *Absalom and Achitophel* under his direction, was afterwards Poet Laureate for many years. He is described as a free, good-natured, fuddling companion, intemperate and improvident, and he died in the precincts of the Mint at Southwark, then a sanctuary for debtors. Tate's Pythagoreanism—his acquaintance with Ovid and Dryden perhaps justifies the description, although there is no direct allusion to the Sage of Samos in the following poem—has a touch of misogyny that is worth investigating. This is the full text of *The Banquet:*

> Dispatch, and to the myrtle grove convey
> Whate'er with Nature's palate suits,
> The Dairy's store with salads, roots and fruits;
> I mean to play the Epicure today!
> Let nought be wanting to complete
>   Our bloodless treat:
> But bloodless let it be: for 'tis decreed
> The grape alone for this repast shall bleed.
> But Love be first expell'd the Company,
> With unmixt Wine our mirth as pure and free,
> From Thoughts of any scornful little She.
> Come Sir, a whetting glass, and do not spare
>   By Jove delicious fare!
> Speak Friends, was ever Monarch's table stor'd
>   Like this our rural board,
> Where, with the blessing of the field, is sent
>   The diet of the Gods, *Content.*

---

[1] Classical forms were also used, of course, for deliberate satire. William Walsh wrote *The Golden Age estored* in 1703 as an Imitation of the Fourth Eclogue of Vergil:

> The time is come, by ancient Bards foretold;
> Restoring the Saturnian age of gold;
> The vile, degenerate whiggish offspring ends,
> A high-church progeny from heaven descends.

e rest is little more than a list of contemporary names; "it now strikes no longer" as Johnson remarks his brief life of this friend of Dryden.

Wine apart, the sentiments are mildly Manichean. That sect, to which St. Augustine once adhered, combined Christian and Eastern elements; it condemned meat-eating and all sex, even in marriage. Or it might be merely a temporal reflection of Christian monasticism which, we noted, often included abstinence from flesh food as well as celibacy, though the British friars do not seem to have looked on the reformed diet as a "bloodless treat"! Women were admitted to the Pythagorean community at Crotona, some became lecturers and one of them, Theano, is reputed to have married the Sage, with whom she figures in Raphael's *School of Athens*.

Tate's lines probably echo the impact of Puritanism on the classical theme that has in Tasso and Spenser become entangled with sensuality. Milton escaped the crisis by retreat to Eden where, according to St. Augustine, Adam and Eve, before the Fall, could have had sexual intercourse without lust, though in fact they did not. Milton says they did and attacks the hypocrites who say otherwise. But his own Garden of Eden is no Spenserian Bower of Bliss! Marvell, we observed in passing, would not have an Eve in his Eden even on St. Augustine's terms:

> Such was that happy garden-state
> While man there walked without a mate:
> After a place so pure and sweet,
> What other help could yet be meet!
> But 'twas beyond a mortal's share
> To wander solitary there:
> Two paradises 'twere in one,
> To live in paradise alone.

The scornful little she contrives to make an unexpected reappearance in the predominantly Christian ballad of Goldsmith's to be quoted presently. But in the Pythagorean fabulists to whom we now turn, woman is quietly dropped.

The main design of Bernard de Mandeville's *Fable of the Bees* a powerful and strangely neglected work first published in 171 and later expanded by prose additions, is "to show the impossibilit of enjoying all the most elegant comforts of life that are to be me with in an industrious, wealthy and powerful nation, and at th same time be blessed with all the virtue and innocence that can be wished for in a Golden Age". Mandeville simply elaborates the argument of the Platonic Socrates (quoted in Chapter 1), and at the end of his Preface declares his own choice: "If laying aside all worldly greatness and vainglory, I should be asked where I thought it was most probable that men might enjoy true happiness, I would prefer a small peaceable society, in which men neither envied nor esteemed by neighbours, should be contented to live upon the natural product of the spot they inhabit, to a vast multitude abounding in wealth and power, that should always be conquering others by their arms abroad, and debauching themselves by foreign luxury at home." In the *Fable* itself, Honesty destroys all the typical features of the luxurious state, and

> Kind Nature, free from gard'ners force,
> Allows all fruits in her own course

and the *Moral* concludes:

> Bare virtue can't make nations live
> In splendour, they that would revive
> A Golden Age, must be as free,
> For acorns, as for honesty.

That this conclusion was something more than a conventional flourish is clear from Mandeville's extensive prose *Remarks* (P): "In the first ages man, without doubt, fed on the fruits of the earth, without any previous preparation. . . . Another piece of luxury the poor enjoy, that is not looked upon as such, and which there is no doubt but the wealthiest in a golden age would abstain from, is their making use of the flesh of animals to eat. . . . I have often thought, if it was not for this tyranny which custom usurps over us, that men of any tolerable good nature could never be reconciled to the killing of so many animals for their daily food, as long as the bountiful earth so plentifully provides them with varieties of vegetable dainties." He "will urge nothing of what Pythagoras and many other wise men have said concerning this barbarity of eating flesh . . ." but he nevertheless spends four pages on another fable, pointing the moral.

This second fable, in prose, is about an argumentative Lion, "one of the breed that rang'd in Aesop's days", and it is interesting to speculate on the origin and purpose of the animal fable which, as the inevitable "moral" shows, was a didactic form. Aesop, who lived in the same century as Pythagoras, and was perhaps familiar with the doctrine of metempsychosis, is sometimes credited with having added the moral element to the anthropological and zoological interest of the African Beast-tale, but the author of *The Light of Asia*, Sir Edwin Arnold, calls the Indian *Hitopadesa* "The Father of All Fables" and holds that Aesop and other fabulists are indebted to adaptations and translations of those didactic tales. "Max Muller", says Ernest Rhys, "even prepared a kind of family tree to show the descent of the modern fables that sprang from this antique stock. . . . This may help to account for that lurking air of hidden meanings and immemorial mythical signs which we find in some fables, recalling a people, wise and childish at once, who had built up a theory of the world ages before Aesop was born."

In the *Hitopadesa* fables, creatures change from one form to another, probably with reference to doctrines of reincarnation, and there is conversation between animals and between creatures and human beings. One begins, "The Crow said to the Rat"—as, long before Aesop, the hawk speaks to the nightingale in Hesiod's *Works and Days*—and another begins, "Said the King to the Birds", reminding us of Plato, St. Francis and Leonardo da Vinci, but still more of Orpheus himself. The theory of the world that India had built up ages before Aesop was born was based upon "the unity of all life" and the fundamental value of the Orpheus myth is its intuition of enchanted harmony between the musician-god and the whole natural order, including the creatures. Indeed, may there not be some ultimate identity of Orpheus and his lute and the divine flute-player, Krishna? "Every sound in nature is an echo of Krishna's flute."

In any case, as we have seen in the poetry of Empedocles, the effect of endowing animals with human characteristics is to emphasise what men and beasts have in common and to establish ethical ties between them. The form of fable moves organically through the theological disputation of Dryden's *The Hind and the Panther* to its culmination in such a tale as John Gay's of *Pythagoras and the Countryman*, where man and animals are held subject to one moral law. When Gay was a small boy, Sir Roger L'Estrange brought out a fine edition of the *Fables of Aesop* and followed it with *Fables and Stories Moralised*. Both Mandeville and Gay may have been influenced by these volumes. Thomas Warton the younger, the Laureate, whose own poetry is quoted later in this chapter, put Gay with Dryden at the head of the poets who have "noble talents for moral, ethical and panegyrical poesy", and the Sage's rebuke to the Clown in this poem certainly rebuts a sophistry used by Chesterfield, to escape his Pythagorean scruples, and later by Benjamin Franklin, who recognised the nature of his rationalisation, and which is still sometimes heard from professing Christians:

> Pythag'ras rose at early dawn
> By soaring meditation drawn,
> To breathe the fragrance of the day,
> Through flowery fields he took his way.
> In musing contemplation warm,
> His steps misled him to a farm,
> Where, on the ladder's topmost round,
> A peasant stood; the hammer's sound
> Shook the weak barn. Say friend, what care
> Calls for thy honest labour there?
>   The Clown with surly voice replies:
> Vengeance aloud for justice cries.
> This kite, by daily rapine fed,
> My hens' annoy, my turkeys' dread,
> At length his forfeit life has paid;
> See, on the wall, his wings display'd,
> Here nail'd, a terror to his kind,
> My fowls shall future safety find,
> My yard the thriving poultry feed,
> And my barn's refuse fat the breed.
>   Friend, says the Sage, the doom is wise;
> For public good the murd'rer dies.
> But, if these tyrants of the air
> Demand a sentence so severe,
> Think how the glutton man devours;
> What bloody feasts regale his hours!
> O impudence of power and might,
> Thus to condemn a hawk or kite,

> When thou, perhaps, carniv'rous sinner,
> Hadst pullets yesterday for dinner!
>   Hold, cried the Clown, with passion heated,
> Shall kites and men alike be treated?
> When heav'n the world with creatures stored,
> Man was ordain'd their sov'reign lord.
>   Thus tyrants boast, the Sage replied,
> Whose murders spring from power and pride.
> Own then this manlike kite is slain
> Thy greater lux'ry to sustain;
> For "petty rogues submit to fate,
> That great ones may enjoy their state."

Not that the subtly Christian image of the "manlike kite" crucified on the barn-door deterred John Gay from being a carnivorous sinner and rhyming *A Receipt for Stewing Veal*, any more than Tate's unsanguinary picnic inhibited him from writing *The Innocent Epicure, or Art of Angling*. In Gay's friend, Alexander Pope, and in James Thomson, we may observe some tremors of embarrassment at this contradiction of precept and practice. Few of the finer spirits of the age were quite without doubts about diet. Sir Isaac Newton, wrote Voltaire—whose own similar views are discussed later in this chapter—"thought it a very frightful inconsistency to believe that animals feel and at the same time to cause them to suffer. On this point his morality was in accord with his philosophy. He yielded but with repugnance to the barbarous custom of supporting ourselves upon the blood and flesh of beings like ourselves, whom we caress, and he never permitted in his own house the putting them to death by slow and exquisite modes of killing for the sake of making the food more delicious." Samuel Johnson conceded that "It is not very easy to fix the principles upon which mankind have agreed to eat some animals and reject others; and as the principle is not evident, it is not uniform".

Pope was in no doubt about the principle, but—like most British poets before Shelley—he equivocated in practice. His principle is the unity of life, and the state of Nature is to be at peace with all creatures, feeding without murder on the bounty of the good earth:

> Look round our world; behold the chain of love
> Combining all below and all above.

See plastic Nature working to this end,
The single atoms each to other tend,
Attract, attracted to, the next in place
Form'd and impell'd its neighbour to embrace.
See Matter next, with various life endued,
Press to one centre still, the general good.
See dying vegetables sustain,
See life dissolving vegetate again:
All forms that perish other forms supply;
(By turns we catch the vital breath, and die)
Like bubbles on the sea of Matter borne,
They rise, they break, and to that sea return.
Nothing is foreign: parts relate to whole;
One all-extending, all-preserving soul
Connects each being, greatest with the least;
Made beast in aid of man, and man of beast;
All served, all serving: nothing stands alone:
The chain holds on, and where it ends, unknown.

Nor think, in Nature's state they blindly trod;
The state of Nature was the reign of God:
Self-love and social at her birth began,
Union the bond of all things, and of man.
Pride then was not; nor arts, that pride to aid;
Man walk'd with beast, joint tenant of the shade;
The same his table, and the same his bed;
No murder clothed him, and no murder fed.
In the same temple, the resounding wood,
All vocal beings hymn'd their equal God:
The shrine with gore unstain'd, with gold undress'd,
Unbribed, unbloody, stood the blameless priest:
Heaven's attribute was universal care,
And man's prerogative, to rule, but spare.
Ah! how unlike the man of times to come!
Of half that live the butcher and the tomb,
Who, foe to Nature, hears the general groan,
Murders their species, and betrays his own.
But just disease to luxury succeeds,
And every death its own avenger breeds;
The fury-passions from that blood began,
And turn'd on man, a fiercer savage, man.

> God loves from whole to parts: but human soul
> Must rise from individual to the whole.
> Self-love but serves the virtuous mind to wake,
> As the small pebble stirs the peaceful lake;
> The centre moved, a circle straight succeeds,
> Another still, and still another spreads;
> Friend, parent, neighbour, first it will embrace;
> His country next; and next all human race;
> Wide and more wide, the o'erflowings of the mind
> Take every creature in, of every kind;
> Earth smiles around, with boundless bounty blest,
> And Heaven beholds its image in his breast.

Pope's didacticism is in earnest. " 'He has writ in the cause of virtue, and done some things to mend people's morals' is the only commendation I long for." His improving sentiments were not exclusively reserved for his own poems and such embroideries of other poets as we observed in his translation of Homer. "At a time when cruelty to animals, of the most unspeakably horrible kind, was exhibited daily, and was held to be no disgrace", writes Edith Sitwell, ". . . [he] wrote an essay, reproaching such cruelty in the most moving terms." She prints the whole indictment, in her admirable life of the poet: ". . . if our sports are destructive, our gluttony is more so, and in a more inhuman manner. Lobsters roasted alive, pigs whipp'd to death, fowls sewed up, are testimonies of our outrageous luxury." Pope also expressed his disapproval of experiments on animals: "he is a very good man; only I'm sorry he has his hands so much imbrued with blood. . . . Indeed, he commits most of these barbarities with the thought of being of use to man; but how do we know, that we have a right to kill creatures that we are so little above as dogs, for our curiosity, or even for some use to us?" But Pope was never altogether consistent, even in preaching. As a youth he was, he says, "no great hunter, indeed, but a great esteemer of the noble sport" of which he wrote in *Windsor Forest*:

> The shady empire shall retain no trace
> Of war or blood, but in the sylvan chase;
> The trumpet sleep, whilst cheerful horns are blown,
> And arms employ'd on birds and beasts alone.

Yet his dream was of the garden of Alcinous, and in his last years at Twickenham he realised it and could write to Swift of a garden almost such as Marvell dreamed of: "I have more fruit trees and kitchen gardens than you have thought of; nay, I have good melons and pineapples of my own growth. . . ." It had "two or three sweet little lawns", wrote Horace Walpole, "opening and opening beyond one another, and the whole surrounded by thick impenetrable woods". But the diet was mixed, the poet fed:

> On broccoli and mutton round the year;
> But ancient friends (though poor, or out of play),
> That touch my bell, I cannot turn away.
> 'Tis true, no turbots dignify my boards,
> But gudgeons, flounders, what my Thames affords:
> To Hounslow Heath I point, and Banstead Down,
> Thence comes your mutton, and these chicks my own:
> From yon old walnut-tree a shower shall fall;
> And grapes, long lingering on my only wall,
> And figs from standard and espalier join;
> The devil is in you if you cannot dine.

—Or, perhaps, if you can dine so? For the poem[1] opens with:

> Let's talk, my friends, but talk before we dine.
> Not when a gilt buffet's reflected pride
> Turns you from sound philosophy aside.

Perhaps the praise of "plain bread and milk" in the same poem, contrasted with orgies where the stomach is "A tomb of boil'd and roast, and flesh and fish" had conjured up awkward recollections of the Golden Age over which Pope had rhapsodized in his all too recent *Essay on Man* when "no murder fed" mankind. By that standard even "broccoli and mutton" was reproached. Had he not written compassionately in the *Essay* of "The lamb thy riot dooms to bleed" that "Licks the hand just raised to shed his blood"?[2]

---

[1] This *Imitation of the Second Satire of the Second Book of Horace* (we have quoted from Horace's original Chapter 2), is a free version into which Pope introduces his own friends and much else, so that we are making no extravagant assumptions in treating the sentiments as his own. This poem is, more legitimately, an extreme example of the "improving" process that we saw at work in Pope's translation of Homer's *Iliad*.

[2] This image, of which there is a prototype in the quoted fragments of Empedocles' poems, is recurrent—largely, no doubt, because of the Christian associations of the Lamb. The challenge is directly taken by up Goldsmith, quoted in this chapter, and in Blake's "Little lamb who made thee . . ."? Compare also:

> So first the harmless sheep doth yield his fleece
> And next his throat unto the butcher's knife.

Shakespeare, 3 *Henry VI*, V, vi, 9. (*footnote continued on next page*)

Dean Swift had no such misgivings. As a guest at Twickenham he could savour the mutton, although he might have been uneasy about the dessert, since he ascribed his deafness to an immoderate indulgence in fruit, an opinion that would have gladdened the heart of Sir Thomas Elyot. We may take the *Epigram on Fasting* as an epitome of Swift's conviction that diet has little or nothing to do with ethics:

> Who can believe with common Sense,
> A Bacon-slice gives God Offence?
> Or, how a Herring hath a Charm
> Almighty Anger to disarm?
> Wrapt up in Majesty divine
> Does he regard on what we dine?

Nevertheless, Swift, like Pope, finds at least a nominal adherence to the tradition useful in a passage of *A Panegyrick on the Dean*, where he outdoes Pope in denouncing the gluttony of the age:

> When Saturn rul'd the Skies alone,
> The *golden* Age to *Gold* unknown;
> This earthly Globe to thee assign'd,
> Receiv'd the Gifts of all Mankind.
>
> .   .   .   .
>
> But, when at last usurping Jove
> Old *Saturn* from his Empire drove;
> Then *Gluttony* with greasy Paws,
> Her Napkin pinn'd up to her Jaws,
> With watry Chaps, and wagging Chin,
> Brac'd like a Drum her oily Skin;
> Wedg'd in a spacious Elbow-Chair,
> And on her plate a treble Share,
> As if she ne'er could have enuff:
> Taught harmless Man to cram and stuff.

Footnote continued from page 173

The Lamb misued breeds public strife
And yet forgives the butcher's knife.
Blake, *Auguries of Innocence.*

He slays the lamb that looks him in the face
And horribly devours his mangled flesh
Shelley, *Queen Mab.*

Whereas in Ovid, quoted at the beginning of this chapter, it is not the Christian Lamb but a Calf
that lies beneath the knife,
Looks up, and from her Butcher begs her life.

She sent her Priests in Wooden Shoes
From haughty Gaul to make ragous.
Instead of wholesome Bread and Cheese,[1]
To dress their Soups and Fricassyes;
And, for our home-bred *British* Chear,
Botargo, Catsup and Caveer.

In *Gulliver's Travels*, which appeared a year before the first volume of Gay's *Fables*, Swift has his own animal parable. The horse-sense of the Houyhnhnms is largely concerned with food. The inferior and semi-human Yahoos—"Upon the whole, I never beheld in all my travels so disagreeable an animal, or one against which I naturally conceived so strong an antipathy"—eat roots "and the flesh of some animals which I afterwards found to be that of asses and dogs, and now and then a cow dead by accident or disease" and are "the only animals in this country subject to any disease" which is "contracted not by any ill treatment they meet with, but by the nastiness and greediness of that horrid brute". Their behaviour is distinctly Bacchanalian. If "you throw among five Yahoos as much food as would be sufficient for fifty, they will, instead of eating peaceably, fall together by the ears, each single one impatient to *have all to itself*... if a cow died of age or accident, before a Houyhnhnm could secure it for his own Yahoos, those in the neighbourhood would come in herds to seize it, and then would ensue such a battle as I had described, with terrible wounds made by their claws on both sides, although they seldom were able to kill one another, for want of such convenient instruments of death as we had invented".

The Houyhnhnms, the master race of horses whose name means "the perfection of nature", who "went upon a supposition that all

---

[1] Pope's "plain bread and milk" and Swift's "wholesome bread and cheese" as symbols of frugal and virtuous fare may have something in common with a passage, interesting for our purpose, in *The Art of Cookery* (1708), a curious work by William King (1663–1712), who was friendly with Swift:

> The tender lettuce brings on softer sleep;
> Eat beef or pie-crust if you'd serious be;
> Your shellfish raises Venus from the sea;
> For nature, that inclines to ill or good,
> Still nourishes our passions by our food.
> Happy the man that has each fortune tried,
> To whom she much has given, and much denied:
> With abstinence all delicates he sees,
> And can regale himself with toast and cheese.

A much less idyllic picture of peasant life on home-made bread, cheese and vegetables is most amusingly drawn in *The Salad*, attributed to Vergil(!), translated in 1799 by William Cowper. Cowper, whose translation of Milton's Pythagorean Elegy to Deodati has been quoted in the last chapter, shows strong sympathy with animals in his own poems and may be counted among the forerunners of nineteenth-century "humanitarian" verse. But he made the monastic distinction in favour of eating fish, as will be seen from a later footnote.

animals had a title to their share in the production of the earth" and in their great assembly were wont to discuss "the various excellencies of *poetry*", dine on oats boiled in milk and graze. Although accidents are not unknown, the Houyhnhnms do not think it possible that disease could affect themselves or even mankind. "That Nature, who worketh all things to perfection, should suffer any pains to breed in our bodies, he thought impossible; and desired to know the reason of so unaccountable an evil. I told him, we fed on a thousand things which operated contrary to each other. . . ."

War preparation, legal practice, doctors, clothes, money economy and digging for "stones" are all heavily satirised and there is a particularly devastating assault upon the dependent food economy: England "produces three times the quantity of food, more than its inhabitants are able to consume, as well as liquors extracted from grain, or pressed out of the fruit of certain trees, which made excellent drink; and the same proportion in every other convenience of life. But, in order to feed the luxury and intemperance of the males, and the vanity of the females, we sent away the greatest part of our necessary things to other countries, from whence in return we brought the materials of diseases, folly, and vice, to spend among our selves." The criticism, incidentally, is not inapplicable to an industrialised island that depends on the other side of the world for food and other primary supplies.

The dietary régime of Gulliver himself, the "gentle Yahoo", was a compromise between the morbid rapacity of the Yahoos and the healthy lacto-vegetarianism of the superior Houyhnhnms. At first he refuses roots and ass's flesh, hay and oats, but later makes dough from the oats and eats it warm with milk. "It was at first a very insipid diet although common enough in many parts of Europe, but grew tolerable by time; and having been often reduced to hard fare in my life, this was not the first experiment I had made how easily nature is satisfied. And I cannot but observe, that I never had one hour's sickness, while I stayed on this island . . . and I often gathered wholesome herbs, which I boiled, or eat as salades with my bread; and now and then, for a rarity, I made a little butter, and drank the whey. . . . I often got honey out of hollow trees, which I mingled with water, or eat it with my bread. No man could more verify the truth of these two maxims: *that, Nature is very easily satisfied;* and *that necessity is the mother of invention.* I enjoyed perfect health of body, and tranquillity of mind; I did not feel the treachery or inconstancy of a friend, nor the injuries of a secret or open enemy . . ." and so on through a long catalogue of the vicissitudes attributed to civilized life.

But, as is artistically appropriate to the satire but may also have been true of the Dean himself, Gulliver's horse-sense bears the Yahoo taint. "I agreed in every feature of my body with other Yahoos, except where it was to my real disadvantage in point of strength, the shortness of my claws, and some other particulars where nature had no part. . . ." He "sometimes made a shift to catch a rabbit, or a bird, by springes made of Yahoos hairs" and when he prepares to leave the island he "laid in a stock of boiled flesh, of rabbits and fowls; and took with me two vessels, one filled with milk, and the other with water". He would hardly have escaped the Yahoo's evil if the voyage had not been a short one. But he arrives next day at New Holland, where he lives for three days on oysters and limpets!

The God of Oliver Goldsmith's gentle Hermit is not, like Swift's, too wrapped up in majesty divine to care on what we dine:

> No flocks that range the valley free
>   To slaughter I condemn;
> Taught by that Power that pities me,
>   I learn to pity them:
>
> But from the mountain's grassy side
>   A guiltless feast I bring—
> A scrip with herbs and fruits supplied,
>   And water from the spring.

The Hermit[1] offers shelter to a wandering youth, with whom he shares his vegetable store. Finding his guest love-lorn, the Hermit, in the best tradition of Marvell and Tate, advises him to "spurn the sex". He then discovers his guest to be a girl, Angelina, who

---

[1] Goldsmith's hermit is Christian rather than classical. More than a century earlier, and before even the appearance of *Paradise Lost*, an authentic Christian Hermit became, as he complains, "the gazing stock of the Nation" not far from London. The title-page of a surviving pamphlet runs:

THE/ENGLISH HERMITE/OR/Wonder of this AGE.

Being a relation of the life of Roger Crab, living neer Uxbridg, taken from his own mouth, showing his strange reserved and unparallel'd kind of life, who counteth it a sin against his body and soul to eate any sort of Flesh, Fish, or living Creature, or to drinke any Wine, Ale or Beere. He can live with three farthings a week.

His constant food is Roots and Hearbs, as Cabbage, Turneps, Carrets, Dock-leaves and Grasse; also Bread and Bran, without Butter or Cheese: His cloathing is Sack-Cloath. (*footnote continued on next page*)

reproaches herself for trifling with the affections of a faithful Edwin. Whereupon the Hermit reveals himself to be that sorrowing swain and, if he dare not promise to make her happy ever after, at least declares that—

> The sigh that rends thy constant heart
> Shall break thy Edwin's too.

Thirty-five years earlier a new strain first sounded in English poetry, a new freshness of approach to Nature mingled with the increasingly artificial classicism of the Augustans. Thomson's feeling for Nature, untypical of the century, foreshadows Wordsworth. In *Spring*, which stands first in *The Seasons*, and was published a few years before Pope's *Essay on Man*, James Thomson recaptures the Pythagorean vision of the Golden Age. When the Scottish minister's son in Thomson asserts himself against the poet, the theme falls suddenly to the bathos of:

> High Heaven forbids the bold presumptuous strain

—as though Swift's divine majesty had unwrapped himself sufficiently to come down on the side of fallen Man and against Eden —and Thomson tries to pass to a description of the joys of angling, only to find himself penning an indictment of senseless cruelty.

In *Summer*, published a year earlier, there is, however, an unspoilt vision of the feast of fruits—the last of the following quotations— which surpasses Milton's in sensuous richness. Thomson is not here imitating the classics, but he is restoring a vital element to the tradition. When the Golden Feast was distinguished from the common yearning for Cockaigne and the disgusting gluttony of the eighteenth century, it was too often set beside the ascetic tradition of the monasteries, as a virtuous austerity. The true tradition is not of frugality but of what Tate called "the diet of the Gods" and Thomson celebrates as glorious abundance for mankind:

Footnote continued from page 177

He left the Army, and kept a Shop at Chesham, and hath now left off that, and sold a considerable Estate to give to the Poore, showing his reasons from the Scripture, Mark 10. 21. Jer. 35.

Wherefore if meate make my brother to offend, I will never eat flesh while the world stands. I Cor. 8. 13.

LONDON/Printed and are to be sold in Popes-head Alley, and at the Exchange, 1655.

In a page of verse at the end of the pamphlet, Crab congratulates himself on having by this means escaped the temptations of the flesh:

> And from wenching I am sunk,
> My bones are kept so bare.

Then spring the living herbs, profusely wild,
O'er all the deep-green earth, beyond the power
Of botanist to number up their tribes:
Whether he steals along the lonely dale,
In silent search; or through the forest, rank
With what the dull incurious weeds account,
Bursts his blind way; or climbs the mountain-rock,
Fired by the nodding verdure of its brow.
With such a liberal hand has Nature flung
Their seeds abroad, blown them about in winds,
Innumerous mix'd them with the nursing mould,
The moistening current, and prolific rain.
        But who their virtues can declare? who pierce,
With vision pure, into these secret stores
Of health, and life, and joy? the food of man,
While yet he lived in innocence, and told
A length of golden years, unflesh'd in blood;
A stranger to the savage arts of life,
Death, rapine, carnage, surfeit, and disease;
The lord, and not the tyrant, of the world.

.   .   .   .   .

Nor yet injurious act, nor surly deed,
Was known among those happy sons of Heaven;
For reason and benevolence were law.
Harmonious Nature, too, look'd smiling on.
Clear shone the skies, cool'd with eternal gales,
And balmy spirits all. The youthful sun
Shot his best rays; and still the gracious clouds
Dropp'd fatness down; as o'er the swelling mead
The herds and flocks, commixing, play'd secure.
This, when, emergent from the gloomy wood,
The glaring lion saw, his horrid heart
Was meeken'd, and he join'd his sullen joy,
For music held the whole in perfect peace:
Soft sigh'd the flute: the tender voice was heard,
Warbling the varied heart; the woodlands round
Applied their choir; and winds and waters flow'd
In consonance. Such were those prime of days.
        But now those white unblemish'd manners, whence
The fabling Poets took their golden age,

Are found no more amid these iron times,
These dregs of life! Now the distemper'd mind
Has lost that concord of harmonious powers,
Which forms the soul of happiness, and all
Is off the poise within; the passions all
Have burst their bounds; and reason, half-extinct
Or impotent, or else approving, sees
The foul disorder.

.   .   .   .

The seasons since have, with severer sway,
Oppress'd a broken world: the Winter keen
Shook forth his waste of snows; and Summer shot
His pestilential heats. Great Spring, before,
Green'd all the year, and fruits and blossoms blush'd
In social sweetness on the self-same bough.
Pure was the temperate air; an even calm
Perpetual reign'd, save what the zephyrs bland
Breathed o'er the blue expanse; for them nor storms
Were taught to blow, nor hurricanes to rage;
Sound slept the waters: no sulphureous glooms
Swell'd in the sky, and sent the lightning forth;
While sickly damps, and cold autumnal fogs,
Hung not, relaxing, on the springs of life.
But now, of turbid elements the sport,
From clear to cloudy toss'd, from hot to cold,
And dry to moist, with inward-eating change,
Our drooping days are dwindled down to nought,
Their period finish'd, ere 'tis well begun.
And yet the wholesome herb neglected dies;
Though with the pure exhilarating soul
Of nutriment and health, and vital powers
Beyond the search of art, 'tis copious bless'd.
For, with hot ravin fired, ensanguined man
Is now become the lion of the plain,
And worse. The wolf, who from the nightly fold
Fierce drags the bleating prey, ne'er drunk her milk,
Nor wore her warming fleece: nor has the steer,
At whose strong chest the deadly tiger hangs,
E'er ploughed for him. They, too, are temper'd high,
With hunger stung and wild necessity,
Nor lodges pity in their shaggy breast.

But man, whom Nature form'd of milder clay,
With every kind emotion in his heart,
And taught alone to weep; while from her lap
She pours ten thousand delicacies, herbs,
And fruits, as numerous as the drops of rain
Or beams that gave them birth: shall he, fair form!
Who wears sweet smiles, and looks erect on Heaven,
E'er stoop to mingle with the prowling herd,
And dip his tongue in gore? The beast of prey,
Blood-stain'd, deserves to bleed; but you, ye flocks,
What have you done? ye peaceful people, what,
To merit death? you who have given us milk
In luscious streams, and lent us your own coat
Against the Winter's cold? And the plain ox,
That harmless, honest, guileless animal,
In what has he offended? he whose toil,
Patient, and ever ready, clothes the land
With all the pomp of harvest; shall he bleed,
And struggling groan beneath the cruel hands
E'en of the clown he feeds? and that, perhaps,
To swell the riot of the autumnal feast
Won by his labour? Thus the feeling heart
Would tenderly suggest; but 'tis enough,
In this late age, adventurous to have touch'd
Light on the numbers of the Samian sage:
High Heaven forbids the bold presumptuous strain,
Whose wisest will has fix'd us in a state
That must not yet to pure perfection rise.
Besides, who knows, how raised to higher life,
From stage to stage, the vital scale ascends.

　　　Now, when the first foul torrent of the brooks,
Swell'd with the vernal rains, is ebb'd away,
And whitening, down their mossy-tinctured stream
Descends the billowy foam; now is the time,
While yet the dark-brown water aids the guile,
To tempt the trout. The well-dissembled fly,
The rod fine-tapering with elastic spring,
Snatch'd from the hoary steed the floating line,
And all thy slender watery stores, prepare.
But let not on thy hook the tortured worm
Convulsive twist in agonizing folds;

Which, by rapacious hunger swallow'd deep,
Gives, as you tear it from the bleeding breast
Of the weak, hapless, uncomplaining wretch,
Harsh pain and horror to the tender hand.[1]

. . . . .

          Here, in eternal prime,
Unnumber'd fruits of keen delicious taste
And vital spirit, drink amid the cliffs,
And burning sands that bank the shrubby vales,
Redoubled day, yet in their rugged coats
A friendly juice to cool its rage contain.
     Bear me, Pomona, to thy citron groves;
To where the lemon and the piercing lime,
With the deep orange, glowing through the green,
Their lighter glories blend. Lay me reclined
Beneath the spreading tamarind, that shakes,
Fann'd by the breeze, its fever-cooling fruit.
Deep in the night the massy locust sheds,
Quench my hot limbs; or lead me through the maze,
Embowering endless, of the Indian fig;
Or thrown at gayer ease, on some fair brow,
Let me behold, by breezy murmurs cool'd,
Broad o'er my head the verdant cedar wave,
And high palmetos lift their graceful shade.
Or, stretch'd amid these orchards of the sun,
Give me to drain the cocoa's milky bowl,

---

[1] Such scruples are by no means general, even among those poets most sympathetic to animals. Cowper, for instance, acknowledges a present of fish from a clergyman thus:

> Peace, therefore, and good health and much good fish,
> To him who sent thee! and success, as oft,
> As it descends into the billowy gulph,
> To the same drag that caught thee!—Fare thee well!
> Thy lot, thy brethren of the slimy fin
> Would envy, could they know that thou wast doom'd
> To feed a bard, and to be praised in verse.

It would be interesting to hear the fish's comment on the honour, as it might have been penned by the author of *The Fish, The Man and The Spirit*—Leigh Hunt. But a poet's sensibility has often less to do with his attitude in such matters than his philosophy. Thomson was still in Pythagorean mood. And even when satirising the Pythagorean doctrine of metempsychosis, in *The Progress of the Soul*, John Donne must needs write:

> Is any kind subject to rape like fish?
> Ill unto man, they neither do, nor wish:
> Fishers they kill not, nor with noise awake,
> They do not hunt, nor strive to make a prey
> Of beasts, nor their young sons to bear away;
> Fowls they pursue not, nor do undertake
> To spoil the nests industrious birds do make;
> Yet them all these unkind kinds feed upon
> To kill them is an occupation,
>   And laws make Feasts and Lents for their destruction

—in which lines it is Man who is indirectly criticised. The full indictment may be read in Samuel Butler' poem, *The Righteous Man* (which reminds us that *Erewhon* is among the vegetarian Utopias!) and Rober Buchanan's *Man of the Red Right Hand*.

And from the palm to draw its freshening wine,
More bounteous far than all the frantic juice
Which Bacchus pours! Nor, on its slender twigs
Low-bending, be the full pomegranate scorn'd;
Nor, creeping through the woods, the gelid race
Of berries. Oft in humble station dwells
Unboastful worth, above fastidious pomp.
Witness, thou best Anana, thou the pride
Of vegetable life, beyond whate'er
The poets imaged in the golden age:
Quick let me strip thee of thy tufty coat,
Spread thy ambrosial stores, and feast with Jove!

James Thomson's contemporary, Thomas Warton, was a poet of comparable qualities who had the distinction of fathering two poets of the same school, Thomas the Younger and Joseph. Between them the Wartons are sometimes given the credit of begetting the Romantic movement, or at least of being the most significant forerunners, half a century before their time—an estimate that is rather hard on Thomson. But the Wartons' poetry certainly foreshadows the Romantic poets and it is interesting to discover that they contribute not only a new spontaneity but a more precise classicism. We have seen that Swift could use the Golden Age as a stalking-horse when intent on satirizing gluttony, without realising how much the traditional food imagery would strengthen his effect, and Alexander Pope's Horatian denunciation of gluttony faded into a bad anti-climax because it got mixed up in the same way. *The Glutton*, by Thomas Warton the Elder, deals with the same theme without confusion and is therefore immensely more effective as an artistic whole, whatever any reader may think about its dietetic precepts:

Fat, pamper'd Porus, eating for renown,
In soups and sauces melts his manors down;
Regardless of his heirs, with mortgag'd lands,
Buys hecatombs of fish and ortōlans;
True judge of merit, most disdainful looks
On chiefs and patriots when compar'd to cooks;
With what delight pigs whipt to death he crams,
Or fatten'd frogs, or essences of hams;

For fifty thousand tongues of peacocks sighs,
Mix'd with the brains of birds of paradise;
Loud ring the glasses, powder'd footmen run,
He eats, drinks, surfeits, still eats, is undone!
See the swoln Glutton in terrific state,
Behind his chair what dire diseases wait;
There tottering gout, and white-tongu'd fever stand,
Big dropsy, with full goblets in his hand,
Asthma thick-panting with short gasps of breath,
And apoplexy, fiercest friend of death.
Sweeter the lonely hermit's simple food,
Who in lone caves or near the rushy flood,
With eager appetite at early hours,
From maple dish salubrious herbs devours!
Soft drowsy dews at eve his temples steep,
And happy dreams attend his easy sleep:
Wak'd by the thrush to neighbouring vales he goes,
To mark how sucks the bee, how blooms the rose;
What latent juice the trodden herbage yields,
Wild Nature's physic in the flowery fields.
With temperance sooth'd each solitary day,
Free, innocent, and easy, steals away,
Till age down binds him in the friendly grave,
No fashion's dupe, no powerful passion's slave.

Warton's point had, however, been made more than half a century
earlier by Abraham Cowley, in a poem written for his friend John
Evelyn who held similar dietary views and expressed them in his
Acetaria. Cowley will not yield unchallenged the glutton's claim
to have the more delectable fare:

When Epicurus to the world had taught
     That pleasure is the chiefest good,
     (And was, perhaps, i'th'right, if rightly understood),
His life he to this doctrine brought,
And in a garden's shade that Sovereign pleasure sought:
     Whoever a true *Epicure* would be,
     May there find cheap and virtuous luxury.
Vitellius his table which did hold
As many creatures as the ark of old—
     That fiscal table to which every day
     All countries did a constant tribute pay—

> Could nothing more delectable afford
>   Than Nature's Liberality—
>   Helped with a little Art and Industry—
> Allows the meanest gardener's board.
>   The wanton Taste no Flesh nor Fowl can choose,
>   For which the Grape or Melon it would lose,
>   Though all th' inhabitants of Earth and Air
>   Be listed in the Glutton's bill of fare.

And Cowley goes on to make the same damaging contrast between the town and the country that was so dear to the Wartons:

> Let Cities boast that they provide
> For life the ornaments of Pride;
> But 'tis the Country and the Field
> That furnish it with Staff and Shield.

But if Cowley had been beforehand with these Pythagorean sentiments, the elder Thomas Warton has clearly anticipated Goldsmith's hermit and, we might say, he is already commending migration back to the deserted village. His ode, *Retirement*, ends:

> Teach me St. James's to despise.
> For what are courts but schools
> For fops or hospitals for fools?
> Where slaves and madmen, young and old?
> Meet to adore some Calf of Gold.

Mammon, as in Spenser, is the villain of the piece. A fragment of a *Satire* ends:

> Still Britons (Justice, Freedom, Conscience sold)
> Own the supreme omnipotence of Gold.

Thomas Warton the Younger—the elder son—can write very agreeable rustic verse when he wishes, as in *The Hamlet*. But his imagery gives us a clue to the fact that his heart was not in the family tradition. " 'Tis thou O Summer mild", he sings in the *Approach of Summer*, ". . . With whom each field's a paradise, And all the globe a bower of bliss." The Spenserian echo is significant, and we are not surprised when this amiable editor of the poetical miscellany, *The Oxford Sausage*, which celebrates the easy-going university life, writes mock-tragically of Eden in his amusing *Panegyric on Oxford Ale:*

> Thus while, improvident of future ill,
> I quaff the luscious tankard uncontroll'd,
> And thoughtless riot in unlicens'd bliss;
> Sudden (dire fate of all things excellent!)
> Th' unpitying bursar's cross-affixing hand
> Blasts all my joys, and stops my glad career.
>
> Thus Adam, exiled from the beauteous scenes
> Of Eden, grieved, no more in fragrant bower
> On fruits divine to feast, fresh shade and vale
> No more to visit, or vine-mantled grot;
> But, all forlorn, the dreary wilderness
> And unrejoicing solitudes to trace.

Or when in the *Prologue on the Old Winchester Playhouse—over the Butcher's Shambles* he writes cheerfully—

> Suet, and sighs, blank verse and blood abound

and gaily makes the inevitable joke about "the pound of flesh" and assures his readers that at "our house" guests would not be so tantalised.

And where his father saw that gold was the curse of the age, the younger Thomas writes eulogistically in *For the New Year,* 1786, that—

> The golden chain of commerce winds

across the deep.

Thomas Warton the Younger was much more a man of the age, and it is anything but accidental that of the trio he was the one who became, in 1785, Poet Laureate, though it would be difficult to find good critical reasons for preferring his poetry to that of his younger brother, Joseph. Joseph Warton's poem *The Enthusiast, or the Lover of Nature,* was written at the age of eighteen—Shelley was two or three years older when he wrote *Queen Mab*—although not published until four years later, 1744. It was therefore written ten years after the collected *Seasons* by James Thomson appeared in 1730, and its author was still alive when William Blake wrote *The Four Zoas* at the end of the century.

Sir Edmund Gosse hailed *The Enthusiast* as "the earliest expression of complete revolt against the classical attitude", which is true enough if one is thinking of the conventional repetition of classical themes for the sake of elegance. But Joseph's later works included a translation of Vergil's *Eclogues* and *Georgics*, an essay on the genius of Pope and an edition of his works, and he was working on an edition of Dryden when he died. Probably some of the poetry of these three on the theme we are considering was well-known to him when he wrote *The Enthusiast*, and he certainly very well understood the values he had inherited from his father's poetry. The poem runs to two or three hundred lines and since our main interest here is in Joseph Warton as an intermediate figure between the Augustans and the Romantics, it will be necessary to begin with a few brief quotations and to identify the allusions before giving the poet a slightly better chance of speaking for himself. Warton begins with a renunciation of cities and the peruked nature of the great estates, reminiscent of his father's rejection of the Court at St. James's and all it stood for:

> To unfrequented meads, and pathless wilds,
> Lead me from gardens deck'd with arts vain pomps.

It is interesting to find an image from Mandeville, in whose *Fable* the bees fly from corrupt society and seek rural innocence in a hollow tree, forswearing splendour for the sake of virtue. Warton writes:

> While from an hollow oak, whose naked roots
> O'erhang a pensive rill, the busy bees
> Hum drowsy lullabies. The bards of old
> Fair Nature's friends, sought such retreats.

That does not exactly promise "complete revolt against the classical attitude" comparable say, with Blake's "The Classics! it is the Classics, & not Goths nor Monks, that Desolate Europe with Wars. . . . Sacred Truth has pronounced that Greece & Rome, as Babylon & Egypt, so far from being parents of Arts & Sciences, as they pretend, were destroyers of all Art. Homer, Virgil & Ovid confirm this opinion, & make us reverence The Word of God, the only light of antiquity that remains unperverted by War." But Warton pursues his description of "the bards of old":

> oft too they met
> In summer evenings, near sequester'd bowers,
> Or mountain-nymph, or muse, and eager learnt
> The moral strains she taught to mend mankind.
> As to a secret grot Aegeria stole
> With patriot Numa, and in silent night
> Whisper'd him sacred laws, he list'ning sat,
> Rapt with her virtuous voice, old Tyber lean'd
> Attentive on his urn, and hush'd his waves.

The emphasis on the didactic purpose of poetry is significant, and Numa is, of course, the recipient in *Metamorphoses* XV of instruction in the Pythagorean philosophy, which makes him worthy to rule Rome.

Joseph is known also to have appreciated Milton, and the Miltonic note is sounded in his eulogy of Nature:

> Can the great artist, though with taste supreme
> Endu'd, one beauty to this Eden add?

He then passes to a paraphrase of Lucretius:

> Happy the first of men!, ere yet confin'd
> To smoky cities; who in sheltering groves,
> Warm caves, and deep-sunk vallies liv'd and lov'd,
> By cares unwounded; what the sun and showers,
> And genial earth untillag'd could produce,
> They gather'd grateful, or the acorn brown,
> Or blushing berry; by the liquid lapse
> Of murm'ring waters call'd to slake their thirst,
> Or with fair nymphs their sun-brown limbs to bathe.

Warton goes on to describe the innocence of women in those happy golden times, which he contrasts with the evils of civilization. It is obvious enough that Warton has painted a much more favourable picture of the first age than is to be found in Lucretius, and it is this antithesis between primal innocence and contemporary urban wickedness that he wants to emphasise, where Lucretius only touched on it.

> Oft near some crowded city would I walk,
> Listening the far-off noises, rattling cars,
> Loud shouts of joy, sad shrieks of sorrow, knells
> Full slowly tolling, instruments of trade
> Striking mine ears with one deep-swelling hum.

The associations are so depressingly familiar to children of the industrial revolution that it is difficult to realise how prophetic are these lines, written in 1740! Forsaking the cities, the poet seeks Contemplation on "some level mead" and there appear to him at night Philosophy, Solitude Serene, Wisdom and Virtue—who is leading Innocence, "a naked boy". Virtue addresses the poet:

> Whoe'er thou art,
> Mortal, by whom I deign to be beheld
> In these my midnight walks; depart, and say
> That henceforth I and my immortal train
> Forsake Britannia's isle; who fondly stoops
> To Vice, her favourite paramour.

The poet too would therefore leave his own country for some place where traces of primal splendour linger on:

> O who will bear me then to western climes,
> (Since Virtue leaves our wretched land)[1] to fields
> Yet unpolluted with Iberian swords:
> The isles of Innocence, from mortal view
> Deeply retir'd, beneath a plantane's shade,
> Where Happiness and Quiet sit enthron'd,
> With simple Indian swains, that I may hunt
> The boar and tiger through savannahs wild,
> Through fragrant deserts, and through citron-groves?
> There fed on dates and herbs, would I despise
> The far-fetch'd cates of luxury, and hoards
> Of marrow-heated avarice; nor heed
> The distant din of the tumultuous world.

The boar-hunt, of course, is an incongruous[2] note inadvertently taken over from Lucretius. Its association with Western climes

---

[1] Compare Goldsmith's *Deserted Village*, written thirty years later, in 1770: "I see the rural virtues leave the land"—and Poetry with them.

[2] "To kill Man-killers, Man has lawful Pow'r" says Pythagoras in Dryden's version of Ovid, so that the sentiment here expressed could be justified in a poem in that tradition. But the emphasis here is rather on the pleasures of the hunt which is no less inconsistent than Pope's admiration of the "sylvan chase".

and Red Indians reminds us rather of Drayton's Virginia voyage. But the significant thing about *The Enthusiast* is the vision of Virtue forsaking Britannia's isle, only a little over a century after Ben Jonson had over-confidently moored the Fortunate Isles to Britain and William Browne had seen his vision of the Golden Age amid *Britannia's Pastorals*. For something like a departure of Virtue from Britain really happened in English poetry during the latter half of the eighteenth century until, stimulated by tendencies and events in revolutionary France, the contrasting voices of Blake and Wordsworth were raised in accents that heralded a new age. We therefore glance next at a development whose roots lie far back in French history and which we may discern in growth through the representative writings of Montaigne and Voltaire before it comes to fruition in Rousseau and Lamartine.

Three hundred years after the great majority of people in Southern France had fallen under the influence of the Cathari, a strictly vegetarian heretical sect, and two centuries after Petrarch had retired to his ascetic solitude in a valley near Avignon, Michel de Montaigne was born in his father's château near Bordeaux. Until he was six he heard and spoke no language other than Latin. The first classical literature to appeal to him was Ovid's *Metamorphoses* and his own later writing is so much indebted to Plutarch and Seneca, he says in his old age, that he "meerely framed of their spoiles" the *Essays* that have delighted the world.

We have noted that *Of the Caniballes*, in the first book of *Essays* was the source of Gonzalo's speech on the commonwealth in *The Tempest*. Montaigne there considers that the lately-discovered primitives could have taught something to Lycurgus (the Spartan whom Plutarch compared with the Roman Numa) and Plato; "for me seemeth that what in those nations we see by experience, doth not only exceed all the pictures wherewith licentious Poesie hath proudly imbellished the golden age, and all her quaint inventions to faine a happy condition of man, but also the conception and desire of Philosophy". But in fact his description closely agrees with the tradition of the Golden Age, except in the matter of diet. The cannibals, as might be expected, did not draw the line at other strange fish and flesh and practised hunting. These attributes Shakespeare rejected.

Yet, in the eleventh essay, *On Cruelty*, and the more famous twelfth essay on *Raymond Sebond*, in his second book of *Essays*, Montaigne writes more than sympathetically of the beliefs of Pythagoras, Plato and his revered Plutarch on the subject of the unity of life and its ethical implications. Pythagoras, he notes, made God a spirit dispersed through the nature of all things; he borrowed metempsychosis from the Egyptians but it has since been accepted by many other nations and "especially of our Druides". He was wont, like Leonardo, to buy fishes and birds and set them free again, and Montaigne here interpolates a quotation from the Pythagorean final book of Ovid's *Metamorphoses*. Plato, he writes, considered that one of the chief glories of the Saturnian Golden Age was that man enjoyed communication with the beasts, "by and from whom he got an absolute understanding and perfect wisdom, whereby he led a happier life than we can doe". The former essay closes with Plutarch's refusal to send to the shambles any ox that had long served him by its labour.

"As for me", Montaigne confesses, "I could never so much as endure, without remorse and griefe, to see a poore, sillie, and innocent beast pursued and killed, which is harmless and void of defence, and of whom we receive no offence at all." There is "a kind of respect, and a generall duty of humanity, which tieth us not only to brute beasts that have life and sense, but even unto trees and plants". This thoroughly Orphic conception leads Montaigne to the vision of the bounteous Nature that surrounds every child: "The earth without labour or tilling doth sufficiently produce and offer him as much as he shall need . . . our common mother nature, hath with great plentie stored us with whatsoever should be needfull for us, yea, as is most likely, more richly and amply, than now adaies she doth, that we have added so much art unto it. The gluttonous excesse, and intemperate lavishnesse of our appetite exceeding all the inventions, we endevour to finde out, wherewith to glut and cloy the same."

"The Hindus", says Rousseau's celebrated contemporary, Voltaire, "in embracing the doctrine of *Metempsychosis*, had one restraint the more. The dread of killing a father or mother, in killing men and other animals, inspired in them a terror of murder and every other violence, which became with them a second nature. . . .

Some have supposed the cradle of our race to be Hindustan . . . a land which produces without culture the most nourishing and most healthful fruits. . . . These peoples need and desire pure and refreshing foods. Nature has lavished upon them forests of citron trees, orange trees, fig trees, palm trees, cocoa-nut trees, and plains covered with rice. . . . In general, the men of the South-East have received from Nature gentler manners than the people of our West. . . . These people are scandalised at seeing us drinking wine and eating flesh, which they themselves abhor"—a fact confirmed from personal experience in Gandhi's *Autobiography*. Elsewhere, Voltaire uses as mouthpiece a Phoenix to account to the Princess of Babylon for the silence of the animals: "It is because men fell into the practice of eating us in place of holding converse with and being instructed by us. The barbarians!" and Voltaire here cites Genesis in a footnote. "It is a horrible crime in the country of the Ganges to kill and eat one's fellows", the Phoenix continues, and the Princess is then conducted to a dining-hall with walls of orange-wood, where shepherds and shepherdesses in long white dresses with golden girdles serve her a hundred dishes "with a hundred delicious meats, among which was seen no disguised corpse".

In the same tale the Princess's lover is questioned by an English lord, "Whether they ate 'good roast beef' in the country of the people of the Ganges. The vegetarian traveller replied to him with his accustomed politeness that they did not eat their brethren in that part of the world. He explained to him the system and diet which was that of Pythagoras, of Porphyry, of Iamblichus; whereupon *milord* went off into a sound slumber." "Pythagoreanism", Voltaire writes again, "is the only religion in the world which has been able to educe a religious feeling from the horror of murder and slaughter." Dealing with Pythagorean and Neoplatonist vegetarianism, he praises the French translation of Porphyry's treatise *Of Abstinence from the Flesh of Living Animals*, and notes that it made few converts.

Rousseau was no versifier but since, as Hume asserted, he had only *felt* rather than thought during the whole course of his life, he may be regarded as a poet rather than as a political economist, and he is in fact often credited with originating the Romantic movement. Since Plato introduced myths into the *Republic* there seems no reason apart from rationalist hostility why Rousseau should not do the same if he found it necessary and provided he understood what he was doing. There is, in fact, a close resemblance between Plato's aetiological myths, discussed in our first chapter, and Rousseau's central and much-derided myth of the State of Nature. Rousseau does understand the extra-temporal nature of his vision too and his statement about it is perfectly clear: "For it is by no means a light undertaking", he wrote in the Preface to his Discourse on *The Origin of Inequality*, "to distinguish properly between what is original and what is artificial in the actual nature of man, or to form a true idea of a state which no longer exists, perhaps never did exist, and probably never will exist; and of which it is, nevertheless, necessary to have true ideas, in order to form a proper judgment of our present state." It is hardly possible to imagine any statement in prose that could more happily epitomise the nature of the Golden Age as the major poets from Hesiod onwards interpreted it, and the extraordinary thing is that so many people have been led to believe that Rousseau's whole conception of the state of Nature was no more than an eccentric notion of his own devising.

Rousseau himself was conscious of the poetic tradition. In the same *Discourse* he writes: "Metallurgy and agriculture were the two arts which produced this great revolution. The poets tell us that it was gold and silver, but for the philosophers it was iron and corn, which first civilized men, and ruined humanity." The poets, however, had equally insisted that the Golden Age was the era before land was ploughed for crops and that war and ruin came most catastrophically in the Iron Age, so that the distinction is not as sharp as Rousseau supposed. His vagueness about the poetic tradition is the measure of the originality of his own conception; but the fact that his was an essentially new vision does not alter the fact that it was a new vision of an old truth, and that Rousseau knew it.

Rousseau was not at all vague about the dietary factor in the tradition. "Savage man", he wrote, "when he had dined, is at peace with all nature, and the friend of all his fellow-creatures." "I see him satisfying his hunger at the first oak, and slaking his thirst at the first brook; finding his bed at the foot of the tree which afforded him a repast; and, with that, all his wants supplied." Rousseau's practical conclusion from this has been mentioned in an earlier chapter, his belief—expressed in *Emile*—that "the indifference of children towards meat is one proof that the taste for meat is unnatural; their preference is for vegetable foods", and he goes on to discuss the Cyclops and the Lotus-eaters in Homer and to quote at length from Plutarch's eloquent essay against flesh-eating. The heroine of his *Nouvelle Héloïse* "likes neither flesh-meat nor ragouts" and but for a partiality to fish would be "a true Pythagorean".

To a large extent, Rousseau practised what he preached. His economy was "less the effect of prudence than that love of simplicity, which, even to this day, the use of the most expensive tables has not been able to vitiate", he wrote in the *Confessions*, "Nothing in my idea, either at that time or since, could exceed a rustic repast; give me milk, vegetables, eggs, and brown bread, with tolerable wine, and I shall always think myself sumptuously regaled; a good appetite will furnish out the rest, if the *maître d'hôtel*, with a number of unnecessary footmen do not satiate me with their important attentions. Six or seven sous would then procure me a more agreeable meal than as many francs would have done since; I was abstemious, therefore, for want of a temptation to be otherwise; though I do not know but I am wrong to call this abstinence, for with my pears, new cheese, bread, and some glasses of Montserrat wine, which you might have cut with a knife, I was the greatest of epicures." "You English", he remarks, "who eat quantities of meat, have an element of barbarity in your inflexible natures." That was his *tu quoque*. For Rousseau's first *Discourse* bore the motto from Ovid, "Here I am a barbarian, because men understand me not". A barbarian who understood the classics in their bearing on human origins, however, and who accepted Mandeville's indictment of civilized societies, though he was inevitably repelled by its author's "cold subtlety of style". For Rousseau was the embodiment of *The Enthusiast, or the Lover of Nature*.

Rousseau was not the only French writer of the revolutionary age who was consciously in the Golden Age tradition. St. Pierre's declared object in his idyllic romance, *Paul et Virginie*, was "to reunite to the beauty of Nature, as seen in the tropics, the moral beauty of a small society of human beings" and this explicitly Pythagorean fable was translated into half a dozen European languages, including English. In the thirteenth century France probably sent Britain the myth of Cockaigne. Now, five hundred years later, she was sending the myth of the Golden Feast, in a pseudo-anthropological form in Rousseau, resembling the account by Lucretius which Joseph Warton had used, and in the form of a didactic romance, first of many blue lagoons, by St. Pierre.

Two years after Rousseau's death a poet was born in France whose early education, he tells us in his *Confidences*, "derived in a large measure from Pythagoras and from the *Emile*". Alphonse de Lamartine's mother was responsible for bringing him up to twelve years of age on bread, milk-products, vegetables and fruit and instilling the example of "the numberless refined and pious people of India, who abstain from everything that has had life". Later on Lamartine reluctantly conformed to the general custom of society but, perhaps as a result of the travels that were the theme of his *Voyage en Orient* in 1835, he wrote three years later an epic poem, *La Chute d'un Ange*, in which he voiced a denunciation of human tyranny and explicit commandments. I am indebted to Marjory Fausset for a translation of the following lines which preserves not only the hexameter form but the spirit of the original:

To sate their hunger, these
Find not enough the fruits that God gives to their store,
And Nature shudders as they impiously ask more
For they are seeking other sustenance in Blood
And in their city now it runs in foul flood.

·   ·   ·   ·   ·

Never shalt thou lift thy hand thy kin to kill,
Never upon earth aught of blood shalt thou spill
Whether of human or of herd, of bird or beast—
Within thy heart a mute cry utters against the feast,
For blood is life, that thou never canst give again.
Feed thou shalt only upon the golden grain
Over thy hills and valleys like the waves of the sea
With reeds of rice rising where the waters be,
Banquet renewed each summer season for the guest,
Roots, ripened fruits on the bough, and flowers expressed
In nectar, overflowing excess of the bee's hoard,
With all the gifts of the earth where sap is stored,
Offering itself to slake thy hunger. Animal flesh
Cries Pity, and Death would build death in thy heart afresh.

ORPHEUS AND THE ROMANTICS

BUT purple night and crimson morning & golden day descending
Thro' the clear changing atmosphere, display'd green fields among
The varying clouds, like paradises stretch'd in the expanse,
With towns & villages and temples, tents, sheep-folds and pastures,
Where dwell the children of the elemental worlds in harmony.
Not long in harmony they dwell; their life is drawn away,
And wintry woes succeed, successive driven into the Void
Where Enion craves, successive drawn into the golden feast.

      .   .   .   .   .

Why is the Sheep given to the knife? The Lamb plays in the Sun.
He starts; he hears the foot of Man; he says: "take thou my wool
But spare my life": but he knows not that winter cometh fast.

      .   .   .   .   .

This was the Lamentation of Enion round the golden Feast.
Eternity groan'd & was troubled at the image of Eternal Death
Without the body of Man, an Exudation from his sick'ning limbs.

The lines are from Night II of *The Four Zoas* by William Blake.
The editors Sloss and Wallis say that Enion "represents a mode of
spiritual enlightenment, so that in mortality she is either a recollection or a hope". There is a Fall in which the children are driven into
the Void and for some there is a realisation of identity with the
supreme spiritual Reality, the experience of Eden, as Blake calls it,
that draws the spirit back to the golden feast celebrated at the end
of the Dream. Blake believed that the experience of Eden was
"rare in mortal life though he himself had known it". "Every two
hundred years has a door to Eden", he writes in *Jerusalem*, and we
remember Mr. Butts standing in the door of the summer-house at
Lambeth, aghast at the sight of the poet and his wife, both naked.
" 'Come in!' cried Blake; 'it's only Adam and Eve, you know!'
Husband and wife had been reciting passages from *Paradise Lost,*

in character, and the garden of Hercules Buildings had to represent the Garden of Eden." "All these things are written in Eden", Blake says in the *Descriptive Catalogue*. "The artist is an inhabitant of that happy country; and if every thing goes on as it has begun, the world of vegetation and generation may expect to be opened again to Heaven, through Eden, as it was in the beginning."

In the Preface to *Milton*, Blake avers, "We do not want either Greek or Roman Models if we are but just & true to our own Imaginations, those Worlds of Eternity in which we shall live for ever in Jesus our Lord" and laments that "Shakespeare & Milton were both curb'd by the general malady & infection from the silly Greek & Latin slaves of the Sword". But the golden feast at the end of *The Four Zoas* is not only Eden but also "their ancient golden age renew'd". Blake is communicating his own vision and not imitating the classics. It is all the more important that what he sees *is* the Golden Age of Hesiod and Ovid as well as the Eden of Milton. Blake's poem is the British incarnation of a universal revelation.

For Blake, "Every thing that lives is Holy", and as *The Four Zoas* developed its final shape he "became less interested in the 'Fall' than in the restoration of ideal unity. . . . Freedom comes only by the saving vision of 'Universal Brotherhood and Love', the Divine Vision of a Christ differing in almost all respects from the Christ of religious orthodoxy . . . the atonement achieved by the Christ of Blake is not of man with God, but of all forms of life in the Universe into the great Unity, sometimes figured as Man, sometimes as the harmony of the Eternals of whom Man is one."

"Rise up, O Sun! most glorious minister & light of day!
Flow on, ye gentle airs, & bear the voice of my rejoicing!
Wave freshly, clear waters, flowing around the tender grass;
And thou, sweet smelling ground, put forth thy life in fruit & flowers!"
Follow me, O my flocks, & hear me sing my rapturous song!
I will cause my voice to be heard on the clouds that glitter in the sun.
I will call, & who shall answer me? I will sing; who shall reply?
For from my pleasant hills, behold the living living springs
Running among my green pastures, delighting among my trees!
I am not here alone: my flocks, you are my brethren;
And you birds, that sing & adorn the sky, you are my sisters.
I sing, & you reply to my song; I rejoice, & you are glad.

Follow me, O my flocks! we will now descend into the valley.
O, how delicious are the grapes flourishing in the sun!
How clear the spring of the rock, running among the golden sand!
How cool the breezes of the valley! & the arms of the branching trees
Cover us from the sun; come & let us sit in the Shade.
My Luvah[1] here hath plac'd me in a sweet & pleasant land,
And given me fruits & pleasant waters & warm hills & cool valleys.
Here will I build myself a house, & here I'll call on his name;
Here I'll return when I am weary, & take my pleasant rest."

So spoke the sinless soul. . . .

"I see the hand that leadeth me doth also lead my flocks."
She went up to her flocks & turnéd oft to see her shining house.
She stop'd to drink of the clear spring & eat the grapes & apples;
She bore the fruits in her lap; she gather'd flowers for her bosom.
She calléd to her flocks, saying: "Follow me, O my flocks!"

The song arose to the Golden feast: the Eternal Man rejoic'd.
Then the Eternal Man said: "Luvah, the Vintage is ripe; arise!
The sons of Urizen shall gather the vintage with sharp hooks.
And all thy sons, O Luvah, bear away the families of Earth.
I hear the flail of Urizen; his barns are full, no room
Remains; & in the Vineyards stand the abounding sheaves beneath
The falling Grapes that odorous burst upon the winds. Arise!
My flocks & herds trample the Corn, my cattle browze upon
The ripe Clusters. The shepherds shout for Luvah, prince of Love.
Let the Bulls of Luvah tread the Corn, & draw the loaded waggon
Into the Barn, while children glean the Ears around the door.
Then shall they lift their innocent hands & stroke his furious nose,
And he shall lick the little girl's white neck & on her head
Scatter the perfume of his breath; while from his mountains high
The lion of terror shall come down, & bending his bright mane
And couching at their side shall eat from the curl'd boy's white lap
His golden food, and in the Evening sleep before the door."

"How is it we have walk'd thro' fires, & yet are not consum'd?
How is it that all things are chang'd, even as in ancient time?
The Sun arises from his dewy bed, & the fresh airs
Play in his smiling beams, giving the seeds of life to grow;
And the fresh Earth beams forth ten thousand thousand springs of life.

[1] "In the ideal state Luvah is 'Prince of Love', the 'mildest gentlest Zoa'."—Sloss and Wallis, II, p. 1?

Blake "looks forward to a perfect age of political and moral anarchy. He is not concerned, any more than Isaiah or Shelley, to give to his picture of an ideal state the precision and particularity of a Utopia. He is a prophet, not a speculative philosopher." "Though reacting to similar impulses, and travelling along the same or parallel roads, though there is often remarkable similarity in their visions and modes of expression, yet in the end Blake is more masculine and not less humane than Shelley. Both rejected the current conventions of their day, believing that therein lay the source of all the ills they saw about them. Both assailed Christianity from the standpoint of a purer doctrine deriving directly from Christ. Both affirmed the righteousness of individual impulses, and proclaimed the gospel of brotherhood and perfect charity."

In March 1812 the Shelleys, reported Miss Nugent, had become Pythagoreans and the poet spoke as one believing in metempsychosis. In 1813 was published *Queen Mab*, in which Shelley contrasts the corruptions and miseries of warring civilization with the glories of Nature. Not humanity but the perversions and enslavements of power have alienated Man from his terrestrial paradise, which he may reclaim at will.

> Look on yonder earth
> The golden harvests spring; the unfailing sun
> Sheds light and life; the fruits, the flowers, the trees,
> Arise in due succession; all things speak
> Peace, harmony, and love. The universe,
> In nature's silent eloquence, declares
> That all fulfil the works of love and joy,—
> All but the outcast Man. He fabricates
> The sword which stabs his peace.

>   Hath Nature's soul,
> That formed this world so beautiful, that spread
> Earth's lap with plenty, and life's smallest chord
> Strung to unchanging unison, that gave
> The happy birds their dwelling in the grove,
> That yielded to the wanderers of the deep
> The lovely silence of the unfathomed main,
> And filled the meanest worm that crawls in dust
> With spirit, thought, and love; on Man alone,

Partial in causeless malice, wantonly
Heaped ruin, vice, and slavery; his soul
Blasted with withering curses; placed afar
The meteor happiness, that shuns his grasp,
But serving on the frightful gulf to glare,
Rent wide beneath his footsteps?

                         Nature!—no!
Kings, priests, and statesmen, blast the human flower
Even in its tender bud; their influence darts
Like subtle poison through the bloodless veins
Of desolate society.

.   .   .   .   .

Here now the human being stands adorning
This loveliest earth, with taintless body and mind;
Blest from his birth with all bland impulses,
Which gently in his noble bosom wake
All kindly passions and all pure desires.
Him, still from hope to hope the bliss pursuing,
Which from the exhaustless lore of human weal
Draws on the virtuous mind, the thoughts that rise
In time-destroying infiniteness, gift
With self-enshrined eternity, that mocks
The unprevailing hoariness of age,
And man, once fleeting o'er the transient scene
Swift as an unremembered vision, stands
Immortal upon earth. No longer now
He slays the lamb that looks him in the face,
And horribly devours his mangled flesh,
Which, still avenging nature's broken law,
Kindled all putrid humours in his frame,
All evil passions, and all vain belief,
Hatred, despair, and loathing in his mind,
The germs of misery, death, disease, and crime.
No longer now the wingéd habitants,
That in the woods their sweet lives sing away,
Flee from the form of man; but gather round,
And prune their sunny feathers on the hands
Which little children stretch in friendly sport
Towards these dreadless partners of their play.
All things are void of terror; man has lost

His terrible prerogative, and stands ·
An equal amidst equals. Happiness
And science dawn though late upon the earth;
Peace cheers the mind, health renovates the frame;
Disease and pleasure cease to mingle here,
Reason and passion cease to combat there;
Whilst each unfettered o'er the earth extend
Their all-subduing energies, and wield
The sceptre of a vast dominion there;
Whilst every shape and mode of matter lends
Its force to the omnipotence of mind,
Which from its dark mine drags the gem of truth
To decorate its paradise of peace.

A very long prose note to *Queen Mab* is the best-known account of Shelley's dietary principles, which were discredited by possibly apocryphal revelations about mutton chops in Thomas Love Peacock's memoir of the poet and amusingly satirised in the character of Mr. Escot the deteriorationist in the same writer's *Headlong Hall*. Other biographers have similarly belittled the importance to Shelley of his conviction that flesh-eating, war and orthodox Christianity were an unholy trinity, a belief he develops as a crucial argument in the little-read *Refutation of Deism* and in a virtually unknown essay *On the Vegetable System of Diet*. The theme, and the underlying affirmation of the unity of life, recurs in many of his finest poems, besides *Queen Mab*. *Alastor* and *Epipsychidion* are quoted later. Here it is enough to mention *The Revolt of Islam*, *Prometheus Unbound*, *Hellas* and *The Witch of Atlas*. The passage from *The Revolt of Islam* is almost a paraphrase of that just quoted from *Queen Mab*:

My brethren, we are free! The fruits are glowing
Beneath the stars, and the night winds are flowing
O'er the ripe corn, the birds and beasts are dreaming—
Never again may blood of bird or beast
Stain with its venomous stream a human feast,
To the pure skies in accusation steaming,
Avenging poisons shall have ceased
  To feed disease and fear and madness,
  The dwellers of the earth and air

> Shall throng around our steps in gladness,
>   Seeking their food or refuge there.
> Our toil from thought all glorious forms shall cull,
> To make this Earth, our home, more beautiful,
> And Science, and her sister Poesy,
> Shall clothe in light the fields and cities of the free!

According to Pliny, Prometheus was the first to slaughter an ox, probably because the use of fire was associated with the cooking of animal flesh to make it palatable. But in Shelley's poem *Prometheus Unbound* the cosmic conflict is between the Furies who "track all things that weep, and bleed, and live" as hounds pursue a wounded fawn, and the great protagonist of humanity who cries, "I wish no living thing to suffer pain", who begs of Earth the common heritage, "Some comfort; flowers, and fruits, and happy sounds, And love, though fleeting", a symbol of peace; who teaches "the hidden power of herbs and springs" whereby disease is banished, and whose final prayer is addressed not to man only but to "Spirits, whose homes are flesh: ye beasts and birds". In this rapturous last act of *Prometheus*, the Earth rejoices in the rule of Love when "Language is a perpetual orphic song". "Orphic" is not accidental here. *Hellas* ends in the same way. Within the space of some fifty lines most of the significant images are brought into the single focus, beginning with Hesperus, Eden and paradise islands—there is even a phrase that might recall Boethius's vision in his death cell—and rising to a final triumphant chorus:

> The world's great age begins anew,
>   The golden years return,
> The earth doth like a snake renew
>   Her winter weeds outworn . . .
>
> A loftier Argo cleaves the main,
>   Fraught with a later prize;
> Another Orpheus sings again,
>   And loves, and weeps, and dies. . . .
>
> Saturn and Love their long repose
>   Shall burst more bright and good. . . .

And *The Witch of Atlas* dwelt in a cave (later used, it seems, by those holy hermits in Dryden's *Don Sebastian*) stored with scrolls:

The works of some Saturnian Archimage,
Which taught the expiations at whose price
    Men from the Gods might win that happy age
Too lightly lost, redeeming native vice;
    And which might quench the earth-consuming rage
Of gold and blood—till men should live and move
Harmonious as the sacred stars above.

This fairest lady, bathed in golden sunlight, has the Orphic magic:

And her low voice was heard like love, and drew
All living things towards this wonder new.

And first the spotted cameleopard came,
    And then the wise and fearless elephant;
Then the sly serpent, in the golden flame
    Of his own volumes intervolved;—all gaunt
And sanguine beasts her gentle looks made tame.
    They drank before her at her sacred fount;
And every beast of beating heart grew bold,
Such gentleness and power even to behold.

The brinded lioness led forth her young,
    That she might teach them how they should forego
Their inborn thirst of death; the pard unstrung
    His sinews at her feet, and sought to know
With looks whose motions spoke without a tongue
    How he might be as gentle as the doe.
The magic circle of her voice and eyes
All savage natures did imparadise.

She is chaste herself and brings lovers together in true marriage, and causes soldiers to dream of beating their swords into ploughshares.

In a lost letter written to the dying Keats on his arrival at Naples in November 1820, Shelley offered "advice as to the adaptation of diet to the climate". Perhaps he had been partly responsible for Keats's vegetable diet at an earlier date? In July of the same year, Mrs. Gisborne noted that a Dr. "Lamb" had abandoned hope of Keats's survival; could this be the same Dr. William Lambe who from 1806, the year after he established a London practice, until his death in 1847, lived wholly on vegetable food? Shelley met Lambe in April 1812 and was strongly influenced by him.

From Keats's letters and early verse one would not surmise much initial inclination for such a régime. Writing to his sister in July 1818 during his tour in Scotland, he avowed, "I can eat a Bull's head as easily as I used to do Bull's eyes—I take a whole string of Pork Sausages down as easily as a Pen'orth of Lady's fingers" and bewailed the oatcakes, milk and eggs which was all he could hope to get morning, noon and night in the Highlands. What Wilson Knight calls Keats's "almost excessive, and indeed at the first not always so subtle, use of taste. His references to eating and drinking contribute, as in Shakespeare's *Antony and Cleopatra*, to the strangely physical impact of his poetry as a whole"—is illustrated by some of the lines on the Mermaid Tavern, which appeared in a letter to Reynolds some months earlier:

> Souls of poets dead and gone,
> What Elysium have ye known,
> Happy field, or mossy cavern,
> Fairer than the Mermaid Tavern?
>   Have ye tippled drink more fine
> Than mine Host's Canary wine?
> Or are fruits of Paradise
> Sweeter than those dainty pies
> Of Venison. O generous food. . . .

That was as near as Keats got to Cockaigne. A year later he wrote to his sister in a different strain: "I should like now to promenade round your Gardens—apple-tasting—pear-tasting—plum-judging—apricot-nibbling—peach-scrunching—Nectarine-sucking and Melon-carving. I have also a great feeling for antiquated cherries full of sugar cracks—and a white currant tree for company." A week or two later this too found expression in his poetry, in the revised *Eve of St. Agnes* and the *Ode to Autumn*:

> And still she slept an azure-lidded sleep,
> In blanchéd linen, smooth, and lavender'd,
> While he[1] from forth the closet brought a heap
> Of candied apple, quince, and plum, and gourd;
> With jellies soother than the creamy curd,
>   And lucent syrops, tinct with cinnamon;
> Manna and dates, in argosy transferr'd

[1] Porphyro—a name with a Neoplatonist ring.

From Fez; and spicéd dainties, every one,
From silken Samarcand to cedar'd Lebanon.

These delicates he heap'd with glowing hand
On golden dishes and in baskets bright
Of wreathéd silver: sumptuous they stand
In the retiréd quiet of the night,
Filling the chilly room with perfume light.

And this, of course, is Keats's imagery for a poem of true, chaste love. Here is the first stanza of the *Ode to Autumn*, written at the same time in September 1819:

Season of mists and mellow fruitfulness!
Close bosom-friend of the maturing sun;
Conspiring with him how to load and bless
With fruit the vines that round the thatch-eaves run;
To bend with apples the moss'd cottage-trees,
And fill all fruit with ripeness to the core;
To swell the gourd, and plump the hazel shells
With a sweet kernel; to set budding more,
And still more, later flowers for the bees,
Until they think warm days will never cease,
For Summer has o'er-brimm'd their clammy cells.

Five days before Keats began to revise *The Eve of St. Agnes*, he wrote to John Taylor a letter in which he makes a distinction between Cain and Abel, to Cain's advantage, anticipating by a year or two the similar emphasis in Byron's *Cain*, presently to be quoted. "Our health, temperament and dispositions", wrote Keats, "are taken more (notwithstanding the contradiction of the history of Cain and Abel) from the air we breathe than is generally imagined. See the difference between a Peasant and a Butcher. . . . The one takes his mingled with the fume of slaughter the other with the damp exhalement of the glebe."

"Talking of Pleasure", he writes to Dilke two or three weeks later, "this moment I was writing with one hand, and with the other holding to my Mouth a Nectarine—good god how fine. It went down soft, pulpy, slushy, oozy—all its delicious embonpoint melted down my throat like a large beatified Strawberry." And two or three weeks after that he wrote to his sister: "I have left off animal food that my brains may never henceforth be in a greater mist than is theirs by nature." This reveals that Keats's first motive for experimenting with his diet was not simply to arrest the progress of bodily disease, but rather—as Thoreau puts it—"that every man who has been in earnest to preserve his higher or poetic faculties in the best condition has been particularly inclined to abstain from animal food, and from much food of any kind". The fatal illness did not in fact begin until the following February, though he had been troubled earlier with an ominous sore throat, to which soft fruit was evidently and deliciously soothing.

But from February 1820 onwards the restricted diet became one of the irritations of serious illness. He is "confined almost entirely to vegetable food", "under an interdict with respect to animal food, living upon pseudo victuals", "feeding upon sham victuals" hoping that " 'tis nothing but debility and will entirely cease on my recovery of my strength, which is the object of my present diet". By November he was at Naples and after a serious relapse early in December he died in February 1821.

For the last year of his short life, Keats's diet was only part of his medical history. But for six months before that it had been something more, part of his joy in living and part of his poetry, as Shelley's vegetarianism was too: body and imagination had sat down to the same table. To the same period as the revision of *The Eve of St. Agnes* and as the lovely *Ode to Autumn* belongs the Vision of the end of the Saturnian time, dreamed by a poet who swears "by the golden age"—*The Fall of Hyperion*.

> on a mound
> Of moss, was spread a feast of summer fruits,
> Which, nearer seen, seem'd refuse of a meal
> By angel tasted, or our Mother Eve;[1]
> For empty shells were scatter'd on the grass,
> And grapestalks but half bare, and remnants more
> Sweet-smelling, whose pure kinds I could not know.
> Still was more plenty than the fabled horn
> Thrice emptied could pour forth at banqueting,
> For Proserpine return'd to her own fields,
> Where the white heifers low. And appetite,

[1] The line is overwhelmingly reminiscent of the meal shared by Raphael in Eden, in Milton's *Paradise Lost*.

More yearning than on earth I ever felt,
Growing within, I ate deliciously,—
And, after not long, thirsted; for thereby
Stood a cool vessel of transparent juice
Sipp'd by the wander'd bee, the which I took,
And pledging all the mortals of the world,
And all the dead whose names are in our lips,
Drank. That full draught is parent of my theme.

And at the last entrance of the hero who has become Keats himself, in the play written at the same time, *Otho the Great*, in the final scene where Keats had shaken himself free from the irksome chains of Brown's melodramatic scenario, Keats wrote: "I should have Orphean lips, and Plato's fancy. . . ." More than any other European poet until Rilke wrote the *Orpheus Sonnets*, Keats in his celebration of the feast of fruits had indeed Orphean lips.

The German poet Friederich von Schiller, like Lucretius and his own French contemporary, Rousseau, believed in an original state of Nature, if not in the mythical Saturnian time. Through the influence of Goethe, Schiller was appointed to the University of Jena in the fateful year 1789, and his lecture there entitled *Thoughts Concerning the First Human Society* agrees closely with Rousseau's *Discourse on the Origin of Inequality*, written thirty-five years earlier for the Academy of Dijon, except that it seeks to conform also to Old Testament tradition. In his biography of Schiller, Carlyle notes that this lecture and its companion pieces are "of the very highest order; full of strength and beauty; delicious to the lovers of that plastic philosophy, which employs itself in giving form and life to the 'dry bones' of those antique events". Man lived at first in the Eden state, says Schiller, and he has to learn to reconstruct by reason the state of innocence he has lost. From knowledge of how plants reproduce he advanced to agriculture, beginning not with wheat but perhaps with rice, since this grows wild in India. In his dealings with the animals "he began with natural and innocent wants. For centuries he may have contented himself with the milk of animals before he undertook to slaughter them." The toiling labourer in the field envied the lot of the shepherd, and when the shepherds presently drove their flocks on to the agriculturists' fields for want of other fodder, the first blows were struck, and now for the first time man "had to wage war against his neighbour". This obviously conforms to the reading of the story of Cain and Abel, which, as we shall see, was to be dramatically treated in England by Lord Byron, and it exactly agrees with Socrates' account of the origin of war in Plato's *Republic*.

But in his poem on *The Eleusinian Festival*, a celebration which was, as we noted, largely influenced by Orphic rites and ideas, Schiller uses a different chronology to convey an advance from primitive hunting and war to the full glory of civilization through the discovery of agriculture. A more strictly Lucretian, or a nineteenth-century evolutionary view is employed, but the central repudiation of blood sacrifice is still an expression of the Byronic conflict of Cain and Abel. The poem opens with a choric verse in praise of Ceres and then passes to a recitative:

> Wind in a garland the ears of gold,
>   Azure cyanes[1] inwoven be:
> Oh how gladly shall eye behold
>   The queen who comes in her majesty.
> Man with man in communion mixing,
>   Taming the wild ones where she went;
> Into the peace of the homestead fixing
>   Lawless bosom and shifting tent.
>
> Darkly hid in cave and cleft,
>   Shy the Troglodyte abode;
> Earth, a waste, was found and left
>   Where the wandering Nomad strove:
> Deadly with the spear and shaft,
>   Prowled the hunter through the land;
> Woe the stranger, waves may waft
>   On an ever-fatal strand.
>
> Thus was all to Ceres, when
>   Searching for her ravished child,
> (No green culture smiling then),
>   O'er the drear coasts bleak and wild,
> Never shelter did she gain,
>   Never friendly threshold trod;
> All unbuilded then the fane,
>   All unheeded then the God!

[1] Cornflowers.

Not with golden corn-ears strewed
  Were the ghastly altar-stones;
Bleaching there, and gore-imbrued,
  Lay the unhallowed human bones!
Wide and far, where'er she roved,
  Still reigned misery over all;
And her mighty soul was moved
  At man's universal fall.

"What! can *this* be man—to whom
  Our own godlike form was given—
Likeness of the shapes that bloom
  In the garden-mount of heaven?
Was not earth on man bestowed?
  Earth itself his kingly home!
Roams he through his bright abode,
  Homeless wheresoe'er he roam?

"Will no god vouchsafe to aid?
  None of the celestial choir—
Lift the demi-god we made
  From the slough and from the mire?
No, the grief they ne'er have known,
  Calmly the celestials scan;
I—the Mother—I, alone
  Have a heart that feels for man!

"Let—that man to man may soar—
  Man and earth with one another
Make a compact evermore,
  Man the son, and earth the mother.
Let their laws the seasons show,
  Time itself man's teacher be,
And the sweet moon moving slow
  To the starry melody!"

Gently brightening from the cloud,
  Round her image, veil-like thrown
On the startled savage crowd,
  Lo! the goddess-glory shone!
Soft the goddess-glory stole
  On their war-feast o'er the dead;
Fierce hands offered her the bowl
  With the blood of foemen red.

Loathing turned the gentle queen,
  Loathing, shuddering, turned—and said
"Ne'er a godhead's lips have been
  With the food of tigers fed.
Offering pure that ne'er pollutes,
  Be to purer beings given,
Summer flowers and autumn fruits
  Please the family of heaven."

And the wrathful spear she takes
  From the hunter's savage hand,
With the shaft of murder,—breaks
  Into furrows the light sand
From her spikéd wreath she singles
  Out a golden seed of corn,
With the earth the germ she mingles,
  And the mighty birth is born!

Robing now the rugged ground—
  Glints the budding lively green,
Now—a golden forest—round
  Waves the mellow harvest sheen!
And the goddess blessed the earth,
  Bade the earliest sheaf be bound,
Chose the landmark for a hearth,
  And serenely smiling round

Spoke in prayer—"O Father King,
  On thine ether-hill divine,
Take, O Zeus, this offering,
  Let it soften thee to thine!
From thy people's eyes away,
  Roll the vapour coiled below;
Let the hearts untaught to pray
  Learn the Father-God to know!"

The art of husbandry once commenced, the chorus proceeds in
the latter half of the poem to deduce from it the improvements of
all social life, though these amount to the antithesis of the Golden
Age as it was seen, for instance, in Chaucer's poem. There is property,
of course, one learns to respect his neighbour's landmarks; the earth

is ploughed; walls and ramparts soar; the hills are chained by empire; the huge pines of the doomed forest fall to make first the rude trunk and then the polished mast of seafaring vessels. But, nevertheless, the central value remains:

> Cast to earth is the gory spear
>
> .   .   .   .   .
>
> In the waste the beast is free,
> And the God upon his throne!

But it was in the masterpiece of Schiller's friend Goethe, the great "Physician of the Iron Age" as Matthew Arnold called him, that the Romantic reunion with an idealised Nature found its fullest Germanic expression. The dedication of *Faust* speaks of the "Orphean lyre" the poet is stringing for his song, and the phrase is a key-note for all that is to come. The great poem opens with its hero's rebellion against the cloistered life of scholarship:

> Instead of nature's living sphere,
> Created for mankind of old,
> Brute skeletons surround thee here,
> And dead men's bones in smoke and mould.

The principal paradisal visions are in the later and more allegorical Part II, but it will help to show how organically the whole poem moves towards them if we take a rapid glance at the food imagery of Part I. In the Prologue in Heaven, the Lord asks Mephistopheles if he knows Faust, and the devil replies:

> He serves thee truly in a wondrous fashion.
> Poor fool! His food and drink are not of earth.

And Faust, walking beyond the merrymaking crowd on Easter Day speaks of how, in seeking to serve God, he has disciplined himself with prayer and fast, like Christ in the wilderness. These are, therefore, the images of salvation, and opposite food images are temptations of a corrupting sensuality. Mephistopheles offers that,

> Rich odours shall regale your smell,
> On choicest sweets your palate dwell

and later Faust reproaches him, still in his own imagery, "Yet food thou hast which satisfieth never". Mephistopheles shows him "fruit that, ere 'tis pluck'd, doth rot". When Faust leaves his study to Mephistopheles, the devil exults:

> Earth's joys o'erleaping, leaveth them behind.
> Him will I drag through life's wild waste,
> Through scenes of vapid dullness, where at last
> Bewilder'd, he shall falter, and stick fast;
> And still to mock his greedy haste,
> Viands and drink shall float his craving lips beyond—
> Vainly he'll seek refreshment, anguish-tost,
> And were he not the devil's by his bond,
> Yet must his soul infallibly be lost!

Auerbach's beer-cellar is a glimpse of this fools' paradise:[1]

> ALL (*sing*):
>
> Happy as cannibals are we,
> Or as five hundred swine.

In the Walpurgis Night orgy, Faust's vision of the apple-tree is an Eden image, with reminiscence of innocent love, promptly fouled by Mephistopheles' obscenity about the rifted tree, and in the ensuing Picasso-esque interlude, the Fiddler's allusion to Orpheus neatly mocks that reformer with memories of Bacchanalian orgies.

Part II opens with Faust reclining upon flowery turf, aroused to find that "Around me everywhere is paradise". The scene changes to the contrasted corrupt imperial Court, where greed for gold, corrupt justices and the usual symptoms of decadence are displayed. Although ruin threatens, the Steward boasts that—

---

[1] The myth of Cockaigne or Schlauraffenland was well-known in nineteenth-century Germany, and recurs in a nightmare form in two very short *Fairy Tales* by the Brothers Grimm that are a sort of prose equivalent to the terrible visions of Bosch and the elder Brueghel and perhaps for that reason are omitted from most popular editions.

Both are titled legends. *The Legend of Sly Monkey Land* tells of ". . . a linden tree on which grew nothing but big flat cakes. Then I saw two dried-up old crones carrying a hundred cartloads of dripping on their backs . . . and saw a stream of honey flowing like water from a deep valley. . . . Then a cock crowed 'Cock-a-doodle-do.' That's the end of the story, Cock-a-doodle-do!" And it is an end that reminds us of John Fletcher's song in which "The stewed cock shall crow, cock-aloodle-loo".

The Legend of Ditmarsch follows next. "I will tell you a story. Listen! I saw two roast fowls flying, and they flew with their backs towards the earth and their stomachs towards heaven. . . ."

The Witch's house of cakes, sweets and gingerbread is a juvenile form of the same myth, found in *Hansel and Gretel*. The Witch will eat Hansel for breakfast when he is fattened, as punishment for nibbling at her house.

The cooks lack nothing;—deer, wild-boar,
Stags, hares, fowls, turkeys, ducks and geese,—[1]
Tributes in kind, sure payment, these
Come fairly in, and none complains.

Mephistopheles promises that "A herd of golden calves anon
Themselves shall tear from out the soil" and meanwhile there is a
carnival masquerade. "The first groups", writes Anna Swanwick,
"bring before the eye some features of the Golden Age, when the
human race, free from selfishness and greed, lived together in joyous
liberty; the peace and plenty, the richness of imagination and of love,
which characterised that idyllic period, are aptly symbolised by the
Olive-branch, the Wheatsheaf, the Fancy-nosegay, and the Budding
Roses in the hands of the Florentine Garden-girls. In the succeeding
group of the Mother and Daughter, this picture of primeval simplicity is contrasted with life under a more conventional aspect. As
civilization advances the fruits of the field no longer suffice for
human nourishment. Fishermen and Bird-catchers are introduced,
and the Wood-cutters appear as representatives of manual toil.
It is not difficult to discern the social classes represented by the
Pulcinelli and the Parasites, while the Drunken Man exhibits the
debasing influence of sensual indulgence." Thus the Gardeners' Song
is of an orchard paradise:

Mark the blossoms calmly sprouting,
Charmingly to wreath your brow;
Fruits will not deceive, I trow,
Taste, enjoy them, nothing doubting.

Magnum bonum, cherries, peaches,
Faces offer sub-embrown'd:
Buy, poor judge the eye is found;—
Heed what tongue, what palate teaches.

[1] A remark in Goethe's *Autobiography* (I, i) may help to show the poet's attitude and its origin: "I call
to mind, also, that I always flew past the adjoining meat-stalls, narrow and disgusting as they were, in
perfect horror."
  Pythagoras, Porphyry says, had such an abhorrence of the slaughter-house that he could never bring
himself to endure contact with, or even the sight of, butchers and cooks.
  Walter de la Mare has a poem about a similar revulsion:

I can't abear a Butcher,
I can't abide his meat,
The ugliest shop of all is his,
The ugliest in the street;
Bakers' are warm, cobblers' dark,
Chemists' burn watery lights;
But oh, the sawdust butcher's shop,
That ugliest of sights!

Luscious fruits to taste invite them
Who behold these rich supplies,
We o'er roses poetize;—
As for apples, we must bite them.

Let us now, with your good pleasure,
Join your youthful choir, in pairs;
And beside your flowery wares,
Thus adorn our riper treasure.

Under leaf-adornéd bowers,
'Mid the merry windings haste;
Each will find what suits his taste;
Buds of leafage, fruit or flowers.

In contrast to this Song, which already foreshadows the *Orpheus Sonnets* of Rilke, after the fishers, bird-catchers and wood-cutters come parasites, flattering and lustful:

There is roasting,
There is brewing,
There is toasting,
There is stewing,
Your true taster
Licks the dish;
Sniffs the roast,
Forebodes the fish;
These for great deeds make him able,
Seated at his patron's table.

In the third act of Part II, Faust achieves his union with Helen, the spirit of Hellenism, and the full vision of Arcadia is vouchsafed:

Our gifts to these are great and glorious:
To every one a goodly land,
Fertile and broad. March on victorious!
Here in the midst we take our stand.

Girt round by waves in sun-light dancing,
Half-island, thee—whose hill-chains blend
With Europe's mountains, widely branching—
Will they in rivalry defend.

Blessed be this land, all lands transcending,
To every race, for evermore,
Which sees my queen the throne ascending,
As erst her birth it hailed of yore.

When, 'mid Eurotas' reedy whisper,
Forth from the shell she burst to light,
Her mighty mother, brothers, sister,
Were blinded by the dazzling sight.

This land, her choicest bloom that layeth
Before thee, waiting thy behest—
Though the wide earth, thy sceptre swayeth,
Oh love thy father-land the best!

What though the sun's keen arrow coldly playeth,
Upon the mountain-summits, jagg'd and bare
Yet where the rock the verdure over-layeth,
The wild goat nibbling, crops its scanty fare;

The spring leaps forth, united plunge the fountains,
And meadow, gorge, and valley, all are green,
On broken pastures of a hundred mountains
Spread far and wide, the woolly herds are seen;

With measured tread, cautious, in line divided,
By the steep edge, the hornéd cattle wend;
Yet for them all a shelter is provided,
O'er many a cave the vaulted rock doth bend!

Pan shields them there, and many a nymph appeareth,
In moist and bushy caverns dwelling free;
And yearning after higher spheres, upreareth
Its leafy branches tree close-pressed to tree—

Primeval woods! The giant oak there standing,
Links bough to bough, a stubborn, tortuous, maze;
The gentle maple, with sweet juice expanding,
Shoots clear aloft and with its burden plays—

And motherly for child and lambkin streameth,
'Mid silent shades, warm milk prepared for them;
Fruit close at hand, the plain's ripe nurture, gleameth,
And honey droppeth from the hollow stem.

Pleasure is here a birthright; vieing
In gladness cheek and lip are found,
Each in his station is undying,
Content and blooming health abound.

And thus to all his father's strength unfoldeth
The gentle child, environed by sweet day.
Amazed we stand; each asks, as he beholdeth:
If gods they be, or men? so fair are they.

So when the part of hind Apollo playeth,
Like him the fairest shepherd-youth appears;
For there where Nature in clear circle swayeth,
Harmoniously are linked her several spheres.

Thus happy Fate hath me, hath thee attended;
Behind us henceforth let the past be thrown!
From God supreme, oh feel thyself descended:
Thou to the primal world belong'st alone.

Thee shall no firm-built fortress capture;
Strong in eternal youth, expands
For us a sojourn, fraught with rapture,
Arcadia, near to Sparta's lands.

Allured to this blest region, hither
Hast fled to brightest destiny:
Thrones change to bowers that never wither;
Arcadian be our bliss and free!

And the Act rises to a final Chorus:

We, amid the wavy-trembling of these thousand rustling branches,
Gently lure with dalliance charming from the root the vital currents,
Up into the boughs; with foliage, soon with lavish wealth of blossoms,
We adorn our tresses, floating in the breeze for airy growth.
Falls the fruit, forthwith assemble life-enjoying folk and cattle,
For the grasping, for the tasting, swiftly coming, onward pressing,
And, as 'fore the Gods primeval, so all bend around us here.

Act IV shows the horrors of war that has meantime overtaken the vainglorious Emperor who did not heed the warnings of the carnival, and the final act sets Faust to the epic and symbolic task of land-reclamation, work that has been impressively realised in the Netherlands in this century. Goethe was profoundly moved by the

Hellenistic expression of what Wagner—not Faust's companion but the composer of *Parsifal*—later derived from Schopenhauer, who was influenced in turn by the Neoplatonists and their Buddhist and Brahminical predecessors. Wagner saw that the "fruit-nourished nations" were innately peaceful (there may be individual exceptions, such as Hitler) while "blood and murdered corpses" was "the only worthy food of these world-conquerors". In our own time the Orphic song in German accents has been heard on Rilke's lips.

While Goethe predicted Nature's triumphant reunion with a purified civilization, something towards which we are perhaps reluctantly moving under compulsion of our own destructiveness, and of which such things as Richard St. Barbe Baker's New Earth Charter are the more positive and visionary omens, in Italy the melancholy poet Leopardi was half contemptuously lamenting the imminent liquidation of all such islands of content by the Moloch of civilization. Since Pythagoras established his community in Southern Italy, and Roman poets sang with varying conviction the praises of a Saturnian Golden Age, echoed by Boethius in his death-cell, Dante had identified the Earthly Paradise with the Christian Elysium and Tasso and Petrarch with a more earthy one. But for a long time nothing had been heard in Italy of the ancient theme until Leopardi raised his voice in a more than Lucretian pessimism about the cheerlessness and transience of the state of Nature which, like Dante, he closely associates with the Christian Eden. As Geoffrey Bickersteth shows in the notes to his translation of Leopardi's *Hymn to the Patriarchs*, the poem passes from Adam and the crime of Cain to the uselessness of the Flood in stemming the iniquity of mankind. Abraham and Jacob remind the poet of the Golden Age:

> A time there was (nor doth the Aonian song
> And rumour's voice regale men's pining ears
> On empty fancies), yea, there was a time
> When these unhappy shores were to our kin
> A haunt delectable, and golden ran
> Our fleeting years. Not that with milk the brooks[1]
> Channelled the slopes of their maternal hills
> In rich cascades; not that the shepherd drove
> The tiger intermingled with his flocks
> To their familiar folds, or led the wolf

[1] This negative phrase is reminiscent of Tasso's *Aminta* Chorus, cf. p. 97.

217

> To gambol with them at the springs; but Man,
> Unconscious of his troubles and his fate,
> Hence lived untroubled; o'er the secret laws
> Of Nature and of Heaven a veil was drawn
> In these old days, a soft illusive mist
> That hid the truth of things: and, well content
> To hope, our bark sailed smoothly into port.
>
> Even so, in the vast Californian woods,
> Yet dwells a happy race whose blood is proof
> Against pale care, whose limbs by no disease
> Are withered; and the forest yields them food,
> The caverned cliffs a home, the swampy dale
> Refreshing drink, and the black day of death
> Draws nigh them unforeseen. Alas for all
> The realms wise Nature rules! Unarmed are they
> Against our savage onslaught. Shores and cave
> And tranquil woods—our mad zeal lays them bare
> And will not be denied, but unto wants
> And woes it knew not educates the race
> Which we have ravished, and drives Happiness
> Naked, in flight, beyond the sunset bars.

Byron, so much admired by Goethe, and a figure of full European stature, was charged with blasphemy and atheism when he published his play, *Cain*, and was hailed by William Blake as Elijah, the spirit of prophecy. Like Schiller in his lecture on the first human society and in his poem on the Eleusinian feast, Byron defends the agricultural against the pastoral man. In the dispute between the first brothers, Cain is championing Eden and Abel is wrong to offer the blood of slaughtered animals to Jehovah, who is still more wrong to prefer it to the offering of fruits.

> CAIN (*standing erect during this speech*):
>
> Spirit! whate'er or whosoe'er Thou art,
> Omnipotent, it may be—and, if good,
> Shown in the exemption of Thy deeds from evil;
> Jehovah upon earth! and God in heaven!
> And it may be with other names, because
> Thine attributes seem many, as Thy works:
> If Thou must be propitiated with prayers,

Take them! If Thou must be induced with altars,
And soften'd with a sacrifice, receive them!
Two beings here erect them unto Thee.
If Thou lov'st blood, the shepherd's shrine, which smokes
On my right hand, hath shed it for Thy service
In the first of his flock, whose limbs now reek
In sanguinary incense to Thy skies;
Or if the sweet and blooming fruits of earth,
And milder seasons which the unstain'd turf
I spread them on now offers in the face
Of the broad sun which ripen'd them, may seem
Good to Thee, inasmuch as they have not
Suffer'd in limb or life, and rather form
A sample of thy works, than supplication
To look on ours! If a shrine without victim,
And altar without gore, may win Thy favour,
Look on it!

.   .   .   .   .

(The fire upon the altar of ABEL *kindles into a column of the brightest flame
and ascends to heaven; while a whirlwind throws down the altar of Cain,
and scatters the fruits abroad upon the earth.)*

ABEL (*kneeling*):   Oh, brother, pray! Jehovah's wroth with thee.

CAIN: Why so?

ABEL: Thy fruits are scatter'd on the earth.

CAIN: From earth they came, to earth let them return;
        Their seed will bear fresh fruit there ere the summer;
        Thy burnt flesh-offering prospers better; see
        How heaven licks up the flames, when thick with blood!

ABEL: Think not upon my offering's acceptance,
        But make another of thine own before
        It is too late.

CAIN: I will build no more altars,
        Nor suffer any——

ABEL (*rising*):   Cain! what meanest thou?

CAIN: To cast down yon vile flatterer of the clouds,
        The smoky harbinger of thy dull prayers—
        Thine altar, with its blood of lambs and kids,
        Which fed on milk, to be destroy'd in blood.

ABEL (*opposing him*): Thou shalt not!—add not impious works to impious
    Words! let that altar stand—'tis hallowed now
    By the immortal pleasure of Jehovah,
    In His acceptance of the victims.

CAIN: *His!*
    His pleasure! what was his high pleasure in
    The fumes of scorching flesh and smoking blood,
    To the pain of the bleating mothers, which
    Still yearn for their dead offspring? or the pangs
    Of the sad ignorant victims underneath
    Thy pious knife? Give way! this bloody record
    Shall not stand in the sun, to shame creation.

So that it is not altogether surprising that Byron, who could later write lightheartedly in *Don Juan*, "But man is a carnivorous production. . . . Although his anatomical construction Bears vegetables, in a grumbling way . . ." would not at one time touch meat, fish or wine. "He appeared, indeed, to have conceived a notion that animal food has some peculiar influence on the character; and I remember one day, as I sat opposite to him, employed, I suppose, rather earnestly over a 'beef-steak', after watching me for a few seconds, he said in a grave tone of inquiry,—'Moore, don't you find eating beef-steak makes you ferocious?'" To John Murray he wrote from Ravenna in 1820, "I have fed at times for two months together on *sheer biscuits and water* (without metaphor)", and of Hobhouse, "I maintain that he is more *carnivorously* and *carnally sensual* than I am. . . ." Biscuits and water make an even more fantastically inadequate diet than the crumbled bread and raisins on which Shelley subsisted at times.

A hundred and thirty years later, in 1949, another poet, Christopher Fry, wrote a play about the return of Christianity to Britain at the end of the sixth century, which includes a scene closely resembling the one just quoted from Byron's *Cain*. Cymen is urged to offer up a Briton captured in battle, and whose life he spared on a mysterious divine impulse, as a blood sacrifice to his Jutish gods. He orders his wife, Clodesuida, to bring him one of the white goats. But instead of this substitute sacrifice he throws down the altar, and almost at once the Messenger appears to bid him to the assembly—

To receive the person and words of Augustine
Exponent of the Christian god.

From the primitive wild man of Lucretius, whose privations were
balanced by the contrary perils of civilization, the savage in Spenser's allegory who defeated the wicked by his primal virtue, and
Shakespeare's Timon who fled from the wicked city to seek re-
demption in the wilderness, the tradition rose to Prospero in
control of a Lucretian Caliban, a Christ in the Wilderness who had
conquered Comus and his rout. In the visions of Blake, in Shelley's
Prometheus and—notwithstanding blood-guilt—to some extent in
Byron's Cain and Goethe's Faust, man is reborn into a new harmony
with Nature, the wilderness flowers again. Fry echoes a Byronic
overthrow of barbarism, but a symbol more significant of the age
is Aldous Huxley's Shakespeare-reading savage, hunted to death by
citizens of a monstrous brave new world. Once more paradise is
regained only to be lost.

If Shelley and Byron tended to incarnate at least some of the more
austere dietary characteristics of the Golden Age of which the poets
had sung for over two thousand years, the solitary Edward Fitz-
Gerald was a more comfortable embodiment of the eighteenth-
century hermits. His diet, consisting mainly of bread and fruit for
the last fifty years of his life, soon brought him more lightness of
spirits but did not reduce his weight below fourteen stone. He was,
however, convinced that "the great secret of all is not eating meat.
To that the world must come." Whether with the amiable
intention of hastening this millennium, or on aesthetic grounds
alone, FitzGerald rendered as "a Loaf of Bread beneath the Bough,
a Flask of Wine, a Book of Verse . . ." lines of *The Rubá'iyát of
Omar Khayyám* of which the literal translation is, "If a loaf of
wheaten bread be forthcoming, a gourd of wine, and a thigh-
bone of mutton . . .!" As the *Observer* exclaimed when Miss Sack-
ville West brought up the point again some twenty years ago:
"How strangely inimical to poetry is the conception of cold
mutton." But, according to Hari Prasad Shastri, FitzGerald's
translation is strangely inimical to Omar by making him out not
more ascetic than he really was but less. "Not a single *rubaii* has
been faithfully translated by FitzGerald", Shastri declares; Omar

"never married, and never drank a cup of wine in his life". According to this view, practically everything in the poem is mystical symbolism. Omar, like the Persian kings of old, may have lived on bread and fresh fruit rather than flesh, as did FitzGerald himself. In discussing the Neoplatonists we remarked on the Golden Age of Yima and other Persian developments within the tradition, and recorded how certain Pythagoreans sought refuge in Persia. FitzGerald's biographer, Wright, prints an extremely interesting memorandum of the poet's, a special reading list including two items on cannibalism, several on health, including a book by Tryon which converted Benjamin Franklin to vegetarianism for a time, Mandeville's *Fable of the Bees* and two Pythagorean items, one of which is probably the life by Iamblichus.

There may therefore be precise reference in Tennyson's description of the "table of Pythagoras" which he briefly shared under FitzGerald's influence, as he describes in the verses that introduce *Tiresias and Other Poems*.

Old Fitz, who from your suburb grange
    Where once I tarried for a while,
Glance at the wheeling Orb of change,
    And greet it with a kindly smile;
Whom yet I see as there you sit
    Beneath your sheltering garden tree,
And watch your doves about you flit,
    And plant on shoulder, hand and knee·
Or on your head their rosy feet,
    As if they knew your diet spares
Whatever moved in that full sheet
    Let down to Peter at his prayers;
Who lived on milk and meal and grass;
    And once for ten long weeks I tried
Your table of Pythagoras,
    And seem'd at first "a thing enskied"
(As Shakespeare has it) airy light
    To float above the ways of men,
Then fell from that half-spiritual height
    Chill'd till I tasted flesh again.[1]

[1] In the present generation, the poet's great-grandson, Hallam Tennyson, already author of one book, is a vegetarian of longer standing, partly as a result of Gandhian influence during relief work in India.

Tennyson evidently preferred the picnic at *Audley Court*:

> There, on a slope of orchard, Francis laid
> A damask napkin wrought with horse and hound,
> Brought out a dusky loaf that smelt of home,
> And, half-cut-down, a pasty costly-made,
> Where quail and pigeon, lark and leveret lay,
> Like fossils of the rock, with golden yolks
> Imbedded and injellied; last, with these,
> A flask of cider from his father's vats. . . .

Sometimes it was not Francis of Audley Court but Francis of Assisi that haunted him: "Are we devils? are we men?" he agonises in *Locksley Hall—Sixty Years After*:

Sweet St. Francis of Assisi, would that he were here again,

He that in his Catholic wholeness used to call the very flowers
Sisters, brothers—and the beasts—whose pains are hardly less than ours!

Chaos, Cosmos! Cosmos, Chaos! who can tell how all will end?
Read the wide world's annals, you, and take their wisdom for your
    friend.

But between God and Nature, it seemed, there was a terrible and final contradiction. Man, he wrote in *In Memoriam*,

> Who trusted God was love indeed
> And love Creation's final law—
> Tho' Nature, red in tooth and claw
> With ravine, shriek'd against his creed—

must be likewise "seal'd within the iron hills", and human life too was as futile as it was frail.

In *The Golden Year*, Tennyson feels that the ideal age must be realised not in the past or the future but in the instant and by each soul:

> Ah, folly! for it lies so far away,
> Not in our time, nor in our children's time,
> 'Tis like the second world to us that live;
> 'Twere all as one to fix our hopes on Heaven
> As on this vision of the golden year. . . .
> Old writers push'd the happy season back,—
> The more fools they,—we forward; dreamers both:

> You most, that in an age, when every hour
> Must sweat her sixty minutes to the death,
> Live on, God love us, as if the seedsman, rapt
> Upon the teeming harvest, should not plunge
> His hand into the bag: but well I know
> That unto him who works, and feels he works,
> This same grand year is ever at the doors.[1]

Tennyson's dismissal of the fools and dreamers of past and future paradises should be read in the light of his own "fall" from a "half-spiritual height". Down to earth realism is all too often a descent from Eden to Cockaigne. An ever-watchful dragon guards the golden apples of the Hesperides from the impatient hands of man.

A similar pattern is discernible in Wordsworth. Just as he believed at first that the French revolution would usher in something like Utopia, so he, and Tennyson too, thought that the Golden Age could very well return to-morrow morning, and even Shelley had visions of a miraculous transformation in which evil would mysteriously and finally evaporate and the world of unspoilt Nature would revive in all its primal splendour. In the early *Descriptive Sketches*, written when the poet was twenty-three, the sight of the "pastoral Swiss" moving like the Patriarchs "as the verdure leads"—a spectacle which carried its own omens of danger, as we have seen but Wordsworth did not—evoked the vision of a still more idyllic past of what Basil Willey has exactly identified as a "Rousseauistic Eden".

> Far different life from what Tradition hoar
> Transmits of happier lot in times of yore!
> Then Summer lingered long; and honey flowed
> From out the rocks, the wild bees' safe abode:
> Continual waters welling cheered the waste,
> And plants were wholesome, now of deadly taste:[2]

---

[1] Robert Browning was less optimistic. At the end of *Balaustion's Adventure*, which is mainly a version of Euripides' *Alcestis*, Browning revives Alcestis and adds:

> So, the two lived together long and well.
> But never could I learn, by word of scribe
> Or voice of poet, rumour wafts our way,
> That—of the scheme of rule in righteousness,
> The bringing back again the Golden Age,
> Which, rather than renounce, our pair would die—
> That ever one faint particle came true,
> With both alive to bring it to effect:
> Such is the envy Gods still bear mankind!

[2] This odd line is reminiscent of Sir Thomas Elyot's *Castel of Helth*.

Nor Winter yet his frozen stores had piled,
Usurping where the fairest herbage smiled:
Nor Hunger driven the herds from pastures bare,
To climb the treacherous cliffs for scanty fare.
Then the milk-thistle flourished through the land,
And forced the full-swoln udder to demand,
Thrice every day, the pail and welcome hand.
Thus does the father to his children tell
Of banished bliss, by fancy loved too well.
Alas! that human guilt provoked the rod
Of angry Nature to avenge her God.
Still Nature, ever just, to him imparts
Joys only given to incorrupted hearts.

Wordsworth was soon disillusioned about the fruits of violent revolution in France but, as A. C. Bradley observed, he continued to believe that Utopia was "a country which he saw every day, and which, he thought, every man might see who did not strive, nor cry, nor rebel, but opened his heart in love and thankfulness to sweet influences as universal and perpetual as the air". Some ten years later, in *The Prelude*, Wordsworth's goal is:

Not in Utopia—subterranean fields—
Or some secreted island Heaven knows where,
But in the very world, which is the world
Of all of us—the place where in the end
We find our happiness or not at all.

This is a long step in the direction of the poem Tennyson was to write a quarter of a century later, *The Golden Year*, when "old writers" are roughly dismissed as fools for placing the Golden Age in the remote past. But it has still a trace of the clouds of glory, and is not unlike that passage from Hesiod quoted in the first chapter where the poet shows that for those who lead the right idyllic life some intimation of the joys of the Golden Age is vouchsafed here and now. Wordsworth's typical human figures, writes Basil Willey, "are those which are most intimately 'engaged' with their natural background . . . and for many a sufferer from the strange disease of modern life, looking up from amongst the dark satanic mills of the industrial age, the authority of the Wordsworthian Nature-religion has seemed absolute. Nevertheless it was probably only relative to a certain passing phase of civilization: for an age, and not for all time . . . perhaps the healing power of Nature is only felt to the full, as Ruskin found, by those who return to it at intervals after being long 'in populous cities pent'. Even to Wordsworth Nature meant most as long as he could retain a sense of *escape* into it; when he had long been domiciled there it lost its glory and freshness." These are wise comments on the shortcomings of enthusiasm for Nature, but it remains true that Wordsworth's desire to merge himself with impersonal natural objects reveals the necessary preoccupation of the poetic consciousness of that age with the gap that had opened up, as Joseph Warton and others had seen, between human urban societies and the natural order, and with the urgent need for a valid reintegration if tranquillity is to be restored. The Wordsworthian warning has largely gone unheeded and its insights are only now being slowly reapproached by the painstaking efforts of the ecologists and pioneers of biological equilibrium. The heart of Wordsworth's certainty is his experience of the unity of all living things, in which we may perhaps see the Romantic expression of the intuition that inspired, more than two thousand years before, the belief in metempsychosis:

> I felt the sentiment of Being spread
> O'er all that, lost beyond the reach of thought
> And human knowledge, to the human eye
> Invisible, yet liveth to the heart;
> O'er all that leaps and runs, and shouts and sings,
> Or beats the gladsome air; o'er all that glides
> Beneath the wave, yea, in the wave itself,
> And mighty depth of waters. Wonder not
> If high the transport, great the joy I felt,
> Communing in this sort through earth and heaven
> With every form of creature, as it looked
> Towards the Uncreated with a countenance
> Of adoration, with an eye of love.
> One song they sang, and it was audible,
> Most audible, then, when the fleshly ear,
> O'ercome by humblest prelude of that strain,
> Forgot her functions, and slept undisturbed.

And in the Preface to *The Excursion*, nearly a decade later, he reiterated:

> Paradise, and groves
> Elysian, Fortunate Fields—like those of old
> Sought in the Atlantic Main—why should they be
> A history only of departed things,
> Or a mere fiction of what never was?
> For the discerning intellect of Man,
> When wedded to this goodly universe
> In love and holy passion, shall find these
> A simple produce of the common day.

But Wordsworth's worship of Nature is extravagant in certain vital respects, and his facile rejection of the visions of the greatest poet-seers of the past is one of the danger-signals. William Blake's delight in Wordsworth's poetry was intense, but he considered the eloquent descriptions of Nature in them as conclusive proof of Wordsworth's own atheism: "I see in Wordsworth the Natural Man rising up against the Spiritual Man Continually, & then he is No Poet but a Heathen Philosopher at Enmity against all true Poetry or Inspiration."

Coleridge, who described one of Wordsworth's recitations as "An orphic song indeed" and meant the comparison with that heathen philosopher as a lavish compliment to his friend, agreed with Wordsworth in seeing no reason why groves Elysian should be a history only of departed things, and was presumably enlightened by the ordeal that underlies *The Ancient Mariner*, as we shall see it interpreted for us presently by Cecil Day Lewis.

At one time in his early manhood, Coleridge with Southey and others proposed to found a community in the "delightful part of the new back settlements of America" in accordance with the enlightened principles collectively called Pantisocracy. The labour of each man for two or three hours a day, it was thought, would suffice to support the colony, and the produce was to be common property.

> Yet will I love to follow the sweet dream,
> Where Susquehanna pours his untamed stream

wrote Coleridge in his *Monody on the Death of Chatterton*, and a dream is what it is usually considered to be. Not even Coleridge's dream, but Southey's who at Oxford had fallen under the spell of Plato's *Republic*. Southey's son, however, thought that the scheme originated not with his father but with Coleridge. At any rate a more recent and considered judgment is that "they had approached the scheme in what a business man,—and this is praise indeed— might have called a practical manner". It was "Coleridge more than any of the others—except perhaps Mrs. Fricker—" says the same writer, "who kept his two feet on solid reality".

But if Coleridge was more practical in this matter than he has been given credit for, it was the dream that ruled him: "The thoughts of the day, and the visions of the night, all centre in America." Inevitably these visions were expressed in his poems, though the two following sonnets are among the least known of his minor works:

> Whilst pale Anxiety, corrosive Care,
> The tear of Woe, the gloom of sad Despair,
> And deepen'd Anguish generous bosoms rend;—
> Whilst patriot souls their country's fate lament;
> Whilst mad with rage demoniac, foul intent,
> Embattled legions Despots vainly send
> To arrest the immortal mind's expanding ray
> Of everlasting Truth;—I other climes
> Where dawns, with hope serene, a brighter day
> Than e'er saw Albion in her happiest times,
> With mental eye exulting now explore,
> And soon with kindred minds shall haste to enjoy
> (Free from the ills which here our peace destroy)
> Content and Bliss on Transatlantic shore.

> No more my visionary soul shall dwell
> On joys that were; no more endure to weigh
> The shame and anguish of the evil day,
> Wisely forgetful! O'er the ocean swell
> Sublime of Hope, I seek the cottag'd dell
> Where Virtue calm with careless step may stray,
> And dancing to the moonlight roundelay,
> The wizard Passions weave an holy spell.
> Eyes that have ach'd with Sorrow! Ye shall weep
> Tears of doubt-mingled joy, like theirs who start
> From Precipices of distemper'd sleep,
> On which the fierce-eyed Fiends their revels keep,

And see the rising Sun, and feel it dart
New rays of pleasaunce trembling to the heart.

And in *The Destiny of Nations* he images the contrasting sacrifices to War and Peace:

Lenient of care, thy songs O Peace! are sweet,
As after showers the perfumed gale of eve,
That flings the cool drops on a feverous cheek;
And gay thy grassy altar piled with fruits.
But boasts the shrine of demon War one charm
Save that with many an orgie strange and foul
Dancing around with interwoven arms
The maniac suicide and giant Murder
Exult in their fierce union.

Not that Coleridge himself could pass for a Pythagorean, like Shelley, Keats, Byron, FitzGerald and Tennyson at some period of their lives. He was "very fond of Vegetables", but "particularly Bacon and Peas.—Bacon and Broad Beans." Coleridge's imagination was, as it were, lost at sea,[1] where in a waste of waters the fatal

[1] In a prefatory note written some thirty years after the scheme and fragments of *The Wanderings of Cain*, which it introduces, Coleridge tells how in 1798 the project was undertaken, only to be abandoned, "and *The Ancient Mariner* was written instead." Years afterwards, "I determined on commencing anew, and composing the whole in stanzas, and made some progress in realising this intention, when adverse gales drove my bark off the 'Fortunate Isles' of the Muses: and then other and more momentous interests prompted a different voyage, to firmer anchorage and a securer port. I have vainy tried to recover the lines from the Palimpsest of my memory: and I can only offer the introductory stanza, which had been committed to writing. . . ."

> Encinctured with a twine of leaves,
> That leafy twine his only dress!
> A lovely Boy was plucking fruits,
> By moonlight in a wilderness.
> The moon was bright, the air was free,
> And fruits and flowers together grew
> On many a shrub and many a tree:
> And all put on a gentle hue,
> Hanging in the shadowy air
> Like a picture rich and rare.

This strange night vision of what should be a sunlit paradisal scene is the only glimpse of the Hesperides vouchsafed to Coleridge's *Argo*.

In the prose précis of the second canto the narrative grows yet more eerie, but the reader of the foregoing pages will hear many strange echoes and will note that Abel has fallen under a curse even more terrible than Cain suffers. Cain is led through a dark forest by his little son Enos, who asks his father why the squirrels will not play with him, although "I groaned to them even as thou groanest when thou givest me to eat". They emerge into a wilderness of sand and rock and "discover nothing that acknowledged the influence of the seasons". The shattered summits of the rocks in this waste land "seemed to prophesy mutely of things that then were not; steeples, and battlements, and ships with naked masts." There they meet a terrible Shape, who smites his breast and cries aloud, "Woe is me! woe is me! I must never die again, and yet I am perishing with thirst and hunger"—words that precisely fit the ordeal of the Ancient Mariner himself—and the Shape is recognised as Abel! "Then Cain raised up the Shape that was like Abel, and said:—'The Creator of our father, who had respect unto thee, and unto thy offering, wherefore hath he forsaken thee?' Then the Shape shrieked a second time, and rent his garment, and his naked white skin was like the white sands beneath their feet; and he shrieked yet a third time, and threw himself upon the sand that was black with the shadow of the rock." Abel, and Cain also, has made no sacrifice acceptable to the God of the dead, who was to be shown to Cain and Enos by Abel in the unwritten third canto.

Coleridge's philosophy was largely transcendental Neoplatonism. His lectures on philosophy in 1818–1819 commence from Thales and Pythagoras. It is likely that more could be learned of his early thought and habits from the complete collection of 55 manuscript notebooks which "preserve an almost continuous record of the inner workings of his varied and powerful intellect"—most of which remains unpublished. These notebooks, with other valuable manuscripts and annotated printed books of Coleridge's, were acquired by the British Museum in July 1951.

shot is fired at the albatross. The meaning of this symbolic central image from Coleridge's supreme poem, *The Ancient Mariner*, has been expounded by a modern poet, Cecil Day Lewis: "A crime is committed against one of God's creatures. . . . The consequences of this crime fall not only upon the perpetrator but, to a lesser degree, upon his companions. A period of deadness and disgust follows: the Mariner cannot begin to atone for his crime against love until he feels love again. . . . Now what does all this say but that one man shooting a bird hits all creation, that the responsibility for every action, and its consequences, fall in some sense upon everyone; that we are all—the living and the dead—members one of another? Coleridge himself gives evidence, when he says that 'He prayeth well, who loveth well both man and bird and beast': and the fact that he later repented of these lines does not invalidate them as witnesses to his theme; it only meant that he felt it an artistic mistake to have stated the theme as a downright moral." Like Wordsworth, Coleridge had felt great joy at communing through heaven and earth with every form of creature.

Coleridge never saw his other Eden on the Susquehanna. But at the end of the century Robert Louis Stevenson saw it on his first day out of New York. He saw the dawn break on a new world, he "beheld the sun, no longer shining blankly on the plains of ocean, but striking among shapely hills and his light dispersed and coloured by a thousand accidents of form and surface, I began to exult with myself upon this rise in life like a man who had come into a rich estate. And when I had asked the name of a river from the brakesman, and heard that it was called the Susquehanna, the beauty of the name seemed to be part and parcel of the beauty of the land. As when Adam with divine fitness named the creatures, so this word Susquehanna was at once accepted by the fancy. That was the name, as no other could be, for that shining river and desirable valley."

It was not near the head of the Susquehanna but along the Concord River that the vision of the earthly paradise was seen afresh by the Alcotts, Emerson, Thoreau and Nathaniel Hawthorne. The purely dietary tradition reached them through the fanatical devotion of an emigré Manchester clergyman, William Metcalfe, via Sylvester Graham, Dr. William Alcott and the colourful Horace Greeley and these New England writers were fully conscious of the traditions of Genesis, Pythagoras, and the ancient Hindu lawgiver who, writes Thoreau, "teaches how to eat". They were not the first Americans to experiment in this way of living. A century before in nearby Boston, young Benjamin Franklin adopted a vegetable diet, resulting, as he claims in the *Autobiography*, in "greater clearness of head and quicker apprehension which usually attend temperance in eating and drinking". Finding that bigger fish eat smaller fish (the subject of a terrifying drawing by Brueghel, by the way), Franklin reckoned this let him out of any obligation, "so convenient a thing is it to be a reasonable creature", he mocks at himself, "since it enables one to find or make a reason for every thing one has a mind to do". And there is a monument at Leominster, also in Massachusetts, where in 1775 Johnny Appleseed was born, the orchard-planting folk hero who went unarmed and barefooted among wild animals and Indians. "Forsaking the diets and practices of blood", writes Henry Bailey Stevens, "he made his way through the wilderness to the frontier cabins of the white man and the tepees of the Indian, crying, 'Look! I have brought you news fresh from Heaven.'"[1] The story has recently been charmingly retold in a Disney cartoon, whose accuracy was ensured by accepting the advice of Johnny Appleseed's descendants.

Thoreau's life in the woods led him to pretty much the same conclusions. He was more of a hermit than FitzGerald and he echoed that poet's belief that the world must come to "a more innocent and wholesome diet. . . . I have no doubt that it is a part of the destiny of the human race, in its gradual improvement, to leave off eating animals, as surely as the savage tribes have left off eating each other. . . . The faintest assured objection which one

[1] Johnny Appleseed was inspired by the writings of that Blake-like eighteenth-century prophet Swedenborg, which he carried about with him. Following the allegorical interpretations of Philo, Clement and Origen, Swedenborg considered that there were human beings on the earth before Adam. C. T. Odhner (*The Golden Age*, Pennsylvania, 1913) gives a full account from Swedenborg's writings of the life attributed to the Preadamites, including the following passage from the *Arcana Cœlestia:*
"The eating of the flesh of animals, regarded in itself, is something profane, for in the most ancient times they never ate the flesh of any beast or bird, but only seeds, especially bread made from wheat, also the fruits of trees, vegetables, milk and its various products, such as butter. To kill animals and eat their flesh was to them a wickedness, and like wild beasts. They took from them only service and use, as is evident from Genesis 1: 29, 30. But in process of time, when men began to be as fierce as wild beasts and even fiercer, they then, for the first time, began to kill animals and eat their flesh; and because man's nature was such, it was permitted him to do this, and is still permitted to this day."
But if flesh-eating was not condemned in fallen man it was not encouraged and to Johnny Appleseed pacifism and vegetarianism were as much a vital part of planting the new Eden as the apple orchards themselves. We may note here that there are several large religious sects in America today whose members are entirely or mostly vegetarian: the Seventh Day Adventists, and the non-Christian Mazdaznans and many Theosophists. Smaller groups of the same persuasion as well as secular vegetarian societies and such vegetarian Christian denominations as The Order of the Cross and a group within the Quaker Society of Friends are, of course, to be found in Britain.

healthy man feels will at length prevail over the arguments and customs of mankind." His purpose was unashamedly didactic: "To what end do I lead a simple life at all? That I may teach others to simplify *their* lives." And Thoreau has successors in the present-day New England writers, Henry Bailey Stevens, Richard B. Gregg —and Scott Nearing, who realised Coleridge's "impracticable" dream and has a well-established vegetarian economy that is self-supporting on an average of four hours' manual labour, with four hours for individual vocational work and four hours' sociability through the year.

Thoreau's dietary convictions were as important a part of his transcendentalism as Shelley's were of his nominal atheism, and Thoreau too was a poet at heart. "Music is the sound of the universal laws promulgated", he writes in *A Week on the Concord*, and follows it with some lines on an Aeolian harp and a quotation from Iamblichus about the music unheard by mortal ears that Pythagoras drew from the universal harmony and made audible to his disciples. "Orpheus does not hear the strains which issue from his lyre", he says again, "but only those which are breathed into it: for the original strain precedes the sound, by as much as the echo follows after. The rest is the perquisite of the rocks and trees and beasts. . . . The poet's body is not fed like other men's, but he sometimes tastes the genuine nectar and ambrosia of the gods, and lives a divine life", and perhaps realising that his own poems hardly achieved that exalted level, he adds:

> My life has been the poem I would have writ,
> But I could not both live and utter it.

Living it meant, among other things, the experience that, as he wrote in *Walden,* "spring is like the creation of Cosmos out of Chaos and the realization of the Golden Age".

"I sold my gun before I went to the woods", Thoreau tells us. . . . As for fowling, during the last years that I carried a gun my excuse was that I was studying ornithology, and sought only new or rare birds. But I confess that I am now inclined to think that there is a finer way of studying ornithology than this. It requires so much closer attention to the habits of the birds, that, if for that reason only, I have been willing to omit the gun." And this daily life in harmony

232

with Nature made him more keenly aware of the artificiality of what passed for luxurious living. "I sat at a table where were rich food and wine in abundance, and obsequious attendance, but sincerity and truth were not; and I went away hungry from the inhospitable board."

Those words were published later in *Walden*, but Emerson must have seen them before he brought out his volume of *Poems* in the year after Thoreau went to the woods. *Forbearance* is surely addressed to him:

> Hast thou named all the birds without a gun?
> Loved the wood-rose, and left it on its stalk?
> At rich men's tables eaten bread and pulse?
> Unarmed, faced danger with a heart of trust?
> And loved so well a high behaviour,
> In man or maid, that thou from speech refrained,
> Nobility more nobly to repay?
> O, be my friend, and teach me to be thine!

Emerson admired but did not imitate his friend Thoreau. Odell Shephard, in his wholly delightful life of Bronson Alcott, has a story about Emerson carving a roast and dilating upon the horrors of cannibalism. "But Mr. Emerson," Alcott finally intervened, "if we are to eat meat at all why should we *not* eat the *best*?" Alcott was the author of fifty *Orphic Sayings*, and his reading turned to Hesiod's *Works and Days*, Iamblichus's *Life of Pythagoras* and, above all, to Coleridge. Shelley's life and his social and political theories also appealed very much to Alcott, who did not care for Shelley's poetry. But Coleridge, especially the *Aids to Reflection*, was his guiding star, and his enthusiasm was probably heightened by meeting in 1836 Dr. William Ellery Channing, who had been closely associated with Wordsworth and Coleridge in England. In this Alcott was typical of the transcendental reformers, all of whom, says Shephard, were affected at the second or third remove by the thought of Coleridge; "almost the only kind of enthusiasm not overtly manifested among them", he adds, "was the erotic".

Coleridge himself was dead some years before Alcott came to England in 1842, where, at the idealist Alcott House School, at Ham Common, near Richmond, he declared that "It is proposed to select a spot whereon the new Eden may be planted. . . . On a survey of the present civilized world, Providence seems to have ordained the United States of America, more especially New England, as the field wherein this idea is to be realized in actual experience . . . a few persons, both in the new country and the old, are uniting their efforts to secure, at the earliest possible moment, and by the simplest possible means, a consummation so sublime, so humane, so divine." "Fruitlands", Odell Shephard believes, "was made, in large part, in England."

Alcott, like Thoreau, had Emerson's admiration. "These men", he wrote in his *Journal* on 8 July 1843, "ought to be maintained in their place by the country for its culture". But spring was not perpetual on the farm at Harvard, the first winter killed Fruitlands after a life of only seven months, though this did not prevent one of its more astonishing pioneers, Samuel Larnel, from subsisting for one year on crackers and then for another year, in the Johnny Appleseed tradition, on an exclusive diet of apples. Louisa May Alcott was about ten years old at this time and, because of her father's strict principles, she had never tasted any but a vegetarian diet. She has preserved her diary, which notes not only the dinners of bread and fruit but also some of the slogans—Orphic sayings, Alcott would perhaps have said—that were issued by the little community. The claims were forthright: "Vegetable diet and sweet repose. Animal food and nightmare." "Pluck your body from the orchard; do not snatch it from the shamble." "Without flesh diet there could be no blood-shedding war." "Apollo eats no flesh and has no beard; his voice is melody itself."

This ephemeral descendant of the Orphic and Pythagorean communities of Southern Italy and Greece was, of course, only one among a vast number of Utopian communitarian experiments in the United States during the hundred and fifty years that ended with the close of the nineteenth century. Many were Owenite, and in the year after the Fruitlands experiment Robert Owen stayed for two days with Bronson Alcott. Others were sectarian, and among them the Shakers were often strictly vegetarian communities, such as the one at Mount Lebanon which, according to the last *Americana*, still exists. There were later failures too, including the fantastic Octagon City project on the Neosho River in south-eastern Kansas, which seems to have given up in the first winter, 1856, like Fruitlands thirteen years earlier, though the fact that a Harmonial Vegetarian Society initiated a similar community venture in the extreme north-east of Arkansas, near the Neosho River, in 1860 suggests that there may have been some continuity in that area. Although not strictly vegetarian, the Heard-Huxley community in California in recent years might be considered a lineal descendant of the Coleridge-Southey scheme, if not also of Fruitlands.

Alcott also helped to plan the Brook Farm community. Nathaniel Hawthorne joined it in 1841 and when he married, in the following year, he and his wife moved to Concord, where they lived in Emerson's old house, in which Hawthorne wrote in the next three or four years the stories and sketches published as *Mosses from an Old Manse*. Ten years later he bought Alcott's house where he lived for the rest of his life. Although Brook Farm did not embody sufficient idealism to satisfy Alcott for long, at the end of September 1841 Hawthorne was writing in his *Notebooks* a lament for animals going to the slaughter that would certainly have pleased him. The cows had given milk to support families, and oxen had toiled in the plough-field, Hawthorne reflected, "Even the young steers, and the little calves, had someting of domestic sacredness about them; for children had watched their growth, and petted them, and played with them. And here they all were, old and young, gathered from their thousand homes to Brighton fair; whence the great chance was that they would go to the slaughter-house, and thence be transmitted, in sirloins, joints, and such pieces, to the tables of the Boston folk."

And in the *Mosses from an Old Manse*, Nathaniel Hawthorne wrote his parable of *The New Adam and Eve*, something which probably could not have been written if Fruitlands and Brook Farm had never been attempted. "We who are born into the world's artificial system", Hawthorne begins quietly, "can never adequately know how little in our present state and circumstances is natural, and how much is merely the interpolation of the perverted mind and heart of man. Art has become a second and stronger nature; she is a stepmother, whose crafty tenderness has taught us to despise the bountiful and wholesome ministrations of our true parent. It is only through the medium of the imagination that we can loosen these iron fetters, which we call truth and reality, and make ourselves even partially sensible what prisoners we are."

Then in a mood half sportive and half thoughtful, as he says, he imagines the heart of a modern city, whose human inhabitants have instantaneously disappeared in some almost atomic disaster. Into it come the new Adam and Eve. Presently they feel a little hungry:

"By a most unlucky arrangement there was to have been a grand dinner party in this mansion on the very day when the whole human family, including the invited guests, were summoned to the unknown regions of illimitable space. At the moment of fate, the table was actually spread, and the company on the point of sitting down. Adam and Eve come unbidden to the banquet; it has now been some time cold, but otherwise furnishes them with highly favourable specimens of the gastronomy of their predecessors. But it is difficult to imagine the perplexity of the unperverted couple, in endeavouring to find proper food for their first meal, at a table where the cultivated appetites of a fashionable party were to have been gratified. Will Nature teach them the mystery of a plate of turtle soup? Will she embolden them to attack a haunch of venison? Will she initiate them into the merits of a Parisian pasty, imported by the last steamer that ever crossed the Atlantic? Will she not, rather, bid them turn with disgust from fish, fowl and flesh, which, to their pure nostrils, steam with a loathsome odour of death and corruption?—Food? The bill of fare contains nothing which they recognize as such.

"Fortunately, however, the dessert is ready upon a neighbouring table. Adam, whose appetite and animal instincts are quicker than those of Eve, discovers this fitting banquet.

" 'Here, dearest Eve,' he exclaims, 'here is food.'

" 'Well,' answered she, with the germ of a housewife stirring within her, 'we have been so busy to-day, that a picked up dinner must serve.'

"So Eve comes to the table and receives a red-cheeked apple from her husband's hand in requital of her predecessor's fatal gift to our common grandfather. She eats it without sin, and, let us hope, with no disastrous consequences to her future progeny. They make a plentiful, yet temperate, meal of fruit, which, though not gathered in paradise, is legitimately derived from the seeds that were planted there. Their primal appetite is satisfied."

It is not Miltonic; but it makes its point. This, exactly, is what Rousseau means by his state of Nature.

Longfellow, the most popular of the New England poets, was at college with Hawthorne, though the two were not then intimate friends. Longfellow, however, reviewed Hawthorne's *Twice-told Tales* in 1837, and thought very highly of it. Two of Longfellow's poems take up, as it were, the image of the shot bird that seems to hover over this era, in Coleridge, Thoreau and Emerson. We may glance first at *The Sermon of St. Francis*, preached to the birds. From the Hindu *Hitopadesa* and Hesiod's *Works and Days* onwards, birds and creatures talk to each other in animal fables. But perhaps the first figure in our tradition of man making godlike speech to the creatures is Orpheus himself whose songs charmed the wild and tame alike. In Plato's *Politicus* Myth, the happy people of the age of Cronus, after eating and drinking their fill of harmless food and drink, "passed the time telling tales one to another and to the beasts". Longfellow's St. Francis is akin to them:

> Around Assisi's convent gate
> The birds, God's poor who cannot wait,
> From moor and mere and darksome wood
> Came flocking for their dole of food.
>
> "O brother birds," St. Francis said,
> "Ye come to me and ask for bread,
> But not with bread alone to-day
> Shall ye be fed and sent away.
>
> "Ye shall be fed, ye happy birds,
> With manna of celestial words;
> Not mine, though mine they seem to be,
> Not mine, though they be spoken through me."

And, significantly, it is *The Poet's Tale* in *Tales of a Wayside Inn*, that deals with the slaughter of the birds, and the nemesis that follows, the fundamental pattern is comparable to Coleridge's, as expounded by C. Day Lewis:

> And so the dreadful massacre began;
> O'er fields and orchards, and o'er woodland crests,
> The ceaseless fusillade of terror ran.
> Dead fell the birds, with blood-stains on their breasts,
> Or wounded crept away from sight of man,
> While the young died of famine in their nests;

> A slaughter to be told in groans, not words,
> The very St. Bartholomew of Birds!
> The Summer came, and all the birds were dead;
>   The days were like hot coals; the very ground
> Was burned to ashes; in the orchards fed
>   Myriads of caterpillars, and around
> The cultivated fields and garden beds
>   Hosts of devouring insects crawled, and found
> No foe to check their march, till they had made
> The land a desert without leaf or shade.
>
> Devoured by worms, like Herod, was the town,
>   Because, like Herod, it had ruthlessly
> Slaughtered the Innocents.

A few farmers "confessed their error", they "repealed the law". In the autumn comes the wind, "lamenting the dead children of the air". Next spring a wagon of singing birds is brought in "from all the country round" by order of the town and loosed "in woods and fields, the places they loved best" and the tale ends:

> And a new heaven bent over a new earth
> Amid the sunny farms of Killingworth.

If this were simply a prophetic lecture on biological equilibrium such as is now eloquently preached by the President of the New York Zoological Society, Fairfield Osborn, in *Our Plundered Planet*, it would be necessary to remark that wanton destruction of insects can be quite as fatal, so that the palm would go to the gracious lady in Shelley's *The Sensitive Plant*, the "Eve in this Eden":

> And all killing insects and gnawing worms,
> And things of obscene and unlovely forms,
> She bore in a basket of Indian woof,
> Into the rough woods far aloof,
> In a basket, of grasses and wild flowers full,
> The freshest her gentle hands could pull
> For the poor banished insects, whose intent
> Although they did ill, was innocent.

After a short *Finale*, the *Tales* proceed to a *Prelude* to Part II, where the Theologian is discovered feeding two fat robins in a cage, captured by the hostler as "vagrants and pilferers"; the hostler has made exactly the same mistake as the farmers of Killingworth. The choice of small bird is reminiscent of Blake's *Auguries of Innocence*:

> A Robin Red breast in a Cage
> Puts all Heaven in a Rage.

The Theologian, or rather Longfellow himself in that character now, sees these robins too as auguries of innocence:

> Two poets of the Golden Age,
> Heirs of a boundless heritage
> Of fields and orchards, east and west,
> And sunshine of long summer days,
> Though outlawed now and dispossessed!—
> Such was the Theologian's phrase.

Next follows the Sicilian's tale of the ill-treatment of a horse, ending:

> "Church-bells at best but ring us to the door;
> But go not in to mass; my bell doth more;
> It cometh into court and pleads the cause
> Of creatures dumb and unknown to the laws;
> And this shall make, in every Christian clime,
> The Bell of Atri famous for all time.
>
> "Yes, well your story pleads the cause
> Of those dumb mouths that have no speech,
> Only a cry from each to each
> In its own kind, with its own laws;
> Something that is beyond the reach
> Of human power to learn or teach,—
> An inarticulate moan of pain,
> Like the immeasurable main
> Breaking upon an unknown beach."
>
> Thus spake the Poet with a sigh;
> Then added, with impassioned cry,
> As one who feels the words he speaks,
> The colour flushing in his cheeks,
> The fervour burning in his eye:
> "Among the noblest in the land,

Though he may count himself the least,
That man I honour and revere
Who without favour, without fear,
In the great city dares to stand
The friend of every friendless beast,
And tames with his unflinching hand
The brutes that wear our form and face,
The were-wolves of the human race!"
Then paused, and waited with a frown,
Like some old champion of romance,
Who, having thrown his gauntlet down,
Expectant leans upon his lance;
But neither Knight nor Squire is found
To raise the gauntlet from the ground,
And try with him the battle's chance.

The Squire who picks it up in the long run is himself a Knight of the same order of chivalry. Sir John Squire's poem on the slaughter-houses at Chicago, *The Stockyard*, is one among many fine poems on a similar theme that have since been written, and of which we may only mention here Thomas Hardy's ode on *Compassion*, Walter de la Mare's *Tit for Tat*, and the names of Ralph Hodgson, Robert W. Service and W. H. Davies. Walt Whitman too had this sense of kinship and compassion.

For three generations the family of John Greenleaf Whittier had been connected with the Society of Friends, and for the Quaker poet the harvest festival is an Eleusinian rite of first-fruits: sometimes the emphasis is on human industry in cultivating the wilderness, sometimes on the divine plenty, as in these verses written for the autumn celebrations of 1858 and 1859:

This day, two hundred years ago,
The wild grape by the river's side,
And tasteless ground-nut trailing low,
The table of the woods supplied.

Unknown the apple's red and gold,
The blushing tint of peach and pear;
The mirror of the Powow told
No tale of orchards ripe and rare.

> To see our Father's hand once more
>   Reverse for us the plenteous horn
> Of autumn, filled and running o'er
>   With fruit, and flower, and golden corn!
>
> Once more the liberal year laughs out
>   O'er richer stores than gems of gold;
> Once more with harvest-song and shout
>   Is Nature's bloodless triumph told.
>
> .   .   .   .   .
>
> And let these altars, wreathed with flowers
>   And piled with fruits, awake again
> Thanksgivings for the golden hours,
>   The early and the latter rain.

But two years later civil war broke out and in *Our River*, Whittier sadly wrote:

> Young eyes that last year smiled in ours
>   Now point the rifle's barrel,
> And hands then stained with fruits and flowers
>   Bear redder stains of quarrel.

Peace and innocence were lost once more, even in the land that seemed to Alcott to be ordained for a new Eden. But still there is a way forward to the same primal paradise. Twenty years later, at the age of eighty-five and with ten more years to live, Whittier wrote the *Garden*:

> Why search the wide world everywhere
>   For Eden's unknown ground?
> That garden of the primal pair
>   May nevermore be found.
>
> But, blest by Thee, our patient toil
>   May right the ancient wrong,
> And give to every clime and soil
>   The beauty lost so long.

America had its Cockaignes as well as its Edens. Whittier had been a staunch protagonist of the anti-slavery cause, but he did not especially yearn to liberate the Negroes into the earthly paradise of John Henry, the lusty, ravenous hero whose adventures have been recorded from speech by Howard W. Odum and Guy B. Johnson of the University of North Carolina:

"One day John Henry lef' rock quarry on way to camp an' had to go through woods an' fiel'. Well, he met big black bear an' didn't do nothin' but shoot 'im wid his bow an' arrer, an' arrer went clean through bear an' stuck in big tree on other side. So John Henry pulls arrer out of tree an' pull so hard he falls back 'gainst 'nother tree which is full o' flitterjacks, an' first tree is full o' honey, an' in pullin' arrer out o' one he shakes down honey, an' in fallin' 'gainst other he shaken down flitterjacks. Well John Henry set there an' et honey an' flitterjacks, an' after while when he went to get up to go, button pop off'n his pants, an' kill a rabbit mo' 'n hundred ya'ds on other side o' de tree. An' so up jumped brown baked pig wid sack o' biscuits on his back, an' John Henry et him too.

"So John Henry gits up to go on through woods to camp for supper, 'cause he 'bout to be late an' he mighty hongry for his supper. John Henry sees lake down hill and thinks he'll git him a drink o' water, 'cause he's thirsty, too, after eatin' honey an' flitterjacks an' brown roast pig an' biscuits, still he's hongry yet. An' so he goes down to git drink water an' finds lake ain't nothin' but lake o' honey, an' out in middle dat lake ain't nothin' but tree full o' biscuits. An' so John Henry don't do nothin' but drink dat lake o' honey dry. An' he et the tree full o' biscuits, too. An' so 'bout that time it begin to git dark, an' John Henry sees light on hill an' he think may be he can git sumpin' to eat, cause he's mighty hongry after big day drillin'. So he look roun' an' see light on hill an' he runs up to house where light is an' ast people livin' dere, why'n hell dey don't give him sumpin' to eat, 'cause he ain't had much. An' so he et dat, too.

"Gee-hee," the speaker justifiably added, "dat nigger could eat!" And it is no surprise that this gastronomical hero "had mo wimmin 'an anybody else, some say mo'n ten [men] 'cause, Lawd, I specs he had mo'n thousand wimmin."

And as Marc Connelly showed in *Green Pastures*, the Negro celestial paradise with its fish-frys and big cigars is not too much of an anti-climax after the pleasures of the terrestrial one.

Scandinavian myths of uncertain date written down in the eighth and following centuries consistently warn that death and disease are his portion who partakes of the food or accepts the love offered by the denizens of the Otherworld beyond the seas. It is interesting to find that even the light verse of more recent times which deals with the fortunes of Scandinavian settlers in the Americas conforms to type. El Dorado, of course, was a fabulous South American country in which gold and jewels abounded, and of which Raleigh and Spanish sixteenth-century adventurers went in search. In the satirical Norwegian song of a century ago, El Dorado is America itself:

O El Dorado! lovely name! It sounds like the clinking of ducats! There, surely, of all countries, must be the land of happiness and peace. There, I know, the trees bear fruit of gold, and golden doubloons fill the mouths of fishes; the fields bring forth golden ears, and golden flowers cover the savannahs.

A merry life one leads there, like a perpetual masquerade mid the palm trees under the glittering stars. There the fields bear their crops without cultivation—never fear—and if you want a fine roast, you have only to lasso a buffalo.

To be sure, you may be risking your life: a redskin may scalp you, or a Yankee thrust his bowie knife in your vitals. But what of that? The gold of California will buy you the splendours of the Mogul. But two things it cannot buy—happiness and peace.

Still more pertinent to the conception of an American Cockaigne is the satirical ballad *Oleana* written by a newspaper editor in 1853 to ridicule the ambitious colonisation project in Pennsylvania initiated by the violinist Ole Bull. The editor and translator of *Norwegian Emigrant Songs and Ballads*, Theo. C. Blegen and Martin B. Ruud, remark that "the strange Utopia of Gyntiana (*Peer Gynt*, Act IV) seems to have been inspired by the story of Oleana. Ibsen, in creating Peer Gynt himself, probably drew to some extent upon the characteristics of Ole Bull."

In Oleana, that's where I'd like to be, and not drag the chains of slavery
   in Norway.
         Ole—Ole—Ole—oh! Oleana!
         Ole—Ole—Ole—oh! Oleana!

In Oleana they give you land for nothing, and the grain just pops out of
   the ground. Golly, that's easy.
The grain threshes itself in the granary while I stretch out at ease in my
   bunk.

And the markets! You just ought to see the potatoes! You can distil at least a quart of whiskey from every one of them.

And Münchener beer, as sweet as Ytteborg's, runs in the creeks for the poor man's delectation.

And the salmon, they leap like mad in the rivers, and hop into kettles, and cry out for a cover.

And little roasted piggies rush about the streets, politely inquiring if you wish for ham.

And the cows, they milk and churn and make cheese just as skilfully as Else my sister.

And the bull doesn't stand around idle; he beats his calves for loafing and shirking.

And the calves, they kill and flay themselves and turn to veal roast faster than you can take a drink.

And the hens lay eggs as big as a storehouse, and the cocks strike the hour like an eight-day clock.

And cakes fairly rain from the skies above you. Good Lord, what wondrous tidbits!

The sun shines faithfully all night long, so that you can see in the dark, just like a cat.

The moon is full every night, that is certain: I am observing it now with a bottle for a telescope.

You bet, they give you two dollars a day for carousing; and if you are good and lazy, they'll probably give you four.

The old woman and the kids, why, they go on the township; if the authorities don't pay they get it on the snout.

You don't have to work to support your bastards; if you did, I shouldn't be sitting here spinning verses.

And we all stalk about in velvet suits with silver buttons, smoking meerschaum pipes which the old woman fills for us.

And she has to sweat and toil and struggle; and if she doesn't do it, she gives herself a beating.

And every last one of us plays upon the fiddle, and dances a merry polka; and that's not so bad!

Aye, go to Oleana, there you'll begin to live! The poorest wretch in Norway is a count over there.

Oh, I'd much rather live in Oleana than drag the chains of slavery over there in Norway.

Finally, we may notice what seems to be the American's own version of Cockaigne, *The Big Rock Candy Mountains*:

One evening as the sun went down
And the jungle fire was burning
Down the track came a hobo hiking,
And he said "Boys I'm not turning.
I'm headed for a land that's far away,
Beside the crystal fountains,
So come with me, we'll all go and see
The big Rock Candy Mountains.

In the big Rock Candy Mountains,
There's a land that's fair and bright,
Where the hand-outs grow on bushes,
And you sleep out every night.
Where the box cars all are empty,
Where the sun shines every day,
On the birds and the bees,
And the cigarette trees,
And the lemonade springs
Where the blue-bird sings,
In the big Rock Candy Mountains.

In the big Rock Candy Mountains,
All the cops have wooden legs,
The bull-dogs all have rubber teeth
And the hens lay soft-boiled eggs.
The farmer's trees are full of fruit
And the barns are full of hay.
Oh I'm bound to go
Where there ain't no snow,
Where they hung the Turk
That invented work,
In the big Rock Candy Mountains.

In the big Rock Candy Mountains
You never change your socks.
And the little streams of alcohol
Come trickling down the rocks.
Where the brakemen have to tip their hats,
And the rail-road bulls are blind.
There's the lake of stew,
And of whisky too.
You can paddle all around 'em
In a big canoe
In the big Rock Candy Mountains.

These examples are of interest because they all share the common quality of modern folk-fantasies. If their poetic quality is much below even the worst of Coleridge's or Whittier's verses, the whole tradition strongly suggests that the conception itself is a cruder form of wish-fulfilment that does not bear examination at a higher imaginative level.

We may note here that W. H. Auden in a poetic commentary on *The Tempest*, introduces a reminiscence of Cockaigne that has more than a little in common with *The Big Rock Candy Mountains*:

> Sing first that green remote Cockagne
> Where whiskey-rivers run,
> And every gorgeous number may
> Be laid by anyone;
> For medicine and rhetoric
> Lie mouldering on shelves,
> While sad young dogs and stomach-aches
> Love no one but themselves.

Shelley's *Alastor*, in solitary communion with all that lives, addressing his invocation to earth, ocean and air, moves in a wholly different dimension of the human spirit:

> If no bright bird, insect or gentle beast
> I consciously have injured, but still loved
> And cherished these my kindred;—then forgive
> This boast, beloved brethren, and withdraw
> No portion of your wonted favour now!

And perhaps there was deliberate thought of Coleridge and his Mariner in Shelley's identification of the ship bound for Eden and an albatross, in *Epipsychidion*:

> A ship is floating in the harbour now,
> A wind is hovering o'er the mountain's brow;
> There is a path on the sea's azure floor,
> No keel has ever ploughed that path before;
> The halcyons brood around the foamless isles;
> The treacherous Ocean has forsworn its wiles;
> The merry mariners are bold and free;
> Say, my heart's sister, wilt thou sail with me?
> Our bark is as an albatross, whose nest
> Is a far Eden of the purple East;

And we between her wings will sit, while Night
And Day, and Storm, and Calm, pursue their flight,
Our ministers, along the boundless Sea,
Treading each other's heels, unheededly.
It is an isle under Ionian skies,
Beautiful as a wreck of Paradise,
And, for the harbours are not safe and good,
This land would have remained a solitude
But for some pastoral people native there,
Who from the Elysian, clear, and golden air
Draw the last spirit of the age of gold,
Simple and spirited.

   .   .   .   .   .

It is an isle 'twixt Heaven, Air, Earth, and Sea,
Cradled, and hung in clear tranquillity;
Bright as that wandering Eden Lucifer,
Washed by the soft blue Oceans of young air.
It is a favoured place. Famine or Blight,
Pestilence, War, and Earthquake, never light
Upon its mountain peaks; blind vultures, they
Sail onward far upon their fatal way:
The wingéd storms, chanting their thunder-psalm
To other lands, leave azure chasms of calm
Over this isle, or weep themselves in dew,
From which its fields and woods ever renew
Their green and golden immortality.

   .   .   .   .   .

    This isle and house are mine, and I have vowed
Thee to be lady of the solitude.
And I have fitted up some chambers there
Looking towards the golden Eastern air,
And level with the living winds, which flow
Like waves above the living waves below.
I have sent books and music there, and all
Those instruments with which high spirits call
The future from its cradle, and the past
Out of its grave, and make the present last
In thoughts and joys which sleep, but cannot die,
Folded within their own eternity.
Our simple life wants little, and true taste
Hires not the pale drudge Luxury, to waste

247

> The scene it would adorn, and therefore still,
> Nature, with all her children, haunts the hill.

The poem is prefaced by an almost prophetic *Advertisement*, written in 1821: "The Writer of the following Lines died at Florence, as he was preparing for a voyage to one of the wildest of the Sporades, which he had bought, and where he had fitted up an old building, and where it was his hope to have realized a scheme of life suited, perhaps, to that happier and better world of which he is now an inhabitant, but hardly practicable in this. His life was singular; less on account of the romantic vicissitudes which diversified it, than the ideal tinge which it received from his own character and feelings. The present poem, like the *Vita Nuova* of Dante, is sufficiently intelligible to a certain class of readers without a matter-of-fact history of the circumstances to which it relates; and to a certain other class it must ever remain incomprehensible from a defect of a common organ of perception for the ideas of which it treats." In July of the following year Shelley and his sailing ship vanished into a thunder-cloud and he was nevermore seen alive.

The way to the Golden Age is not, after all, by seafaring. What Shelley and the others were seeking was Plato's True Surface of the Earth, or that other island, Dante's purgatorial mountain crested with the terrestrial paradise. On that shore, perhaps, the spirit of Shelley landed. For those who live still in what Wordsworth called "the world of all of us", books and music, and the union of them which is poetry, may call the future from its cradle and the past from its grave, as Shelley said, and as they do in the timeless legend of the Golden Age. If we clip the wings of vision the olive branch of peace and plenty will grow unplucked on those mysterious heights.

There are still what Blake called "doors to Eden". The nonagenarian sage Bernard Shaw, who died in 1950 as peacefully as the long-lived people of Hesiod's Golden Age and their actual successors Pindar and Cornaro, was—like Blake—often closest to tradition when he seemed to conventional minds most revolutionary. "Vegetarianism to Shelley," Shaw wrote towards the end of his long, vigorous life, "like marriage and atheism, was a form of poetry." Reading Shelley, he said, made him change in early manhood to the bloodless diet on which he lived his last half-century; "I must have been the only man who took his poetry seriously." This obeisance to the Life Force in other creatures certainly meant as much to Shaw as a similar observance did to FitzGerald but there are almost no direct references to it in his plays and prefaces. In 1949 I asked him to leave us something comparable to the essays on the same theme by Plutarch, Porphyry, and Shelley himself. His last play for living actors contains it.

Thirty years earlier he had gone *Back to Methuselah* for the image of Eden that closes on Eve's prophecy of a time to come when "there shall be no more digging, nor spinning, nor fighting, nor killing" and forward *As Far as Thought can Reach*, not to the cloud-capped towers and gorgeous palaces but to the simplicities and sanctities of "a sunlit glade at the southern foot of a thickly wooded hill". Like the Hindu sages, he found peace not in a city but among trees, in communion with the creative life of Nature. Shaw had followed Byron in throwing the primary blame on Abel, whose bad example converts Cain to the cult of bloodshed. Flesh-eating has literally bred war in the world in this great myth, as Pythagoras knew and Sir Arthur Keith and other modern experts quoted in my Anthropological Epilogue are coming to believe. "Then came my great idea: why not kill him as he killed the beasts? I struck; and he died, just as they did. Then I gave up your old silly drudging ways, and lived as he had lived, by the chase, the killing, and by the fire. Am I not better than you? stronger, happier, fiercer?" As in Coleridge's strange vision, Abel was with Cain in the wilderness that killing had made, where no seasons are acknowledged and nothing grows.

In the last preface he wrote, Shaw has described his purpose in *Farfetched Fables*. "Being unable to put everything in the heavens above and on the earth beneath into every page I write, as some of my correspondents seem to expect, I have had to leave some scraps and shavings out; and now I gather up a few of them and present them in the childish form of Farfetched Fables. Philosophic treatises, however precise and lucid, are thrown away on readers who can enjoy and sometimes even understand parables, fairy tales, novels, poems, and prophecies. Proverbs are more memorable than catechisms and creeds." We are being offered a mixture of philosophy

and fairy tale, parable, poem and prophecy. And, I think, something
else besides—a counterpart of the final play of Shakespeare's, the
master poet whose position relative to Shaw is the subject of the
little puppet play that formed the Shavian epilogue.

The brief glimpses of moments in the fabulous future of the Isle
of Wight, in *Farfetched Fables,* culminate in the sudden appearance
of a youth, clothed in feathers like a bird, an experimental reincarnation by one of the Disembodied and also, surely, a deliberate
Ariel on the Shavian Unexpected Isle. He too was about to break
his staff and sink his book. And the Fourth Fable—like *The Tempest*
again—has a vanishing banquet, a witty variation on the Shakespearian theme. When the Fables were performed at the little
Watergate Theatre in the Adelphi where Shaw once lived, there
was not a dramatic critic in London who did not see at a glance
that this was senile Shavian nonsense, nor one, as far as I know, who
recognised the parallel with *The Tempest*. The Play of Ideas has long
been a critical cliché. The history of ideas remains as deeply sub-
merged as Prospero's book. To follow the clue of Shaw's Fourth
Fable in that volume would take us also to the Aereal Paradises of
the Superior Daemons of the Cambridge Platonists, and the angel
Raphael's description of ambrosial feasts akin to Eden, which
Shaw's great Puritan predecessor Milton based upon them.

The Diet Commissioner is dictating part of his book on *Human
Diet*, a chapter headed *Living on Air:*

> The British themselves, influenced by a prophet whose name has come
> down to us in various forms as Shelley, Shakespear, and Shavius, had
> already, after some centuries of restricted cannibalism in which only
> fishes, frogs, birds, sheep, cows, pigs, rabbits, and whales were eaten,
> been gradually persuaded to abstain from these also, and to live on plants
> and fruits, and even on grass, honey, and nuts: a diet which they called
> vegetarian. Full stop. New paragraph. Ahem!
> As this change saved the labor of breeding animals for food, and
> supported human health and longevity quite as well, if not better, than
> the eating of dead animals, it was for some time unchallenged as a step
> forward in civilization. But some unforeseen consequences followed.
> When cattle were no longer bred and slaughtered for food, milk and
> butter, cheese and eggs, were no longer to be had. Grass, leaves, and
> nettles became the staple diet. This was sufficient for rude physical health.
> At the Olympic Games grass eating athletes broke all the records. This

was not surprising, as it had long been known that bulls and elephants, fed on grass and leaves, were the strongest, most fertile, most passionate animals known.

But the population, living in the letter of the Biblical assertion that "all flesh is grass"—there is already one voluntary modern Nebuchadnezzar, Mr. Bransom—is ferocious, though not to the point of mass homicide. Wars have ended and the diet of leaves and grass is producing not supermen but supergorillas. A Russian woman proposes living on water and air. Truth is stranger than fiction: the claims made in this Fable were in fact urged on Shaw by Barbara Moore-Pataleewa, who said she lived without even corn or herbs but, like the phoenix, on fruit juices alone. Shaw's statement of the case is a judicious modernisation of the angel Raphael's:

There is substance, called matter, everywhere: in fact, the universe consists of nothing else; but whether we can perceive it, or eat and drink it, depends on temperature, rate of radiation, and the sensitiveness of the instruments for detecting and measuring it. As temperature rises, water changes from solid ice to liquid fluid, from liquid fluid to steam, from steam to gas; but it is none the less substantial even at temperatures that are quite immeasurable and hardly conceivable. It followed logically that living on air is as possible as living on flesh or on grass and chopped carrots, though as men cannot live under water, nor fishes out of it, each phase of substance has its appropriate form of life and diet and set of habits. Such creatures as angels are as possible as whales and minnows, elephants and microbes.

The Russian woman claimed that she had lived for months on air and water, but on condition that the air was fresh and that she took the hardest physical exercise daily. It was already known that the vigils and fasts of saints did not weaken them when their spiritual activity was intense enough to produce a state of ecstasy.

So, this future historian chronicles, the dietary elevation of man-kind is accomplished, the Shavian fire-eaters adapt themselves to the lower element of air, presumably synthesising chlorophyll from sunlight as naturally as the plants do now:

The world became a world of athletes, artists, craftsmen, physicists, and mathematicians, instead of farmers, millers, bakers, butchers, bar tenders, brewers, and distillers. Hunger and thirst, which had for centuries meant the need for bread and onions, cheese and beer, beef and mutton, became a search for knowledge of nature and power over it, and a desire for truth and righteousness. The supergorilla became the soldier and servant of Creative Evolution.

So begins the transition to the disembodied awareness that materialises in the final Fable as the feathered man whose name, by the way, is also Raphael. So the Shavian vision and the Shakespearian come in the end to much the same thing:

> Our revels now are ended. These our actors,
> As I foretold you, were all spirits, and
> Are melted into air, into thin air:
> And, like the baseless fabric of this vision,
> The cloud-capp'd towers, the gorgeous palaces,
> The solemn temples, the great globe itself,
> Yea, all which it inherit, shall dissolve,
> And, like this insubstantial pageant faded,
> Leave not a rack behind. We are such stuff
> As dreams are made on.

Shaw's countryman and contemporary, W. B. Yeats, found a door to Eden in his long journey through Eastern and Celtic wisdom. One of the *Last Poems,* a thin volume also containing verses on Pythagoras, opens in what Wordsworth called "the world of all of us"—

> A bloody and a sudden end
>   Gunshot or a noose,
> For Death who takes what man would keep,
>   Leaves what man would lose.

As Blake would say, the Spiritual Man sees through the eyes of the Natural Man, in the last stanza of this lament over the death of an old whore:

> The priests have got a book that says
>   But for Adam's sin
> Eden's Garden would be there
>   And I there within.
> No expectation fails there,
>   No pleasing habit ends,
> No man grows old, no girl grows cold,
>   But friends walk by friends.
> Who quarrels over halfpennies
>   That plucks the trees for bread? . . .

To Yeats, as to Bran many centuries before him, a stranger-woman had brought a branch of the apple tree from the far land.

The Orphic music too had sounded for him. He contemplated "poems spoken to a harp" in *The Idea of Good and Evil*, and it was music played by an old fiddler in a train near Sligo that brought the voices to him out of *The Celtic Twilight*:

I seemed to hear a voice of lamentation out of the Golden Age. It told me that we are imperfect, incomplete, and no more like a beautiful woven web, but like a bundle of cords knotted together and flung into a corner. It said that the world was once all perfect and kindly, and that still the kindly and perfect world existed, but buried like a mass of roses under many spadefuls of earth. The faeries and the more innocent of the spirits dwelt within it, and lamented over our fallen world. . . . It said that if only they who live in the Golden Age could die we might be happy, for the sad voices would be still; but alas! alas! they must sing and we must weep until the Eternal gates swing open.

"Buried like a mass of roses under many spadefuls of earth. . . ." And so it was too that Sean O'Casey felt it, in the golden transfiguration of the loungers and shrivelled flower-sellers of the grimy city in *Red Roses for Me*.

The Orphic music is still heard. When Rainer Maria Rilke, for whom Orpheus was the ideal poet, and who "understood the continuity of the universe . . . recognised the kinship between his own life and the life of animals and birds and trees and plants", saw in a shop window a little engraving of Orpheus with his lyre, the *Orpheus Sonnets* he grouped around it were "the record of a vision, or intuition, into what the old Greek philosophers called the Nature of Being".

Fruits are the food in Heaven to which Orphée, Eurydice and the window-mender Heurtebise sit down at the end of Jean Cocteau's play, and in Anouilh's, which is showing in London as I write in 1951, Orpheus and Eurydice will not leave their little paradise to dine as the world does at the restaurant. Their love-feast must be only fruit, wine and bread, and Orpheus insists on *real* fruit, not just the American kind. "True tears," says Jean-Louis Barrault,[1] are "the tears that come at the sound of Orpheus' lyre." He writes also of reading *The Golden Verses of Pythagoras* and living

---

[1] Jean-Louis Barrault, *Reflections on the Theatre*, translated by Barbara Wall (Rockliff) 1951.

for two early years on a scant and mainly Pythagorean diet.

Anouilh may have been thinking of a letter about the *Orpheus Sonnets* written by Rilke in 1925: "Now there come crowding over from America empty, indifferent things, pseudo-things, dummy-life . . . a house, in the American sense, an American apple or vine, has nothing in common with the house, the fruit, the grape into which the hope and pensiveness of our forefathers would enter. . . . The animated, experienced things that share our lives are coming to an end and cannot be replaced. We are perhaps the last to have still known such things."

This Orphic intuition of a growing and disastrous cleavage between life and its total natural environment goes deeper than anything in Wordsworth. "No view of life could be less anthropocentric than Rilke's", says J. B. Leishman. At the end of the twelfth of the *Orpheus Sonnets*, Rilke asks a central question:

> Does the farmer, anxiously arranging,
> ever reach to where the seed is changing
> into summer? Does not Earth bestow?

And the following sonnet sounds a note that Europe has scarcely heard since Orpheus sang, a poem that Keats might have lived to write:

> Banana, rounded apple, russet pear,
> gooseberry. . . . Does not all this convey
> life and death into your mouth? . . . It's there! . . .
> Read it on a child's face any day,
>
> When it tastes them. What infinity!
> Can't you feel inside your mouth a growing
> mysteriousness, and, where words were, a flowing
> of suddenly released discovery?
>
> Dare to say what "apple" has implied!
> Sweetness, concentrated, self-repressing,
> slowly yielding to the tongue's caressing,
>
> growing awake, transparent, clarified,
> double-meaning'd, sunshine-full, terrestrial:—
> O experience, feeling, joy,—celestial!

ANTHROPOLOGICAL EPILOGUE

WERE the earliest human societies peaceful and were they pastoral? W. J. Perry considers it "an error, as profound as it is universal, to think that men in the food-gathering stage of history were given to fighting. All the available facts go to show that the food-gathering stage of history must have been one of perfect peace."

Elliot Smith explicitly joins hands with the poets: "All the available evidence seems to point clearly to the conclusion that until the invention of the methods of agriculture and irrigation on the large scale practised in Egypt and Babylonia, the world really enjoyed some such Golden Age of Peace as Hesiod has described."

But it was not so much the transition from tree to field that ended the age of perfect peace as the change from a mainly agricultural to a mixed pastoral economy. Where the former is literally rooted to the ground it cultivates, the latter is not only free to migrate but often compelled to do so by the desolation that over-grazing brings about. The acquisition of some more fertile or less damaged area increasingly came to mean the forcible displacement of some peaceful human community.

Edward Gibbon saw the distinction clearly enough: "The thrones of Asia have been repeatedly overturned by the shepherds of the North, and their arms have spread terror and devastation over the most fertile and warlike countries of Europe. On this occasion, as well as on many others, the sober historian is forcibly awakened from a pleasing vision, and is compelled with some reluctance, to confess that the *pastoral* manners, which have been adorned with the fairest attributes of peace and innocence, are much better adapted to the fierce and cruel habits of military life." He contrasts "the happy savages who dwell between the tropics . . . plentifully nourished by the liberality of Nature" with the shepherds of the North "reduced to their flocks and herds", and raises the question whether "the common association of carnivorous and cruel" has some basis of truth, "how far the temper of the human mind may be affected by the use of animal or of vegetable food". Sir Arthur Keith, discussing the origins of agriculture, likewise declares that it "tended to favour and select men of a pacific nature, whereas pastoralism bred warlike qualities".

It is not remarkable, therefore, to find W. W. Greg saying that even in English pastoral poetry of the seventeenth and eighteenth centuries the idea of the Golden Age is "not wholly coincident with that of pastoral". But the constant literary association of which the same authority writes is so all-pervading that it may be helpful here to call in Aldous Huxley to put asunder what man has erroneously joined together. "The relations between social organizations and individuals who live under them is symbolically expressed by the word 'shepherd', as applied to the priests and rulers, who like to think of themselves as God's earthly representatives, and even to God Himself. The metaphor is of high, but not the highest, antiquity; for it was first used by the herd-owning, land-destroying, meat-eating and war-waging peoples who replaced the horticulturists of the first civilization and put an end to that Golden Age of Peace, which not long since was regarded as a mere myth, but is now revealed by the light of archaeology as a proto- and pre-historical reality. By force of unreflecting habit we go on talking sentimentally about the Shepherd of His people, about Pastors and their flocks, about stray lambs and a Good Shepherd. We never pause to reflect that a shepherd is 'not in business for his health', still less for the health of his sheep. If he takes good care of the animals, it is in order that he may rob them of their wool and milk, castrate their male offspring and finally cut their throats and convert them into mutton." Tamburlaine was, after all, a typical shepherd!

Reflecting, as his countryman Thoreau might have done, on the root causes of the Second World War, Fairfield Osborn, President of the New York Zoological Society, wrote: "The uncomfortable truth is that man, during innumerable past ages, has been a predator —a hunter, a meat-eater and a killer. The branching-off point in the evolution of man from that of the anthropoid ape was marked by the development of living habits in the primitive ancestors of man which have proved far from an unmixed blessing for the human race. Man, at an early stage, became a hunter and a killer while his nearest relatives in the animal world most similar to him physiologically remained vegetarians, and at no time, even to the present day, have depended upon the lives of other living creatures for their own survival. It is unlikely that all primitive human beings were predatory, and consequently it is probable that considerable groups of primitive people were plant and fruit eaters, especially those living in tropical or sub-tropical regions. But the explosive, dominant groups, which appear to have made the strongest impact on the course of human civilization, particularly those living in the temperate zones, resorted in the earliest times to hunting, combat and killing."

Orpheus and his lute charmed animals and trees into a single natural harmony, in which wild animals and tame, hunter and hunted, were at peace, as they are also in the Eden myth. Even if we admit some foundations of brazen fact for the poets' vision of a Golden Age, is there any evidence at all that the creatures likewise enjoyed some primal paradise of mutual aid? Osborn's argument points to it. The carnivores, he says, are a minority party among the larger and higher mammals, not more than one per cent. of the animal populations of Africa and North America as they existed before humanity began to upset all the "natural" balances. (Recent experiments in a Moscow Zoo are said to show that species considered incorrigibly hostile may be brought up harmlessly together. Some day the lion may lie down with the lamb, and the habit might even extend to human beings of different political convictions.) Osborn concludes that "unless man respects it, nature will not work for him", that he must not wantonly destroy life but accept "the relatedness of all living things". Thomas Hardy had long since pointed out that a first consequence of evolutionary theory is a vast expansion of our moral obligations to other creatures, and Herbert Spencer in *Social Statics* decided that in practice, "the behaviour of men to the lower animals and their behaviour to each other, bear a constant relationship". Some such insight is dramatically expressed in Flaubert's *Légende de St. Julien,* where the hunter hero shoots a fawn, its mother and finally the stag, who nevertheless approaches the killer, "and with flashing eyes and solemn tone, as of a just judge, he spoke three times, while a bell tolled in the distance, 'Accursed

one! ruthless of heart! thou shalt slay thy father and mother also.' "
This terrible prediction is fulfilled.

"It is probable", says J. M. Marrack, in the first words of his book
on food and planning, "that man's ancestors lived on fruits, leaves
and green roots, as do the great apes to-day. If so, men have eaten
unnatural diets since the dawn of history." But not all men. The
example of the Jainas, still numbering well over a million, is discussed in a note to the first chapter. Another nutritionist, F. Le Gros
Clark, currently estimates that—apart from the masses living at or
below subsistence level—"about fifteen per cent. of the world's
inhabitants do not at present consume meat for religious reasons"
and that more than ninety per cent. of human energy is derived
directly from vegetable foods, rather than indirectly from animal
foods, with milk accounting for another five per cent.

Such scattered but convergent testimony from the scientists is
belated evidence in support of the poets that cannot be lightly
dismissed. For the synthesis we may well turn to Henry Bailey
Stevens' book, *The Recovery of Culture*, of which an English edition
is pending. He finds the cause and occasion of man's branching off
from biological normality in the Ice Ages, and the surviving centre
of "primate culture" somewhere in the vicinity of Java, from whence
radiated traditions of these immemorial ways of living that strongly
influenced the dawn of civilization and left indelible traces in the
religions, languages, arts and customs of the world as well as in the
hearts of men.

Man was once united with Nature. Under some climatic compulsion he began to wound the earth, to tyrannise over the animals, to
destroy vegetation, to ruin topsoil, to uproot himself by travel and
seafaring (and now by flying), a restlessness of which was born that
fatal short-term attitude of irresponsibility which issues in the vicious
extractive "economy" from which we are now suffering, a wastage
of primary global resources aggravated by a dangerous multiplica-
tion of human numbers and by the spiritual and physical devastation
of total war.

Always the dream of his original state haunted him, and perhaps
in memory he transfigured it to something more beautiful than it
was, through a golden haze he glimpsed something of priceless
value to life on earth. That dream alternated with gross wish-

fulfilment fantasies of the Cockaigne type. Not only did an Eden or Golden Age archetype persist in imagination through the course of European civilization, there were from time to time eruptions of original man, seen by visionaries as rising above civilization while retaining certain crudities. He is a rough-and-ready but human figure, not a simpering Arcadian pretender. He has peace of mind. He is at peace with mankind. And both those beatitudes are contingent on a third. He is at peace with the creatures, with Nature and with whatever creative forces are working through that Orphic harmony of life in all its infinite diversity.

REFERENCES

PROLOGUE.

MASSINGHAM W. J., *The Golden Age*, Preface, vii   .   .   xv
COURTHOPE, W. J., *History of English Poetry*, II, p. 1   .   .   xv
BOWRA, C. M., *The Creative Experiment*, p. 24 .   .   .   xvi
SIDNEY, SIR PHILIP, *An Apology for Poetry*, ed. Needham, 8–25 .   xvi
ELIOT, T. S., *The Waste Land*, I, 19–24   .   .   .   xviii
HUXLEY, ALDOUS, *Themes and Variations*, pp. 259–260 . . xviii–xix

BIBLIOGRAPHICAL NOTE

BOAS, G., and LOVEJOY, A. O., *Primitivism and Related Ideas in Antiquity*, xi   xxi

CHAPTER 1
Orpheus

PINDAR, *Pyth*. IV, Antistrophe viii   1
BROWNING, ROBERT, *Easter-Day*, vii   .   .   .   1
GRAVES, ROBERT, *The Golden Fleece*, p. 146   .   .   2
PRESTON, W., trans. *Argonautics* (1803) III, pp. 21–24   .   2–3
MORRIS, WILLIAM, *The Life and Death of Jason*, Book X, 464–555; Book XIV, 91–95, 491–672, 707–709, 760–762 .   .   3–12
Homer

POPE, ALEXANDER, Preface, trans. *Iliad*   .   .   .   12
ROUSSEAU, J. J., *Emile*, (Everyman Library ed. p. 118)   .   12
POPE, ALEXANDER, trans. *Iliad*, XIII, 9–16; *Odyssey*, IV, 763–778; VI, 47–56; VII, 143–158   12–14
Hesiod

ELTON, C. A. trans. *Works and Days*, I, 145–264, 303–330 . 15–19
Orphism

RUSSELL, BERTRAND, *History of Western Philosophy*, pp. 29, 33, 35 . 20
GUTHRIE, W. K. C., *Orpheus and Greek Religion*, qu. Gold Plates . 21
GUTHRIE, W. K. C., *op. cit.*, pp. 197–198 . .   .   21
ARTICLE, "Orpheus" in *Enc. Brit.*   21
Hinduism, Buddhism, Jainism

MANU, "Ordinances," qu. in *Bible of the World*, p. 81   .   22
KEITH, A. BERRIEDALE, *A New Theory of Human Evolution*   .   22
RYDER, ARTHUR W., trans. *Shakuntala*, Int. xx   .   .   23
Mahabharata, III. Story of Savitri   .   .   .   23
Bhagavad Gita, XVII, 7–10   23
GUÉNON, RENÉ, trans. Marco Pallis, *Introduction to the Study of Hindu Doctrines*, pp. 45–46, 50, 49–50 .   .   .   23–24
ARNOLD, EDWIN, *The Light of Asia*, V   .   .   .   24–26
MAGNUS, *Dictionary of European Literature*   .   .   24
TAGORE, RABINDRANATH, qu. *Vegetarian News*, 1924, p. 282   .   24
URWICK, E. J., *The Message of Plato*, pp. 13–14   .   .   26

Pythagoras
    GUTHRIE, W. K. C., *op. cit.* 26
    Enc. Brit. 26
    IAMBLICHUS, *Life*, trans. Taylor ed. 1926, pp. 77, 30, 32, 58, 59, 98, 107–108, 135 26–28
    Golden Verses, Shrine of Wisdom edition, undated, pp. 9, 10, 12 . 29

Empedocles
    DIOGENES LAERTIUS, *Lives*, VIII, 54. Loeb ed. II, 369–371 . . 30
    LEONARD, W. C., trans. *Empedocles*, frag. 77–78, 128, 130, 136, 137, 139 30–31
    Enc. Brit. 32

Pindar
    Olympian Odes, trans. Moore
        I. a.ii. e.ii. s.iii. 37–38
        II. s.iv. a.iv. s.v. 33–34
        VII. a.iii. e.iii. s.iv. a.iv.; (Turner) s.v. a.v. . . 36–37
    Pythian Odes, trans. Moore
        IV. a.viii. 34
        X. a.ii. e.ii. s.iii. 35–36
    STEWART, J, A., *Myths of Plato*, pp. 66, 108 . . . 32–33
    GUTHRIE, W. K. C., *op. cit.*, p. 236 32
    Enc. Metropolitana, qu. in Bohn ed. *Pindar*, p. xi . . 32
    PALEY, F, A., *Odes of Pindar*, pp. xxi, xxvi–xxvii . . 35
    MYERS, E., do., p. 176 34
    HOMER, trans. Pope, *Iliad*, II, 813–822 . . . 36

Eleusis
    HARRISON, JANE, *Prolegomena to the Study of Greek Religion*, pp. 462, 545, 539 39

Aeschylus
    GUTHRIE, W. K. C., *op. cit.*, pp. 233, 234 . . . 39

Euripides
    GUTHRIE, W. K. C., *op. cit.*, p. 237 . . . 39
    Fragment in Athenaeus iv, trans. Howard Williams, *Ethics of Diet*, ed. 1883, 32n. 39
    Fragment in Jane Harrison, *op. cit.*, pp. 478–479 . . 39
    Hippolytus, trans. Gilbert Murray, pp. 50, 39 . . 39–40
    Bacchae, trans. Gilbert Murray, pp. 42–43, 63–64, 76, 34 . 40–41

Aristophanes
    Frogs, trans. J. H. Frere, I, 1301–1319 . . . 41–42
    GUTHRIE, W. K. C., *op. cit.*, pp. 196–197 . . . 42

Athenaeus
    Deipnosophistae, trans. C. B. Gulick, vi, 267–270 . . 42–43

Plato
    Republic
        II, 372, trans. Cornford, pp. 59–60 . . . 49–50
        X, 3–4, trans. Davis (Bohn edition, II), pp. 289–290 . 47–48
        613–621, trans. Stewart, *op. cit.*, p. 149 . . 46

Chapter 1, Plato, (cont.)
    Laws

IV, 6, trans. Burges (Bohn, V), p. 135 46
VI, 22,   do.   pp. 243–245 . . . 47
VIII, 13,   do.   p. 280 47
    23,   do.   pp. 310–311 . . . 47
Politicus, trans. Stewart, *op. cit.*, pp. 183–185 . . 45
Cratylus, trans. Burges, III, pp. 310–311 . . . 46n
Critias, trans. Davis, II, pp. 421, 425, 422, 420, 422, 428–429 . 51–52
STEWART, J. A., *op. cit.*, pp. 65–66, 68, 352, 302, 452, 453, 455 . 44–49
GUTHRIE, W. K. C., *op. cit.* 44
RUSSELL, BERTRAND, *History of Western Philosophy*, p. 111 . . 44
Antipater
    Greek Anthology, qu. in Lord Neaves ed. Blackwoods, p. 119 . 53

CHAPTER 2
Saturnalia

FRAZER, J., *The Golden Bough*, abr. pp. 583, 584 . . . 54–55
SENECA, qu. in Howard Williams, *op. cit.*, p. 32. and *Epist.* 108 . 55–56
JUVENAL, *Satire*, XV 55
Neoplatonists
JOSEPHUS, qu. in Howard Williams, *op. cit.*, p. 73 . . . 56
PLUTARCH, *Essay* do., p. 46. *Lives*, Dryden rev. I, pp. 91, 115; II, pp.
    313–314; and qu. Meyer and Nutt, *Voyage of Bran*, i. 284n. . 57–58
FIRDAUSI, qu. in Carnoy, *Myth. All Races*, VI, pp. 304–305 . 59
SCHOPENHAUER, *Fragments*, Sec. 7: Neoplatonists . . 59n
VOLTAIRE, *Viande* in *Phil Dict.* 60
Lucretius
DUFF, J. D., xvii, xviii, Munro's *Lucretius* . . . 60–61
LEONARD, W. E., trans. of *The Nature of Things*, I, p. 31; IV, p. 158;
    V. pp. 225–229 62–64
Vergil
1 *Georgic*, trans. T. F. Royds, 11. 147–192 . . . 65–66
2 *Georgic*, do. 11. 643–648 66
    The first phrase is the translation by W. F. Jackson Knight,
    Roman Vergil, p. 273
4 *Eclogue*, trans. T. F. Royds, 11. 4–72 . . . 66–68
KNIGHT, W. F. JACKSON, *op. cit.*, pp. 122, 123, 54 . . 65–68
Horace
Secular Hymn, trans. A. F. Murison, p. 163 . . . 68
16 *Epode*, do., pp. 188–192 69–71
Ars Poetica, do., p. 426 71
Poet's Desire, do., *Odes* I, xxxi, p. 43 . . . 71
2 *Satire*, Book II, do., pp. 257–258 71–72
Ovid
Metamorphoses I, trans. A. Golding . . . 73–74
Elegy to Ceres, trans. Marlowe 75
The Cerelia, trans. John Gower 75
    (From *Selected Works*. ed. J. C. & M. J. Thornton, pp. 134–137,
    19, 115–118.)

Milton
   Paradise Lost, V, 291–505 abridged   139–143
   Paradise Regained, I, 303, 339; II, 150, 320; IV, 576   .   .   147–152
   Comus, 69, 706, 976   152–154
   Sixth Latin Elegy, trans. Cowper, *Complete Works*, 1876, p. 695   .   154–155
   On the Morning of Christ's Nativity, xiv   .   .   .   155
Marvell
   The Garden, in *Poems*, ed. G. A. Aitken, Muses Library, p. 98   155–156
   Garvin, Katharine, letter in *T.L.S.* 11th August, 1950   .   .   156

CHAPTER 6
Restoration Comedy
   GREEN, J. R., *Short History*, p. 607   157
   HUDSON, W. H., Introduction to Dryden's Dramatic *Poesy*, etc., viii   157–158
Dryden
   Fables, Preface, pp. 278, 267, ed. Sargeaunt, 1913   .   .   .   158–159
   To the Memory of Anne Killigrew, p. 179   .   .   .   158
   Metamorphoses, XV, 73–154, 668–720, pp. 496–497, 504–505   .   160–163
   Don Sebastian, V, i, in Mermaid ed. vol. ii   .   .   163–164
   JOHNSON, *Lives of the Poets*, Chandos ed. p. 150   .   .   158
   JULIAN, in Howard Williams, *op. cit.*, p. 75   .   .   159
   CHESTERFIELD, *The World*, No. 190, in Williams, *op. cit.*, p. 140   .   160
Tate
   The Banquet in *Poems*, ed. 1684, p. 65   .   .   .   165
   MARVELL, A., "The Garden" in *Poems*, Muses Lib., p. 100   .   166
Fable
   MANDEVILLE, B. DE, *Fable of the Bees*, ed. D. Garman, pp. 24, 27,
      39, 41, 134, 136, 137, 139   166–168
   RHYS, E., *Fables* (Everyman Library) Int., x, xii   .   .   168
   ARNOLD, E., qu. Rhys, *op. cit.*, ix   168
   Hitopadesa, fables in Rhys, *op. cit.*, pp. 109-150   .   .   168
   AVYAKTANANDA, SWAMI, *The Flute of Krishna* in *India Through the
      Ages*, p. 69   168
   GAY, J., *Pythagoras and the Countryman*, in *Fables*, XXXVI   .   169–170
   VOLTAIRE, *Elemens de la Philosophie de Newton*, qu. in Howard
      Williams, *op. cit.*, p. 145.   170
   JOHNSON, S., quoted in Press, untraced   .   .   .   170
Pope
   Essay on Man, III, 7–26, 147–168; IV, 361–372   .   .   170–172
   Windsor Forest, 371–374   172
   Imitation of Horace, Satire, 2, II, 138–148, 4–6, 15, 70   .   173
   SITWELL, E., *Alexander Pope*, 1948 ed. pp. 20, 235, 88, 49   .   172
   WALPOLE, qu. Sitwell, *op. cit.*, 161, 214   .   .   .   173
Swift
   Epigram on Fasting, in *Poems*, ed. H. Williams, III, p. 949   .   174
   A Panegyrick on the Dean, do., III, pp. 894–895   .   .   174–175
   Gulliver's Travels, A Voyage to the Houyhnhnms   .   .   175–177

References

American Edens
FRANKLIN, B., *Autobiography*, pp. 18, 38–39 . . . 231
STEVENS, H. B., *The Recovery of Culture*, p. 160 . . . 231
THOREAU, H. D., *Walden*, in *Selected Works*, ed. H. S. Canby,
pp. 392, 388, 385–386, 452, 463; *Week*, 134–135, 215, 216, 217 231–233
EMERSON, R. W., *Forbearance*, in *Works*, ed. 1881, I, p. 446 . 233
ALCOTT, A. B., in O. Shephard, *Pedlar's Progress*, pp. 441, 323,
326, 357 233–234
ALCOTT, L. M., *Life, Letters and Journals*, ed. E. M. Cheney, ch. 3 234
HAWTHORNE, N., *Notebooks*, ed. R. Stewart, p. 77 . . 235
The New Adam and Eve, in *Mosses from an Old Manse* . . 235–236
LONGFELLOW, H. W., *The Sermon of St. Francis*, in *Poetical Work*,
O.U.P., 1925, p. 331 237
Tales of a Wayside Inn, do., pp. 396–397, 399, 402 . . 237–240
WHITTIER, J. G., *Song of Harvest*, in *Poetical Works*, ed. W.
Garrett Horder, O.U.P., 1911, p. 239 240–241
For an Autumn Festival, do., p. 241 241
Our River, do., p. 245 241
The Garden, do., p. 258 241

American Cockaignes
ODUM, H. W. and JOHNSON, G. B., *Negro Workaday Songs*, 1926,
pp. 221–240 242
BLEGEN, THEO C. and RUUD, M. B., *Norwegian Emigrant Songs
and Ballads*, 1936, pp. 143–144, pp. 176–198 . . . 243–244
Big Rock Candy Mountains, qu. in Berneri, M. L., *Journey Through
Utopia*, 1950 245
AUDEN, W. H., *The Sea and the Mirror*, in *For the Time Being*, p. 13 246

Irish Edens and Golden Ages.
SHAW, G. B., *Back to Methuselah*, in *Complete Plays*, 1931, pp. 869, 938 249
Farfetched Fables 249–252
YEATS, W. B., *John Kinsella's Lament for Mrs. Henry Moore*, in
Last Poems, p. 70 252
The Idea of Good and Evil, p. 16, qu. Stewart, *op. cit.*, p. 393n. . 253
The Golden Age, in *The Celtic Twilight*, pp. 173–175 . 253
O'CASEY, SEAN, *Red Roses for Me* 253

European Orphism
RILKE, R. M., *Sonnets to Orpheus*, I, xii, xiii, trans. J. B. Leish-
man, and Int., pp. 27, 16, 13, 10 253–254
COCTEAU, JEAN, *Orphée* 253
ANOUILH, JEAN, *Eurydice*, (trans. as *Point of Departure*) . . 253
BARRAULT, J-L., *Reflections on the Theatre* . . . 253

ANTHROPOLOGICAL EPILOGUE
PERRY, W. J., *Children of the Sun* 255
SMITH, G. E., *The Evolution of Man*, p. 131 . . . 255
GIBBON, E., *Decline and Fall of The Roman Empire*, xxvi . . 255–256
KEITH, A., *A New Theory of Human Evolution* . . . 256
GREG, W. W., *Pastoral Poetry and Pastoral Drama* . . . 256
HUXLEY, A., *Themes and Variations*, p. 54 . . . 256

Date Due

AP 24'65			
AP 27'65			